THE PHANTOM PUNCH

THE PHANTOM PUNCH

The Story Behind Boxing's Most Controversial Bout

ROB SNEDDON

Down East Books

Camden, Maine

Published by Down East Books
An imprint of The Rowman & Littlefield Publishing Group, Inc.
4501 Forbes Boulevard, Suite 200, Lanham, Maryland 20706
www.rowman.com

Unit A, Whitacre Mews, 26-34 Stannary Street, London SE11 4AB, United Kingdom

Distributed by NATIONAL BOOK NETWORK

British Library Cataloguing in Publication Information Available

Library of Congress Cataloging-in-Publication Data
Library of Congress Cataloging-in-Publication Data Available
ISBN 978-1-60893-365-5 (cloth : alk. paper)

∞™ The paper used in this publication meets the minimum requirements of
American National Standard for Information Sciences—Permanence of Paper for
Printed Library Materials, ANSI/NISO Z39.48-1992.

Printed in the United States of America

For Sam Michael,
who believed in Lewiston more than Lewiston did.

Contents

Introduction

In 2009 someone with the handle okano186 posted a ten-second YouTube clip from the second Ali–Liston fight, at Lewiston, Maine. "The infamous phantom punch shown in slow motion," okano186 wrote. "Do you still think Liston dived?"

The video seemed to have the desired effect on a couple of viewers. "I came here to see if it was faked or not, believing it probably was," wrote one. "Now I realize it was definitely a short, legit punch Liston didn't see. I call this KO legit."

For the most part, however, the video did little to sway people. As of this writing the clip has had almost 700,000 views and generated almost 700 comments. Most said, in effect, that the clip confirmed what the viewer believed. Here's a sampling:

The punch landed. It just didn't have the power to KO a bantamweight much less Charles Sonny Liston.

Clear hit to the temple, face shook, POINT CONCLUDED.

If you think that punch was hard enough to knock Liston out, then you're a fool that clearly does not know anything about boxing, the history of our country, or the culture of the times.

Looked like a straight right to the temple to me . . . lights out.

He took a dive—it's clear as day. I don't know how anyone could dispute that.

It's pointless to call it a dive when he clearly took a hard punch to the face. You can see the shockwave through his entire body.

A shockwave through his entire body? Are we watching the same video? Lol. It doesn't matter. This fight is history.

[Yes], this fight is history . . . and look at the views it has. Dumbass.

1

Typical Internet stuff. But I've seen that same basic argument play out face to face, between the unlikeliest adversaries. Take, for example, an exchange between retired Maine state trooper Normand Bureau and his wife, Irene.

I interviewed the Bureaus on a rainy summer morning in 2014. We sat in their living room on a quiet Lewiston street, not far from the building once called the Central Maine Youth Center but now called the Colisée. It was about two months before the Bureaus' sixtieth wedding anniversary. Normand said that they had been together through "seven kids, eighteen grandkids, and five or six great-grandkids." (I liked the lack of specificity on that last one.)

Normand joined the Maine State Police in 1959. One of his more memorable details was the Ali–Liston fight on May 25, 1965. Normand's regular beat was patrolling the Maine Turnpike. But because he lived in Lewiston and had spent so much time at the Central Maine Youth Center—first as a hockey player, later as president of the Lewiston–Auburn Hockey Association—he was a logical choice to work security at the fight. His lieutenant, who also lived in Lewiston, told the other troopers on the detail, "You want to know anything, go see Norm."

I asked Irene if she had been at the fight too. "No," she said. "I was right here."

By "here" she didn't just mean the same house on the same Lewiston street—she meant the same *room*. "I listened to it on the radio," Irene said.

The day of the fight Normand reported to the arena at about nine in the morning. Rumors of impending violence had Lewiston on edge. One report had it that supporters of the late Malcolm X, who had been assassinated in February, were going to take out Muhammad Ali, who was loyal to Malcolm X's chief rival, Nation of Islam leader Elijah Muhammad. Fred Brooks, president of the closed-circuit TV company that was broadcasting the fight, gave the rumor credence by taking out a $1 million insurance policy on Ali's life. He even made a dark joke about it. "If I could assure the people an assassination," he said, "I could sell a million tickets."

The threats, whether real or imagined, put pressure on the security detail. "I checked every room in the place," said Normand, "and then I went up to the rafters. They had four cameras up there that had been set up a couple of days before. I was the guard for that, so I stayed up there all day. They brought me my lunch. And after the fight I waited until everybody was out of the arena before I went home, around midnight."

During the fight—all two minutes and fifteen seconds of it—Normand had the same vantage point as the primary camera for the closed-circuit broadcast. "What the camera saw," he said, "I saw."

Watch the okano186 clip on YouTube, in other words, and you're seeing the phantom punch from the same angle that Normand Bureau saw it in person and in real time. I pressed for details, but as far as Normand was concerned, the details were irrelevant. "There was only one question," Normand said. "Did he hit him or didn't he hit him? That's all everybody was talking about behind those cameras."

And what did Normand think? "I think Liston took a fall," he said. "That's stayed in my mind forever. I still say [Ali] didn't hit him."

Irene, who had been listening quietly, suddenly spoke up: "You don't think so?" She sounded incredulous.

"I don't think so." Normand's words suggested equivocation but his tone did not.

Irene stared.

"That's my opinion!" Normand said.

"Ohhh-kay," Irene said.

I laughed. "So you think he *did* hit him?" I asked Irene.

"Mmmm-*hmmm*," she said.

Normand Bureau had spent more than twenty years in police work. His keen powers of observation and insight into human behavior had helped him solve tragic missing-child cases, had helped him crack stolen-car rings. His detective work had received national recognition among his peers and later earned him the Maine State Police's highest honor for retirees, its "Legendary Trooper" award.

Plus, he saw the fight with his own eyes.

Irene heard it on the radio.

Yet her opinion was set in cement. Irene Bureau believed that Muhammad Ali's knockout of Sonny Liston was on the level. She was right and her husband was wrong.

Normand gave a dismissive groan. It was time to change the subject.

A nd so it's gone, from living rooms to barrooms to chat rooms, for fifty years. In 2014 *ESPN* magazine listed the phantom punch as one of twenty-five candidates for the title "The Greatest Sports Conspiracy in the History of the Universe." And whatever you believe happened that night at the Central Maine Youth Center, you'll find an expert to back you up.

Looking for some fresh insight, I forwarded the okano186 clip to Dr. William Heinz, a medical orthopedist who specializes in sports-related concussions, and who co-founded the Maine Concussion Management Initiative. He emailed this response: "There was a rotational component to the hit, which could explain why it only took one hit to take [Liston] down. Rotational hits tend to be the worst for concussions."

His conclusion: "Either Liston was a very good actor, or [the knockout] was real."

Contrast that with this assessment from Nick Tosches, whose 2000 book *The Devil and Sonny Liston* is the definitive Liston biography: "When Sonny lay down in the first round, he showed less acting ability than in the episode of *Love American Style* in which he later bizarrely appeared."

And then there's this, from Terry Nilon. Terry's uncle, Jack Nilon, managed Sonny Liston during Liston's brief reign as heavyweight champion, and his father, Bob Nilon, was president of Inter-Continental Promotions, which presented the Lewiston fight. "I know what everybody thinks," Terry told me. "Everybody thinks [Liston] threw the fight. And maybe he did. Maybe people got to him and said, 'You're going down.' But I can tell you this, and I can tell you with total clarity: My father and uncle didn't know anything about it. They came home in a state of shock. In a thousand years they wouldn't have believed Sonny Liston would go down in the first round, whether it be through Muhammad Ali or some other reason. It's just one of the great mysteries."

Whatever drove Liston down—whether it was the phantom punch or something else—in hindsight his fate seems as inevitable as Lennie

Small's in *Of Mice and Men*. Really, what people saw in Lewiston that night was less a boxing match than one of those elaborate domino-toppling demonstrations. One tile tapped the next and the next and the next, fanning out in complex patterns—some falling forward, some backward—until the whole thing came down. And it was Ali's "phantom punch" that set the intricate chain reaction in motion.

First, as okano186's clip clearly shows, the punch did indeed connect—even though many people didn't see it, either ringside or on the broadcast. (To further confuse the issue, Ali whiffed with his immediate follow-up, a left hook. I think that's the "phantom punch" that fooled a lot of viewers.) The sequence began when Liston threw a left jab, his signature punch. Ali ducked away from it, and the punch barely reached his chest. Liston's awkward forward momentum, combined with Ali's quick downward counterpunch, added up to a legitimate knockdown.

But was it a legitimate knock*out*? To have any hope of answering that, you have to follow the line of dominoes from Maine down to Miami, where Ali and Liston had met for the first time exactly fifteen months earlier, and from there all the way back to the last vestiges of the plantation days in the American South.

You also have to forget much of what you think of when you think of Muhammad Ali.

Ali has been regarded as "The Greatest" for so long that it's hard to conceive of a time when he wasn't even considered a true contender. But that was the case before his first title fight with Sonny Liston, at Miami Beach Convention Hall on February 25, 1964. Liston was generally regarded as invincible, with good reason. At the time some "heavyweights" were less than six feet tall and weighed as little as 175 pounds—not even the size of an average major league shortstop today. Liston stood 6' 1" and had an ideal fighting weight of around 212 pounds. Just as important was how his height and weight were proportioned. Liston had oxlike shoulders. His fists were fifteen inches around—so large that he needed custom-made gloves. His punches were like blows from a jackhammer, striking with maximum force every time. And he delivered them without remorse.

That last characteristic was, no doubt, a function of the kind of life that Liston had led. He was born sometime around the start of the Great Depression (the exact date is uncertain) and grew up in rural Arkansas, one of twenty-five kids fathered by an incurable hard case named Tobe Liston. Sonny learned to box while serving a term for armed robbery at one of America's roughest prisons, the Missouri State Penitentiary. And he turned pro in the mid-'50s, a time when heavyweight boxing was thoroughly corrupt. That meant that there was always a criminal element lurking somewhere in his life, and there were too many ambiguous connections to guys with names like Blinky. Throughout his career Liston had regular run-ins with the cops, many of which were nothing more than harassment based on his reputation. That fueled his anger. He dragged a lot of baggage into the ring with him.

The results were frightening. Liston didn't just batter his opponents, he shattered them—psychologically as well as physically. To see stark evidence, go to YouTube and find his December 1961 fight with Albert Westphal in Philadelphia.

Anyone could see that it was a mismatch before it even began. Howard M. Tuckner of the *New York Times* likened Westphal, a master baker from Germany, to "an oversized wiener schnitzel." (The lack of political correctness in 1960s sportswriting can be jarring.) Liston was about five inches taller and almost twenty pounds heavier.

Liston had predicted that he would make quick work of his opponent ("Eastphal or Westphal, that boy's gonna fall") and made good on that prediction less than two minutes into the first round. He landed a right hook that looked as if it had not just knocked Westphal out but also knocked him dead. Westphal slumped to his knees, toppled face-first onto the canvas, then lay motionless. "They could have counted fifty over him," Tuckner noted. When he regained his faculties Westphal said that his mind and body were intact "but my soul not so."

That's what Sonny Liston did to his opponents.

Liston had been reduced to fighting the likes of Albert Westphal because he had already dispatched every other viable heavyweight at that time except one—the titleholder, Floyd Patterson.

Patterson, whose popularity was the polar opposite of Liston's, staked out a moral high ground in avoiding a showdown. After beating Ingemar Johansson in March 1961, Patterson expressed concern about Liston's Mob connections. "I'm not looking to be bumped off," he said. Liston's counterpunch: "As far as I'm concerned Patterson is just afraid to fight me. . . . That's his way of avoiding me."

Liston had a point. Since claiming the vacant title in 1956, Patterson had fought just eight times—including three consecutive bouts with Johansson, in which Patterson lost the title, regained the title, and defended the title. During that same span Liston had fought eighteen times, against tougher competition (Westphal excepted).

By 1962 Patterson had run out of excuses. He had to fight Liston. Liston, who outweighed Patterson by twenty-four pounds, knocked the champion senseless in the first round at Chicago's Comiskey Park on September 25. Patterson was so humiliated that he left town wearing a fake beard. Ten months later they fought a contractually obligated rematch in Las Vegas. Few bettors were interested in Patterson, even at 7–1 odds. Liston kayoed him in the first round again.

Next in line was Muhammad Ali—or Cassius Clay, as he was still known. Merit appeared to have little to do with Clay's getting a title shot. He was simply, as Arthur Daley wrote in the *New York Times*, "the next victim in the Sonny Liston Hit Parade."

Clay, who had won a gold medal in the oxymoronic light-heavyweight division at the 1960 Olympics in Rome, was 19–0 as a pro. But, like Patterson, he had compiled his impressive résumé against a string of lesser opponents. His most recent bout had been against Henry Cooper, a 185-pound "British bleeder," at London's Wembley Stadium. Cooper scored a hard knockdown in the fourth round before Clay rallied for a TKO in the fifth.

Clay, just twenty-two, had insinuated himself into the heavyweight title picture as much through his antics as his fight acumen. He had earned the nickname the "Louisville Lip" for his boastful ways (he was already proclaiming himself "the greatest") and a bit of show-biz shtick: predicting in rhyme the round in which he would KO his opponent. Few boxing experts took him seriously. The odds were the same as they were for the second Liston–Patterson fight, 7–1.

In the days leading up to the fight Clay tormented Liston mercilessly. Everyone could see that he was putting on an act. The class clown was tweaking the class bully. But nearly everyone—including Sonny

Liston—missed the point. Most observers concluded that Clay's brashness was an overcompensation. At the weigh-in—when Clay pushed his outlandishness to new heights—the Miami Beach Boxing Commission's chief physician, Dr. Alexander Robbins, said, "This is a man who is scared to death. He is living in mortal fear."

Liston clearly believed that. He'd become so accustomed to knocking out his opponents without breaking a sweat that he had barely trained for the Clay fight. Which is just what Clay had hoped he would do. Liston expected to win an easy sprint. Instead, Clay made him run a grinding marathon.

Liston wasn't ready for it. By even the most conservative estimate, Liston was at least a decade older than Clay. His age showed. He'd had a knee injury that delayed the second Patterson fight, and was receiving treatments for bursitis in his shoulders.

But it wasn't just quickness and conditioning that set Clay apart from everyone else who had fought Sonny Liston. It was the way he was able to slip punches, his head bobbing like a pigeon's. He held his hands low—one of the reasons so many experts thought he stood no chance—inviting Liston's lethal jab, and then rescinding the invitation with a snap of his head. And then he would counterpunch, landing sharp, stinging blows repeatedly.

As the rounds wore on, Liston's breathing grew heavy, his face puffy. His left arm went numb. Clay had suckered him, and the psychological impact was devastating. It would have bothered Liston far less if Clay had knocked him cold with a first-round haymaker. Then Liston could have attributed the outcome to the puncher's chance that every contender has in theory. But to have his face systematically sliced and diced for six rounds was humiliating. He could neither catch that smart-mouthed punk nor stop him, and *everybody could see that.*

At the start of round seven, Liston remained on his stool. His corner claimed that an injury to his left arm made it impossible to continue.

Clay did a triumphant jig and then turned to the press at ringside. "Eat your words!" he yelled.

Many people suspected a fix. This was a backhanded show of respect for Liston. How could America's most intimidating ex-con get his ass kicked by a slapstick comedian? But it was also a product of the zeitgeist. Stories of Liston's criminal past, and of congressional investigations into boxing's sordid power structure, had dominated fight coverage for years. A deep cynicism had taken hold, similar to the public's attitude toward major league baseball in the wake of the steroids era. Any fight that didn't go according to form in the 1960s raised eyebrows, just as the performance of any baseball player who puts up outsized statistics does today.

The press and the politicians reinforced these suspicions in the aftermath of Clay's staggering upset. "There was no evidence that Liston had injured his arm," Harold Kaese wrote in the next day's *Boston Globe*. "He had thrown a great many lefts, especially in the fifth round, his best. Why did he quit? Because, perhaps, boxing is such a rotten, manipulated sport."

Florida's state attorney demanded copies of Liston's medical records, and members of Inter-Continental Promotions were paraded before yet another senate subcommittee to explain some questionable business practices.

In hindsight, the doubters look foolish. For one thing, Liston *had* injured his arm. A team of doctors diagnosed a torn left biceps tendon. More to the point, the press, almost to a man (there were no women sportswriters then), failed to recognize that Cassius Clay had pulled off a masterpiece, in both strategy and execution.

The backlash to the Miami Beach fight got worse when Clay confirmed that he had joined the Nation of Islam, and then changed his name to Muhammad Ali. In terms of public relations, he might as well have called himself Muhammad Antichrist.

All that negativity festered for fifteen months. By the time Ali and Liston met again, in Lewiston, the American public expected the worst. Many in the crowd at Lewiston thought that's what they got. Fred Gage, a local reporter who was covering the fight for WLAM radio, said the hostile reaction originated with a group of students from nearby Bates College—many of whom, apparently, had gotten in free. (Promoters later acknowledged that they had handed out 1,510 complimentary tickets; paid attendance was just 2,434.) "All the Bates kids were sitting together," Gage recalled almost fifty years later. "And as soon as it was over they started yelling, 'Fix! Fix! Fix!'"

They reacted so swiftly, said Gage, "It was almost as if they had prepared for it."

The reaction was similar at theaters around the country, where the fight was shown on closed-circuit TV. (Home pay-per-view was still in its infancy.) In California's Oakland Coliseum, the crowd "jeered only half-heartedly," wrote Sid Hoos of the *Hayward Daily Review*. "It was as though they expected to be cheated."

It wasn't just the spectators who were susceptible to the power of suggestion. Ali was, too. The cries of "Fix!" set him off. "I wanted the world to know I wasn't satisfied with [Liston] falling," he said afterward. "I wanted the world to know I had nothing to do with them thinking it was a fix."

Ali had been worried that all the talk of assassination attempts might rattle Liston and cause him to do something foolish. "You're going to scare Sonny," Ali had told reporters the day before the fight. "That man don't have the mind like I do. . . . I can cope with [the rumors]. But don't go scaring Sonny."

And now, in the first round, there was Liston, floundering on the canvas after a blow that Ali himself didn't think, in that dangerously charged moment, was sufficient to knock him out. Catcalls resounded through the tiny arena. Ali had burned to showcase his greatness; instead he felt as if he had been duped into participating in a bad vaudeville performance.

That ripped a hole in his pride. So instead of retreating to a neutral corner, as the rules required, he stood over Liston, yelling at him to get up and continue. (That's why he looks so angry in Neil Leifer's famous *Sports Illustrated* photo.)

The last dominoes fell quickly now, in all directions. When Liston hit the canvas, knockdown timer Francis McDonough was on the opposite end of the ring. McDonough started his stopwatch and signaled the count by banging a gavel at ringside, one blow per second.

That's what he was supposed to do. But it was not McDonough's responsibility to count Liston out. According to Maine Boxing Commission rules, the referee, former heavyweight champion Jersey Joe

Walcott, was the only person who had that authority. McDonough was basically just a human metronome, providing a steady one-beat-per-second rhythm so Walcott could keep an accurate count. If Walcott reached ten before Liston got up, the fight would be over.

Ali's refusal to go to a neutral corner complicated things. Walcott had the right—actually he had the duty—to suspend the count until Ali complied. There was precedent for this; in 1927 referee Dave Barry had correctly suspended the count for four seconds in the famous Jack Dempsey–Gene Tunney fight until Dempsey retreated to a neutral corner. Aided (perhaps) by the additional time, Tunney beat the ten count and went on to win.

To suspend the count, Walcott had only to look at McDonough and wave his arms with the palms down, like a football official signaling an incomplete pass. But he didn't. Nor did he ever make the chopping motion, in time with the gavel, that would have indicated he had begun the count. Instead he blundered after Ali, looking like a diffident parent trying to rein in his unruly child at the grocery store. Ali added to the scene's cartoonish aspect by cantering around the ring. At one point he suddenly jumped straight up, apropos of nothing.

The exasperated McDonough, given no indication that the referee could even hear the banging gavel, finally gave up altogether. Liston then staggered to his feet. Walcott, after wiping Liston's gloves, actually allowed the fight to resume. McDonough then implored Nat Fleischer, the seventy-seven-year-old editor of *Ring* magazine, to help him get Walcott's attention. In response to Fleischer's shouting, Walcott *turned his back on the fighters* and walked across the ring. It looked like a classic bit of campy wrestling theater: The hapless referee gets distracted, allowing the heel to pull a dirty trick.

It was bad enough that Walcott abandoned his post. He then compounded this error by abdicating his responsibility as the sole official with the authority to end the fight. "He's out!" Fleischer declared. And so, based on nothing more than a crusty old magazine editor's say-so, Walcott ran back, stepped between Ali and Liston, and called a halt.

The last domino had dropped. A self-fulfilling prophecy had come to pass. All the bad prefight publicity—the Mob owned Liston, Ali was a Black Muslim, Lewiston had no business hosting a world heavyweight title fight—led the closed-circuit TV people to fret about ticket sales at theaters nationwide, which in turn led them to fan a rumor that radicals connected with Malcolm X were going to kill Ali during the fight, which may well have frightened Sonny Liston to the point where he faked being knocked out so he could escape before the bullets flew, but which looked to the fans at ringside like he was taking the anticipated dive for the Mob, which led them to immediately chant "Fix! Fix! Fix!", which enraged Muhammad Ali to the point where he refused to go to a neutral corner, which caused the celebrity referee—who had been endorsed by both the Ali and Liston camps because, as a former heavyweight champion, he would bring credibility to the role and assuage fears that a small town like Lewiston wasn't up to the challenge of hosting a world heavyweight championship—to lose control of the bout and make it appear that the whole thing was a horribly orchestrated put-up job, held in a small town that wasn't up to the challenge of hosting a world heavyweight championship.

So, yes: The Ali–Liston bout in Lewiston had the most chaotic conclusion in heavyweight boxing history. But that doesn't necessarily mean that the outcome was contrived.

I contend that the chaos suggested the opposite. No one could have planned a mess like that. And even if Liston *did* take a dive, it didn't work. Twenty seconds after Liston hit the canvas, Walcott still hadn't counted to one, let alone ten, Ali was jumping around like a lunatic, and the crowd was spitting venom. At that point Sonny Liston was probably as befuddled as anyone else. So he stood up and squared off to fight again—and *then* Walcott said he was kayoed.

Later, when talking with Floyd Patterson, who visited him in his dressing room, Liston seemed determined to retain his dignity. Patterson, referring to the disguise he had worn on his way out of Chicago, told Liston, "You'll know now why I wore the beard. They ask all kinds of questions, and what can you answer?"

Liston's response: "I don't care. I won't wear a beard. I got up to fight again."

That would seem to provide a definitive answer as to whether or not he took a dive. But at different times Liston also offered the following explanations of what happened in Lewiston:

- "[Ali] was crazy. I didn't want anything to do with him. And the Muslims were coming up. Who needed that? So I went down. I wasn't hit."

- "I didn't quit. I got hit and hurt good. Clay's hand caught me high on the left cheekbone and I felt all screwed up. . . . It wasn't the hardest punch I ever took, but it was hard enough."

- "I just went down. I was waiting for the referee to pick up the count. Only he didn't."

- "I lost because Nat Fleischer said I lost."

- "Clay caught me cold and the count was messed up, and that's all there was to it. Clay knocked me down with a good punch. Anybody can get caught cold in the first round, before you even work up a sweat. And when I was down, Clay stood right over me. No, I never blacked out, not for a second. But I wasn't gonna get up, either, not with him standing over me. See, you can't get up without putting one hand on the floor, so I couldn't protect myself. He [could have] hit me on the way up."

The truth was malleable in Liston's massive hands. Maybe not even he fully understood what happened that night in Lewiston. And even if he did, we'll never know. He's been dead since sometime around the last day of 1970. Liston's wife, Geraldine, found his body in their Las Vegas home on January 5, 1971, when she returned from a weeklong trip. The cause of death was uncertain—drugs may or may not have been involved—and it was unclear whether he had died before or after the clock struck midnight to begin the new year.

That was a final, fitting twist. Sonny Liston had lived his life in such murky circumstances that even the years on his tombstone were just his survivors' best guesses.

So why write a book about a fight from fifty years ago that lasted barely two minutes and ended in a controversy that will never be resolved? For one thing, it's an opportunity to clear up the many lingering misconceptions—and build a solid circumstantial case for the most plausible explanation of what happened that night in Lewiston. It's also an opportunity to explain how the fight ended up in Lewiston in the first place, a vital part of the story that's never been fully told before.

I gathered that story's biggest bones in the fall of 2004 while researching an article for *Down East* magazine. My first stop was the Central Maine Youth Center, now called the Colisée. Scaffolding masked the exterior when I visited on a blustery Monday morning; the city had recently begun a $4 million renovation. The lighting inside was dim, and noise from the heavy equipment out front rumbled through the concrete-block walls. It was a building conducive to echoes.

At the time the Colisée was home of the Quebec Major Junior Hockey League's Lewiston MAINEiacs. I walked the perimeter of the ice rink, trying to match my vantage point to Neil Leifer's famous photo. It was harder than I'd thought it would be. Modern sports-marketing graphics, such as the MAINEiacs logo at center ice, clashed with the stark scene in my head. As I strained my mind's eye, trying to superimpose images of the past on the present, I thought of an old joke: *I went to a fight and a hockey game broke out.*

It was fitting that I would channel Rodney Dangerfield. In fight circles, Lewiston got no respect. Never mind that the city had punched well above its weight and landed a world heavyweight title fight— the smallest town to do so since Shelby, Montana, hosted the Jack Dempsey–Tommy Gibbons bout on the Fourth of July in 1923.

But Lewiston's coup was spun from the start not as an accomplishment for the town but as a diminishment of the fight. Even some local residents felt that way. "Lewiston is really nothing," a restaurant counterman named Ray LeCompte told the *Boston Globe*. "We're out in the sticks. A fight like this belongs in a big town like Boston, in a big building."

The fight was supposed to have been in Boston, but Massachusetts politicians ran it out of town, citing many of the same vague improprieties that had plagued the Clay–Liston bout in Miami Beach. When the second fight ended in a travesty that confirmed America's worst suspicions, Lewiston became guilty by association—the horse the fight rode in on. "Everybody kinda blamed it on us," said John Michael, whose father, Sam Michael, was the local co-promoter who had brought the fight to town. "It was a shoot-the-messenger kind of thing."

The media didn't even pretend to treat Lewiston fairly. "A dreadful little Maine back-tree town," columnist Jimmy Breslin called it. Even before the fight some Lewistonians were chagrined by the way the town was portrayed. Norman Thomas, longtime sports editor of the *Lewiston Evening Journal*, said many visiting reporters "show the signs of having been told, 'Get us a good story and MAKE IT FUNNY.'"

Together, all those Lewiston datelines during May 1965 painted an unflattering portrait. The most egregious distortion was that, as the "Fight Doctor," Ferdie Pacheco, later put it, "We were in a state where they knew nothing about boxing."

This was simply not true. Maine in general, and Lewiston in particular, had a rich boxing history. And few people in America had better connections in the fight game than Sam Michael. He had put on his first fight before Ferdie Pacheco was even born. It was a charity event that Sam had put together when he was still in high school, in 1922.

There couldn't have been a better time and place for a budding promoter to come of age. As Bill Bryson noted in *One Summer: America, 1927*, "People in 1920s America were unusually drawn to spectacle." This was the decade that gave birth to the modern sports celebrity. Babe Ruth, Red Grange, Jack Dempsey—all became larger than their already outsized lives.

But the Roaring Twenties fell silent with startling suddenness on October 29, 1929. Black Tuesday. Life suddenly got much tougher for millions of Americans, including Sam Michael. He thought big, but his circumstances were small. During the 1940s alone, Sam and his brother Joe promoted 126 fights in Lewiston. Some were at the local armory, but most were at Lewiston's City Hall Auditorium. That might seem strange today. Most people now think of city hall—when they think of it at all—as a place to cast a ballot or dispute a water bill. But many town halls built in the Victorian Era served as centers of local culture as well as government. People gathered for speeches, concerts—and boxing matches.

Lewiston City Hall, built in 1892, was an ideal venue for prize-fighting. The auditorium had 1,800 seats on the floor, with room for another 672 spectators in the galleries. "It was just like something out of those old black-and-white movies," said John Michael, who was about six years old when his father took him to his first fight at City Hall Auditorium. "The place seemed to be packed. You had the bright light over the ring, hanging down from the ceiling with a shade on it. I remember sitting at ringside with my dad, and there was a bar there, like a tire iron or a crowbar or something. And he let me ring the bell. He said, 'You ready? Go ahead and ring the bell!' So I took the crowbar and went *Ding!*"

Read the names of those who fought at Lewiston City Hall, and you feel like donning a fedora and sparking a cigar. You had Flash Boucher and Slasher Porter. Buster Beaupre and Busy Baker. Napoleon James and Romeo Rivard. Sailor McKinnon and Gunboat Steeves. Johnny Priest and Tommy Lawless. Smitty Hicks and Skeeter Corson. Cannonball Cote and Torpedo Reed. Big Boy Chabot and Pee Wee Martin. Mexican Joe Rivers and Young Al Cortez. Duke Demers and Ducky Dean and Lucky Griffin. Battling Murphy and Baby Tiger Flowers and Evan "Uppercut" Roy. Red Butts, Whitey O'Dell, Blue Nose Parent and a bunch of kids: Frisco Kid and Kid Beau Jack and Chick Kid Cloutier and Kid Norman and Kid Victory and Kid Bouthot, who once scored a TKO of Kid Roy.

The bouts weren't always tidy. Once, a guy named Stan Ketchell won a match despite being knocked cold; Smitty Hicks tagged him after the bell and was disqualified. Another time, three of the bouts on a five-fight card lasted less than two minutes each. Boxing was the riskiest sport to promote. Once that opening bell rang, every detail was beyond the promoter's control—including the length of the match. A baseball game lasted nine innings. A football game lasted sixty minutes. But a fight could end like *that*.

Take what happened during the main event at Lewiston City Hall on September 23, 1946, a scheduled eight-rounder between Al "Shiner" Couture and Ralph Walton. The two had some history; during a bout at City Hall in December 1944, Walton committed several fouls before being disqualified for attempting to knee Couture in the groin. "In the rematch, we almost had it out in the aisle before we got in the ring,"

Couture told the *Hartford Courant* years later. "The guy wanted at me, and I wanted at him."

That should have made the rematch a promoter's dream. But Walton—perhaps distracted by the prefight altercation—forgot to put in his mouthpiece. His corner man yelled to him just as the opening bell rang. "He turned and froze," Couture told the *Courant*. "Bang. I nailed him."

KO.

BoxRec.com, the closest thing to an official record of this wild and undisciplined pastime, lists the time of the bout at fourteen seconds, including the ten count. But according to local legend, the fight lasted just ten-and-a-half seconds. If that's true, then Sam Michael would have the dubious honor of having promoted the shortest fight in the history of professional boxing as well as the most notorious one. Both of them right there in Lewiston.

L ewiston City Hall also hosted fights of a different kind. Sam got involved in his share of those too. In 1956 he became Lewiston's industrial development director—what would now be called the director of economic development. It was an unusual career move but an intriguing one. Sam had no experience in politics or government—although, at age fifty, he had just finished law school. (He never did open a practice. "I'm guessing that would have been too boring for him," John said.) Basically, instead of promoting the likes of Shiner Couture and Cannonball Cote, he would promote the City of Lewiston itself.

That decision said a lot about Sam Michael. Given his résumé and his obvious ambition, he could have gone elsewhere and done well for himself. But he didn't want to leave. He felt at home in Lewiston and wanted to try to help the town reverse the slow decline that had begun when the textile industry headed south after World War I. For the vast majority in Lewiston, life had always been hard—even "the good old days" had meant working sixty hours a week in dirty, dangerous factories and living in crowded tenement houses. But that very closeness, and the shared hardships, had also forged strong bonds. Only someone who had lived a long time in Lewiston, that "dreadful little Maine back-tree town," could understand its appeal.

Like the old ice arena, Lewiston's Victorian city hall—where Sam Michael orchestrated so many fights of one kind or another—still stands. While visiting one day, I asked Phil Nadeau, the deputy city administrator, what had become of the auditorium. He took me up to the top floor, which looked at first glance like standard retrofitted office space: partitioned cubicles beneath a suspended ceiling. But there was another level above that, where the insulation and heating ducts were. It was accessible only by a dark stairwell. We ascended through the gloom—and there it was: the tin ceiling of the old City Hall Auditorium, in all its peeling, decayed splendor. The abandoned galleries sat on either side.

It was here, in this hidden-away place, that Sam Michael had taken the first tentative steps that eventually lured Muhammad Ali and Sonny Liston to Maine.

I had a feeling like déjà vu—except that the vague familiarity I felt was for a time before I was born and a place I had never seen. My goal in writing this book was to create a similar sensation. I wanted to convey what it felt like to be in Lewiston during that surreal month of May 1965, when the heavyweight championship of the world came to town.

—Rob Sneddon, February 2015

PART ONE

CHAPTER ONE

Welcome to Lewiston, Where Life is Harder than It Looks

Maybe it was his encounter with the old Frenchman that made Sam Michael want to live in Lewiston. Maybe that tapped into something comforting that made him feel grounded again.

Sam had bounced around since graduating from trade school. He'd worked at a service station operated by the Reo Motor Company, makers of the Reo Speed Wagon. He'd spent time in the Pacific Northwest installing apple-canning equipment. Now he was back in his hometown of Lowell, Massachusetts, working as an installer for a textile-machine manufacturer that dispatched him to factories around New England. That's what brought him to the Lombard Watson shoe factory in Lewiston, Maine, where he watched the old Frenchman operate some sort of trimmer. The Frenchman worked with a fluidity that came from years of practice. Sam enjoyed watching him.

"Hey," Sam said, "I'd like to be able to do that."

"Here, kid," the Frenchman said. "Try it."

So Sam did. The machine snatched the shoe out of his hands and threw it at the ceiling.

The Frenchman laughed. "Harder than it looks, isn't it, kid?" he said.

Yes, Lewiston might just be the place for Sam. It was far enough from home to give him his independence. (He was one of fourteen kids.) But it was also familiar. Like Lowell, Lewiston was an old textile town with a French Canadian heritage—only more so. Since the late

1860s, when laborers began pouring in from Quebec and New Brunswick to work in the mills that had sprouted along the Androscoggin River, few cities had been better suited to a specific group of immigrants. Entire neighborhoods, known collectively as *Le Petite Canada*, spoke French. They had their own newspaper, *Le Messager*. Newcomers arriving by rail from Montreal stepped off the train at the Grand Trunk Station and into a neighborhood where the language, the names on the shops, and even the smells evoked the land they'd left behind. The eclectic architecture, including touches of French Imperialism on the imposing mill buildings, looked like old Europe. And although Sam wasn't French Canadian—his parents were Lebanese—he was comfortable with the culture.

So: Lewiston it was. Sam moved there at the height of the Roaring Twenties, right around the time he reached his own roaring twenties. He would call either Lewiston or Auburn, its sister city across the Androscoggin, home for the rest of his life.

Sam started at Lombard Watson as a shoe-edge trimmer. But he always had more than one job. Always had an angle. Always looked for an edge. When the Depression hit, he opened a pawnshop at 276 Lisbon Street, right in the heart of town.

And, from the beginning, he scouted out the local boxing scene. That was another thing he liked about Lewiston. Like Lowell, it was a good fight town. Sam was never a boxer himself. He had a way of letting you know that he *could* throw a punch if you pushed him too far. But he preferred to talk. Negotiating; that was his thing. Now, if only he could find the right fighter to manage.

What did Sam see in this kid? He was a loser. In eleven bouts since turning professional—if you could call it that—Maurice "Lefty" LaChance had won just three times, with five defeats and three draws. It was not a record that should have appealed to an ambitious fight manager—particularly when there were so many other up-and-comers to choose from. Boxing had a special appeal during the Depression. All over America, aspiring Cinderella Men fought in grim, smoky halls for a few extra dollars and a modicum of self-esteem.

Maine had more than its share. In Lewiston, the mills were in
decline even before the crash of '29. There were plenty of working-class
French Canadian or Irish immigrants willing to climb into the ring
and try to earn a living doing what they had once done for free, at the
taverns around town. Some, figuring they had little left to lose, fought
an ungodly number of times. By the time he was through, Paul Labbe
Jr., a Quebec native who fought out of Lewiston under the name Paul
Junior, claimed a career record of 476–17.

And some of them started ungodly young. Maybe that's what Sam
saw in Lefty LaChance (a "southpaw," in the language of the sports section), from Lisbon Falls, just along the Androscoggin. *Potential.* Lefty
was a featherweight, wiry as a sack of coat hangers. And, like Sam,
who had promoted his first boxing match back in Lowell while still in
his teens, Lefty was precocious. He was just fourteen when he had his
first pro fight. It was at an anarchic little place called the Punchbowl,
in Lewiston's Dominican Block. Built in the nineteenth century in the
heart of Lewiston's Franco-American district, the Dominican Block was
a Queen Anne-style brick building at the corner of Lincoln and Chest-
nut streets. It was originally a Catholic school, but by the Depression a
guy named Pa Kearns had turned it into a school of hard knocks.

Kearns had promoted boxing events throughout the Lewiston–
Auburn area for several years before landing in the Punchbowl. His
primary motivation might simply have been to give his son, Young Pa
Kearns, a place to fight legally. In any case, his promotions were not
just unvarnished but also unsanded. At one Kearns production, in New
Auburn in 1928, K.O. Peletier rushed Al Nadeau with such gusto at
the opening bell that the ropes broke, causing a delay. Later that night,
to fill out the card, Pa Kearns himself had to substitute for a no-show.
(His opponent was someone named Newsboy Charlifou.) For all that,
the *Lewiston Evening Journal* called it "easily the best show the Auburn
promoter has ever put on."

The night Lefty LaChance made his debut, in April 1936,
"Flash Dutil was picked from the crowd to referee," the *Evening
Journal* reported. LaChance lost that bout, to Kid Miller. He had
two more fights at the Punchbowl that year and lost both of those

as well—including a first-round knockout at the hands of Harold Gooldrup, who went by the name "Frisco Kid" even though he lived in Auburn.

LaChance later recalled that his first fight paid a dollar—in quarters. "If you come next week," Pa Kearns allegedly told him, "I'll give you $1.50."

Lefty's first official victory came at age fifteen in Lewiston City Hall "against some kid from Waterville who was doing well. I beat him in four rounds and got a five-dollar bill. I was hooked."

In those days Lefty trained in a friend's garage. "We had to push four cars out and then push them back in after we had finished," he later recalled. "That helped build muscles."

Once Lefty teamed up with Sam, he began to distinguish himself in Maine's congested featherweight division. By the spring of 1941, at age nineteen, he had gone unbeaten in nineteen straight bouts. That earned him a shot at the Maine state title against Old Town's Henry LeGasse, a regular on Bangor's busy fight scene since 1933.

That bout, at Lewiston's City Hall Auditorium on April 17, 1941, was noteworthy for another reason. It was Sam Michael's first promotion of record. No doubt frustrated by the often shoddy level of area boxing programs, he had decided that he could do better himself. (He addressed the conflict of interest inherent in promoting a bout headlined by his own fighter by having Chick Hayes, a longtime Portland boxing impresario, serve as official matchmaker.)

This was the review of Sam's debut as a fight promoter in the next day's *Evening Journal*:

LEWISTON FIGHT FANS SEE NOVEL PROGRAM
A fight card which started on time, had no substitutes, and presented a great battle in every bout was the tasty dish pushed out to Lewiston–Auburn boxing fans last night at City Hall. It was the first show staged by Sammy Michaels *[sic]* . . .

The article also noted that Sam would have to work hard to win over jaded fight fans: "Lewiston folks have to 'be shown' as the result of some of the boxing adventures staged here."

The report mentioned, in passing, that Lefty LaChance was Maine's new featherweight champion.

The next two years streaked past in a rush of color and growing excitement. Sam continued to promote occasional matches at City Hall Auditorium. LaChance, his rising star, almost always got top billing. Sam also took Lefty on the road, with bouts in Boston, New York, New Jersey, and Connecticut. Finally, on April 9, 1943, LaChance fought Rhode Island's Tony Costa for the New England featherweight title. A win could catapult Lefty to a national ranking.

The fight was in Lewiston. Due to the high level of local interest, the bout was held not at city hall but at the armory, which had a larger capacity. The *Lewiston Daily Sun* reported that a "record-breaking crowd of nearly 5,000 people" turned out for "one of the best fights seen in here in years."

Cars and buses jammed the streets, and the concession stand ran out of Cokes. Food items included Italian sandwiches, which *Evening Journal* reporter Rose O'Brien claimed "blended beautifully with the smoke." O'Brien said the pall was so thick that "you were doing good to see the ring . . . let alone trying to get a squint of the rafters."

O'Brien also wrote this: "Nobody saw Sam Michael breathe during the twelve-round final."

The fight was close. Costa had a slight advantage in round one, landing a few more feeling-out punches than LaChance did. (LaChance, who had been forced to take a week off before the fight because he'd suffered a cut eye in a sparring session, was rusty.) Round two looked even until Lefty landed a hard right to the body, followed by his signature left hook to the chin. LaChance caught Costa with another left hook in the third, bloodying his nose, but Costa recovered and outpunched Lefty the rest of the way to win the round. LaChance won the fourth by a slight margin.

And so it went. Going into the last round, LaChance was ahead on the *Evening Journal* scorecard, six to five. The paper scored round twelve even. "From our bench on the Sabattus Street side of the Armory, LaChance earned the verdict but by a margin so undernourished that we wouldn't have been surprised had the officials called it a draw," said the paper's unbylined reporter.

But all three judges scored LaChance the winner. At age thirty-seven, after harboring aspirations in the boxing game for more than twenty years, Sam Michael was managing a fighter with a legitimate shot at a world title.

On August 16, 1943, Phil Terranova, a tough New Yorker destined for the World Boxing Hall of Fame, fought reigning champion Jackie Callura for the National Boxing Association featherweight title in New Orleans. Callura was leading after seven rounds, but Terranova surprised him with a furious combination in the eighth to win by knockout.

Five weeks later, at the Outdoor Arena in Hartford, Connecticut, Terranova fought Lefty LaChance. In what *Ring* magazine called "a thrilling fight from start to finish," LaChance won a unanimous ten-round decision. Sam's man had beaten a world featherweight champ.

Then, in a sequence that would typify the rest of Sam's boxing career, things went awry.

The Terranova–LaChance fight was a nontitle bout. But the custom—and Sam's expectation—was that Terranova would grant LaChance a rematch, this time for the belt. There were complications, however. It had been almost two years since Pearl Harbor. World War II still raged, with no end in sight. LaChance had been called up to serve and was set to report to Parris Island, South Carolina, to join the Marine Corps in October. That left the status of the Terranova rematch—and of Lefty's relationship with Sam—in doubt.

On the way home from Hartford after the Terranova fight, Sam and Lefty stayed at Sam's mother's house in Lowell. A reporter for the *Lowell Sun*, Frank Moran, caught up with them the next day and wrote an especially fawning piece. Sam, Moran wrote, "is a great fellow, has an unusually pleasant personality, and is a true sportsman."

The article said little about LaChance's title prospects. Instead, both LaChance and Sam said that Lefty's highest priority was to serve his country. "There are millions of guys just like me sacrificing their lives," said LaChance. "I'm no better than they are, and I feel that my place is with them. I'm supposed to be a fairly good fighter. I intend to find out if I really am."

Said Sam, "Lefty is like a son to me. I'll miss him plenty, but I want him to take part in the greatest fight of his career."

With a young wife (Jeanne) and an infant daughter (Doris) to support, Lefty wanted one last payday before leaving for the Marines. So he agreed to fight Newark, New Jersey's Ike Williams, a devastating puncher whom the Associated Press later named the fourth-greatest lightweight of the twentieth century. It was a reckless move; LaChance jeopardized his status as a top featherweight contender by fighting above his weight class against an opponent capable of inflicting real damage. (A newspaper report several months later intimated that LaChance took the fight without Sam's knowing.)

The fight, scheduled for ten rounds at Boston's Mechanic's Hall, got off to a promising start for Lefty. In the third, he landed a hard left to Williams's stomach. The *Boston Globe*'s Clif Keane, employing textbook 1940s boxing prose, reported that "the Newark Thunderbolt was on queer street."

But Keane also wrote that LaChance was "badly outclassed." And when Williams returned from queer street, still standing and with his senses intact, the difference in class showed. In the fourth, Williams hit LaChance with an overwhelming barrage, finishing with a right to the head that "poured in over LaChance's covered body," Keane wrote.

The upshot was a brutal knockout. LaChance was a mess when he went off to the Marines.

Still, Sam tried to arrange a title bout with Terranova. He cleared what would seem to have been the biggest hurdle by securing permission from the Marine Corps for LaChance to fight. But a higher authority intervened. The National Boxing Association decreed that Terranova had to fight a rematch with Jackie Callura before LaChance could get his chance. The Terranova–Callura rematch was scheduled for December 27, meaning Lefty wouldn't get a title shot until sometime in 1944.

Given the uncertainty of the war, there was no telling where LaChance would be by then. So, with his fighter in the Marine Corps and his career in limbo—and with his country facing its greatest threat in his lifetime—Sam Michael decided to enlist in the Army, at age thirty-eight. That winter, the *Lowell Sun* wrote that Sam had "withdrawn, temporarily, from the sports picture. He is now helping Uncle Sam with Word War II, being stationed at Fort Knox in Kentucky with a medical unit. . . . We know he's done a great job guiding [Lefty]

LaChance from a novice into a ranking position in the boxing world and we know he'll do just as good a job for Uncle Sam. He's a good boy!"

But just as Sam was going into the military, LaChance was getting out. An examination had found that problems with his feet and his ears—whether from the Williams bout or those early beatings at the Punchbowl or the cumulative effect of all those punches at such an early age—had rendered him unfit for service. Following his honorable discharge he went back to Lewiston and resumed his boxing career on his own. Sam, on the other hand, passed his physical ("with very high rating," the *Evening Journal* reported) and stayed in for the duration.

Sam and Lefty eventually reconnected, but the moment had passed. Lefty was never again a contender. And although he was still relatively young when he retired, at twenty-eight, he had been a professional boxer for half his life and had fought 218 times. He won 140 bouts and lost sixty-two, with sixteen draws. He had been knocked out thirty-five times.

Like many Lewiston-area boxers, Lefty remained close to Sam for the rest of his life. In 1987, when Lefty was inducted into the Maine Sports Hall of Fame, Sam was his presenter. During his induction speech, Lefty said the Terranova fight in September 1943 was the high-light of his life.

CHAPTER TWO

Every Heavyweight Champ and His Brother

After the war Sam poured most of his energy into promoting rather than managing. Staking everything on a single fighter was too risky. If your guy got hurt or waylaid for some other reason, you were out of luck. And the odds of getting a title shot were just too long.

Sam turned forty in January 1946. He had been married and divorced and was ready to reset his life. His days of chasing the boxing dream across New England and beyond were over. Better to try to entice boxing dreamers to Lewiston instead.

Monday night became Fight Night. Sam staged forty-one cards at City Hall Auditorium in 1946, and two others at the armory. In addition to the fights, Sam also promoted music shows, wrestling matches, barnstorming basketball troupes, and other entertainment spectacles. (One of the acts that Sam and his entertainment partner, Sam Ruttenberg, once brought to Lewiston was the Will Mastin Trio, featuring a young dancer named Sammy Davis Jr. The Trio had a weeklong engagement at a place called the Beacon Ballroom, aka the French Casino. The two Sams had to put the three entertainers up in a private home because at that time, before World War II, none of the local hotels would accept black guests. Sam Michael and Sammy Davis Jr. turned heads around town when they went out for an ice cream together.)

But even with—or perhaps because of—Sam's relentless promotion, local boxing produced diminishing returns. How many times could Lewistonians watch the same shopworn fighters? Sam tried to inject new blood into the sport by conducting annual youth tournaments.

He commissioned something called the Michael Trophy, with the idea of awarding it each year to the city's most promising amateur. But only diehard fans wanted to track unknown contenders through the ranks. And at $1.80 per head, there weren't enough diehards to make weekly boxing matches profitable.

In April 1948 Sam and his brother Joe opened a luncheonette on Court Street in Auburn. And in June Sam got married again, to Doris DeCoster, a New England Telephone and Telegraph employee who was eighteen years his junior.

All of which probably explains why in May 1948 Sam abruptly dropped his regular Monday night boxing cards. Over the next five months he promoted just two bouts while remaining mum on his next move. On October 21, *Evening Journal* sports editor Norman Thomas reported in his "Sport Sandwich" column that Sam "will only operate when he can get main bouts that are especially promising."

Such as?

Five days later, the headline over the *Evening Journal*'s sports section blared the answer:

JOE LOUIS TO FIGHT AT ARMORY ON NOVEMBER 5

As always, Sam aimed high. If the idea was to bring in big names, why not bring in the biggest? Boxers didn't get any bigger than Joe Louis in the 1940s. Louis hadn't lost in twelve years and had held the heavyweight title since knocking out Jimmy Braddock in 1937. He had surpassing power, with a dozen first-round knockouts. One of those had happened at Yankee Stadium in 1938 against Max Schmeling, pride of the Nazis.* At a time when casual racism still pervaded even the best-lit corners of American life, Louis's victory over the symbol of Hitler's evil

---

* Although he was a native German who later served in the Luftwaffe, Schmeling was not in fact a Nazi. To the contrary; he risked his life to save several Jews from Nazi persecution. He became good friends with Louis and later realized that losing that 1938 title bout might have been the best thing that ever happened to him. "Just imagine if I would have come back to Germany with a victory," he said in 1975. "I had nothing to do with the Nazis, but they would have given me a medal."

regime made it "acceptable" for white America to cheer for him. The *Evening Journal*'s take was typical: "Joe, as you readers well know, has always been a credit to his race. He's been a clean living chap who has demonstrated to the public that a top notch mit man doesn't have to be a rough-coarse type."

Louis fought sparingly as he aged. He'd had just four championship defenses in the past two years, all in New York. Not even Sam Michael was idealistic enough, in 1948, to think that Lewiston could host a Joe Louis title fight—or any heavyweight title fight. But back then it was common for the heavyweight champ to barnstorm the country in between title bouts, staging exhibition matches. Sam wagered that plenty of Lewistonians would pay handsomely—top tickets were $4.80—to see the great Joe Louis, in his imposing and exotic (for Maine in the 1940s) brown flesh, right there in their hometown.

So Sam devoted much of his energy in the fall of 1948 to turning Lewiston into Louiston. The Champ's four-round exhibition bout with Boston's Willie James would highlight a card at the armory on the first Friday in November.

As usual, Sam's instincts were correct. And as usual, his luck was lousy.

On Wednesday, November 3, while the *Chicago Tribune* was making erroneous headlines (DEWEY DEFEATS TRUMAN), the *Lewiston Evening Journal* carried news of Joe Louis's impending arrival. The champ was scheduled to fly into Portland at noon on Thursday. From there he would visit the Healy Asylum (a Roman Catholic orphanage) and the Lewiston–Auburn Children's Home, and perhaps address an assembly at St. Dominic's High School. In addition, the *Evening Journal* reported, "Numerous local sports fans and citizens have volunteered to take the champion on brief hunting trips during his stop here. Promoter Michael has been besieged by local people who wish to entertain the champion at their homes."

But Thursday brought only bad news. Sam got a call from Louis's tour manager, Harry Mendel, informing him that Louis had a cold and would have to postpone the visit a week. The following Monday, Louis suffered a small cut in an exhibition bout in Boston. The next night in New Haven, the cut got bigger. Louis's physician, Dr. Clarence Hogan, ordered the champ to skip Lewiston again—indefinitely, this time.

It was a gut punch. "The advance sale was by far the largest that has ever been seen here," the *Evening Journal* reported. "The actual cash in hand was enough to take care of the guarantee to be paid to the champion. . . . [It] was certain to make the evening's cash return the largest in the history of the Maine fight game. It is one of those breaks which put gray hair on the promoters' heads."

Lewiston was bumped to the last date on Louis's barnstorming tour: December 20. The Monday before Christmas. That wasn't nearly as good as the first Friday in November, but it was better than nothing.

And even that date proved problematic.

Louis was supposed to fly out of New York's LaGuardia Field on Sunday afternoon, December 19. But a blizzard brought almost twenty inches of snow to New York that day and shut the airport down. To his credit, Louis didn't give up. He booked a 9:00 p.m. train out of Grand Central Station. He rode all night through the diminishing snow (about ten inches in Boston, just a dusting in Maine), arriving at Portland's Union Station at 6:05 Monday morning.

Sam was waiting. He picked up Louis and Mendel, along with Marshall Miles, Louis's manager; Manny Seamon, Louis's trainer; and Kiah Sayles, Louis's longtime confidant, and drove them all to Lewiston, where they checked in at the DeWitt Hotel, the city's finest.

It was a long day. Louis kept his promise to visit Healy Asylum (a photo of the Champ surrounded by a crescent of suspendered boys led the *Daily Sun*'s sports section the next day) and also made several other stops, including the *Evening Journal* office.

And still Sam's troubles weren't quite over. A news report that day alleged that Louis owed the IRS a significant amount of back taxes. Louis issued a terse denial before the fight and left the armory without comment afterward. In between, he belted poor Willie James with uncharacteristic vigor for an exhibition match, even opening a cut over James's right eye in the second round. "He's mad," Mendel said at ringside. "That's why he's hitting that kid so hard."

The paid attendance of 3,600 was short of the sellout Sam might have had in November. But those who came got their money's worth. Norman Thomas reported that Lewiston gave Joe Louis "the greatest ovation any fighter ever drew forth when he paraded down from the dressing room and into the ring."

Joe Louis announced his retirement on March 1, 1949. Ezzard Charles beat Jersey Joe Walcott for the vacated title that June. Facing money problems, Louis came out of retirement to challenge Charles in September 1950.

For the first time since 1936, Joe Louis lost. The heavyweight title belt's luster faded.

In March 1951 Charles beat Walcott again. Just four months later they met for a third time. Walcott—a Camden, New Jersey, native whose nickname could well have been Journeyman Joe Walcott—won the title in a startling upset.

Six months later Sam brought Walcott to Lewiston for a five-round exhibition bout against Jack Burke of Pittsburgh. This time there were no problems to speak of. Walcott put on a good show for a crowd of 3,400 at the armory on Saturday night. "He displayed the fighting style that carried him to the top, a prancing, herky-jerky, hippity-hop manner that probably is not duplicated in any ring in the world today," wrote *Daily Sun* reporter Ted Taylor. He also "tossed in a lot of clowning."

Purely from a PR perspective, it was hard to imagine a boxing promotion turning out any better. For years afterward Jersey Joe Walcott and Lewiston would form a pleasant association in Sam's mind.

That would abruptly change.

On March 19, 1952, just two months after Walcott's visit, Sam brought another nationally known fighter to town. He wasn't the heavyweight champion—yet. But his time was so ripe that the *Evening Journal* announced his arrival this way:

FUTURE WORLD'S MIT CHAMP HERE FOR EXHIBITION

Rocky Marciano was 39–0, with all but five victories having come by knockout. Five months earlier he had kayoed an aging Joe

Louis—becoming just the second boxer to knock the Brown Bomber out. Clearly it was only a matter of time before he belted his way to the belt.

Marciano was from Brockton, Massachusetts, another tough New England fight town. He had hitchhiked to Portland one summer to work for a contracting company for eighty cents an hour. Lewiston fight fans would *love* a guy like that. (Marciano was also white, which the *Evening Journal* pointed out with an indelicacy typical of the time. Marciano, the paper wrote "looks like a future world's champion after the colored boys get through making a little money for themselves.") So when Sam and his promotional partner at that time, John Rogers, had a chance to bring Marciano to the City Hall Auditorium as he kicked off a barnstorming tour through Maine, of course they agreed.

A story the day before the fight identified Marciano's opponent as "Pete Fuller, son of ex-governor [Alvan T.] Fuller of Massachusetts."

"Pete wanted to be a professional boxer," the story went on, "but followed to his parents' desires and remained an amateur. Very capable with his mits, he trains with the pros and keeps in great fighting condition."

On the facing page an ad listed ticket prices ($1.80–$4.80) and the start time (8:45). It made no mention of Marciano's opponent. A story in the next day's *Evening Journal* said that Fuller would be Marciano's "sparring partner."

The exhibition was well received. Ted Taylor, writing in the *Daily Sun*, said it was better than either the Joe Louis or Joe Walcott matches. "Marciano and Fuller apparently are familiar with each other's styles," Taylor wrote, "and most of last night's spectators were agreed that's a good way to have it if it's going to look like a fight."

Norman Thomas also gave the exhibition a positive review, but with a cryptic twist. He described Marciano's opponent as "a 'Pete Fuller,' but definitely not ex-Governor Fuller's son."

Duncan MacDonald of the Maine Boxing Commission also noticed that Marciano's opponent was not, in fact, *that* Pete Fuller.

A small story in the Boston *Post* solved the mystery. Marciano's eighteen-year-old brother, Sonny Marchegiano (he retained the original spelling of the family name), revealed that he was "Pete Fuller." Said Sonny, "The cards were up advertising Peter Fuller when we found out he couldn't appear without ruining his amateur standing. So I filled in. The people liked it. We gave them a show."

Last-minute substitutes and assumed names were not unusual in local boxing, going back to the days of Pa Kearns vs. Newsboy Charlifou. Subs were particularly common in exhibition bouts; during Jersey Joe Walcott's appearance at the armory earlier that year, Jack Burke had been a last-minute fill-in for Walcott's sparring partner, Harry Wills. But people had paid to see Walcott, not Wills. Nothing was at stake anyway, so it was no big deal.

This time, however, the Maine Boxing Commission decided to make it a big deal. They summoned Rocky Marciano, the world's top heavyweight contender, back to Maine for a hearing at Augusta in April. Sam was also ordered to appear, along with Rogers, before MBC chairman Julius Greenstein of Portland; commissioner MacDonald of Bangor; and commissioner John Magee of Brunswick.

At the hearing, Marciano admitted that it was his idea to box his brother. He said he wasn't trying to deceive anyone; he just tried to offer a solution when Fuller backed out at the last minute. He told the commission that Sam "seemed to think it was all right."

Marciano said he didn't want Sonny's name used "because my mother doesn't appreciate his fighting and I didn't want any press account of it."

He added: "We gave them a very good show. I punched [Sonny] as hard as I punched Joe Louis."

The commissioners were unswayed. They suspended Marciano's Maine boxing license for thirty days. And because the MBC was a member of the National Boxing Association, the suspension was effective nationwide. It would begin following Marciano's scheduled bout with Bernie Reynolds in Providence on May 12.

Sam, who refused to testify at the hearing because he didn't like the ground rules (he wouldn't be allowed to offer an explanation—he could only answer whatever questions the commission deigned to ask) had his matchmaking license suspended six months for "deception and fraudulent misrepresentations." But unlike Marciano, he fought back. The previous fall he had enrolled at Portland Law School. This would be a good opportunity to practice some of what he had learned.

On May 1 Sam issued a statement of his intent to challenge the Maine Boxing Commission in court. Although he admitted that he'd had a lapse of good judgment, he said he had done so with no bad intent. Further, he contended that because the bout was an exhibition and not a true contest, he had not violated any MBC rule.

Sam's statement said:

> If I have been guilty of violating a law or a rule of the Boxing Commission, *"Fiat Justitia, rual coelum,"* meaning "Let right be done though the heavens should fall."
>
> As an individual who has been identified with sports promotions, and with every phase of boxing for thirty years or more, I feel that to permit the Commission's broad assertion of "deception and fraudulent misrepresentations" to go unchallenged is a reflection upon my integrity and character. I have held licenses as a referee, promoter, manager, and second in all of the New England states, as well as in other states, such as New York, New Jersey, in some Southern states, and out west in California, Oregon, and Washington, and never at any time during all these years was I ever called to appear before any of these commissions for violating any rules, or [for] unethical practices.
>
> As a law student, and as a reasonably prudent man, I am aware that there is a fundamental presumption that public officers perform their duty and do not abuse their discretion or exceed their lawful authority. However, in the instant case, the Commission has gravely erred . . . with the result that my good name together with the names of other honorable and upright and well known men has been besmirched idly with charges of "deception and fraudulent misrepresentations."
>
> These charges should be clearly proved in order to be of any avail. . . . I have, therefore, instructed my attorney, Benjamin J. Arena, to take the necessary steps, and to arrange if possible for an early hearing so that I may have the opportunity of clearing my name.

The hearing was held in Augusta on June 13, 1952, before Superior Court Justice Edward P. Murray. Special Assistant Attorney

General Herbert Sawyer represented the Maine Boxing Commission. None of the commissioners themselves saw fit to attend.

Sawyer started by outlining the MBC's case. Or at least he tried to; Justice Murray interrupted and told him to skip the speechmaking and call his witnesses. First up was Sonny Marchegiano.

Sawyer asked Sonny how he had been introduced during the Maine barnstorming tour. Sonny said he couldn't remember.

Next, Portland promoter Chick Hayes testified that he had prepared the press releases identifying Marciano's sparring partner as "Pete Fuller." He said he had received the information from Sam's partner, John Rogers, who had heard it from Marciano's people. Hayes said he assumed that "Pete Fuller" was ex-governor's Fuller's son, a popular amateur, so that's what he told the press.

When it was his turn to speak, Arena, like Sawyer, tried to summarize his case. He began by stressing what appeared to be a salient point: "It was a boxing exhibition, not a boxing contest."

Sawyer objected. Justice Murray sustained. "Excluded," he said.

Arena then asked Hayes to describe what had taken place during the Portland stop on the tour. The Marciano/Marchegiano brothers boxed four rounds, said Hayes, "in an exhibition."

Justice Murray rebuked Hayes and told him that he couldn't say "exhibition" either. So Hayes simply described all the attributes of an exhibition without saying the word. He categorized what took place between Rocky and Sonny in their Maine matches as "four two-minute rounds with no decision and [both boxers] wearing big sixteen-ounce gloves."

He also testified that no commission member ever asked to see either brother's license. When he reiterated to Arena that he had simply assumed "Pete Fuller" was the amateur fighter from Boston, Sawyer interrupted: "Then you were duped!"

That brought a loud objection from Arena, and Justice Murray halted the exchange. He had trouble making himself heard above the commotion.

A little later Sawyer charged that Sam's only purpose in asking for a public hearing was to embarrass the commission. Arena: "They ought to be embarrassed!"

Again Justice Murray stepped in like a referee and sent the combatants to neutral corners.

Finally, when Arena began his closing statement, Justice Murray cut him off: "Don't argue anymore. I can't see that the state has made out a case."

He ordered Sam's suspension lifted.

In his report on the case, Norman Thomas wrote: "Let's have some new boxing commissioners here in Maine. Let's have some who have the courage of their convictions, have nothing to hide, and have the good manners and courage to appear when their high and mighty rulings are questioned."

Boxing promotions in Maine were not for the timid.

Six months after being suspended by the Maine Boxing Commission, Rocky Marciano knocked out Jersey Joe Walcott in Philadelphia to become heavyweight champion of the world. He retired undefeated in 1956, with a record of 49–0.

As a tribute, the Maine Legislature encouraged the state's boxing commission to expunge Marciano's suspension.

Commissioner Duncan MacDonald refused.

CHAPTER THREE

A Different Kind
of Promotion for a
Different Kind of Fight

The Marciano experience dimmed Sam's enthusiasm for local boxing promotions. The growth of televised boxing during the 1950s extinguished it. TV had already killed Sam's interest in music promotion. Much as he enjoyed bringing the Dorsey brothers and Guy Lombardo and other big-name acts to Lewiston, he cashed out when such shows sank into the red. (Driven by a passion for music, Sam's show-biz partner decided to go it alone and suffered heavy losses, confirming the wisdom of Sam's philosophy: "Never fall in love with a promotion.")

At fifty, Sam was ready for a career change. He had just finished law school. He had five kids and owned a house on Summer Street in Auburn. He had become a prominent citizen; among other organizations, he belonged to St. Philips Church, the American Legion, the Lions Club, the Elks, and the Police Athletic League. He cared about his adopted hometown and worried about its future.

Like many other northern industrial cities, Lewiston owed its development to an economy that wasn't far from feudalism. During the city's boom years as a textile center, from 1850 through World War I, a small group of wealthy businessmen, many from out of state, owned not only the mill buildings but also the tenements that housed the workers. They controlled the rights to waterpower from the Androscoggin River. And, as the city's predominant source of tax revenue, they wielded substantial influence in local government. So while a select few got rich from Lewiston's mills, thousands of others lived lives of grim subsistence. Still, for a French Canadian immigrant, the mills provided the only practical, stable means to feed, clothe, and house a large Roman Catholic family.

The dangers of monolithic local economies became apparent throughout America during the twentieth century. Whenever an economic colossus collapsed, so did the surrounding town. It happened when the steel mills closed in places like Youngstown, Ohio, and when auto plants shut down in places like Flint, Michigan.

In Lewiston the economy didn't so much collapse as sag—slowly but inexorably, over several decades. After World War I, cheap labor and more efficient technology in Southern mills bled business away from New England. Booming employment during World War II masked the problem, but then the entropy resumed. Maine lost an estimated 10,000 textile jobs between 1946 and 1959. After decades of steady growth, Lewiston's population declined for the first time.

To try to stem the tide, Lewiston decided to appoint an industrial development director. They picked Sam Michael.

It was an inspired choice. Rather than use his connections and his considerable powers of persuasion to hawk tickets for Bob Cousy's barnstorming team or Slapsie Maxie's Revue or some other trifle, Sam could use them to entice new businesses. Lewiston wasn't merely hungry for growth, it was famished. In December 1956, when Sam started his new job, the economic climate was as bleak as the encroaching winter. Dirty ice clotted the Androscoggin. A cold wind whistled past vacant brick buildings. And Continental Mills had just announced it would lay off 400 of its 1,100 workers.

The *Lewiston Evening Journal* wholeheartedly endorsed the new hire:

> Appointment of Samuel Michael as director of Lewiston's Industrial Development Department brings a man to this post who has wide experience in varying types of promotional work. . . . His personality qualifications also should be of assistance to him in his efforts to attract worthwhile industries to Lewiston. "Sam"—as Michael generally is called by all who know him—has proved himself able to "get along" with most people, and that is not always easy in the type of promotion he has supervised, since the public often is a difficult creature to please.

Sam soon found that, if anything, the public was even more difficult to please in the public-service sector. To make matters worse, many
Lewistonians had developed a posture of cringing retreat. The idea that
the city could actually *prosper* was beyond them. Worn down by years
of layoffs, cutbacks, and belt-tightening, their reflexive response was to
dig in their fingernails to try to slow the decline. Their best hope was to
preserve what little they had left. Where Sam wanted to invest dollars,
they wanted to pinch pennies—and they weren't shy about saying so.
Among the enemies Sam made was a chronic malcontent named Ernest
Malenfant, an alderman whose miserly ways made Silas Marner look
like Andrew Carnegie. Once, Malenfant proposed eliminating additional
compensation for members of the Zoning Board of Appeals who also
served on the Zoning Board itself. The move would save the City of
Lewiston all of $525 out of an annual budget of $4.5 million while effectively discouraging any public servant from taking on additional duties.

Sam was also dismayed when some of the new businesses he per-
suaded to come to town got a hostile reception. The president of one
new arrival, a company that made plastic heels for the shoe industry,
was summoned to a public hearing to face noise complaints from neigh-
boring residents—even though the company was in compliance with
all relevant regulations and zoning laws. The *Daily Sun* described what
followed as "the most explosive argument to take place at a city board
meeting in many years." It concluded with the company president
storming out, threatening to pull his business out of town. "Good riddance!" an alderman yelled after him, punctuating the exchange with a
slur. (The company president was Jewish.)

Sam was stunned. He had nothing against candid, even heated con-
versations. But there was a place for them—and a town meeting wasn't
it. That's one of the reasons he relished his time at the Elks Club, where
guys from every corner of the Lewiston melting pot could get together
and give each other shit and laugh and play cards and just generally
come to understand and respect each other's point of view. Tossing
out chickenshit insults at a public forum just created hard feelings and
made the town look bush league.

What bothered Sam most was that so many of those petty
exchanges ended up in the paper. If the myopic politicians didn't grasp
how bad that made Lewiston look, the newspapermen certainly should

have. When a reporter named Richard Kisonak printed some withering remarks that alderman Malenfant made about Sam's expense account, that was the breaking point. Next time Kisonak came sniffing around Sam's office at city hall, Sam tried to throw him the hell out.

Of course, *that* made the papers, too.

B ut there was another side to local politics. Lewiston was the focal point of Maine's vitalized Democratic movement. (As one political observer noted, you couldn't call it *re*vitalized because the state had never had a substantial Democratic base before.) At that time Maine was one of the most conservative states in America. Except for 1912, when Teddy Roosevelt's Bull Moose Party had cleaved the GOP's base, Republican presidential candidates had carried Maine in every election since the party's founding. That included 1936, when Maine and Vermont had the distinction (either dubious or distinguished, depending) of being the only states to vote against FDR and the New Deal.

Amid that deep-seated conservatism, Lewiston had a liberal history. When a wave of distressed Irish immigrants, displaced by the potato famine, descended on the city in the 1850s, Lewiston instituted welfare programs to assist them, including a New Deal-style system of public-works projects. A century later, the state's most prominent Democrat, Edmund Muskie, was a graduate of Lewiston's Bates College. Muskie was elected governor in 1954 and senator in 1958. Frank Coffin, a Lewiston native and another Bates graduate, was chairman of Maine's Democratic committee from 1954 until 1956. When Coffin was elected to the U.S. House of Representatives, another Lewistonian, Alton Lessard, replaced him as committee head.

Sam Michael was another prominent Lewiston Democrat. To call him progressive was to damn his chronic optimism with faint praise. He believed, in defiance of all obvious evidence, that Lewiston was on the verge of great things. And despite many fits and starts and stops and turns, Sam made impressive progress as Lewiston's industrial development director, at least for a time. 1959 was the high point. That year Paragon Glass, which manufactured Christmas bulbs among other products, came to town from New Jersey. Sam knew that, to ensure a healthy future, he had to expand Lewiston's economic base beyond the traditional textile and shoe industries. Paragon Glass, which moved into a 40,000-square-foot building that a consortium of Lewiston business-men had built on spec, was a good first step. But the real leap occurred in July, when Raytheon, a pioneer in the field of guided-missile technology, announced that it would build a 116,500-square-foot semiconductor plant in Lewiston. The new plant could create as many as 2,000 jobs. Lewiston had won out over several other New England cities, including Fall River and Worcester.

This wasn't some mom-and-pop sewing shop relocating to a vacant building in the mill district. This was a burgeoning technology company that was breaking ground on a brand-new plant out by the Maine Turnpike.* And Raytheon specialized in electronics—a field with a limitless future in the waking moments of the Space Age.

"The Maine industrial renaissance has begun," Sam said, addressing a luncheon of 165 people at the DeWitt, a century-old hotel at the corner of Pine and Park streets that was as classy as any in America in its day. (The menu included "Fresh Electronic Compote" and "Hot Transistor Rolls" along with traditional Maine fare like lobster salad and french fries made with native potatoes.) "It will not stop today and it will not stop tomorrow."

The *Evening Journal* applauded Sam for his "bulldog assiduous-ness," adding that "there is no reason why Maine cannot become the 'boom state' of the Northeast, particularly if additional electronics plants are located here."

As the 1950s drew to a close, things could not have looked much better for the City of Lewiston, Sam Michael's Industrial Development Department, and Maine's Democrats. In addition to two Democratic congressmen—Edmund Muskie and Frank Coffin—in Washington, Lewiston could count on three more years of support from a Democratic governor, Clinton Amos Clauson.

---

* Despite its reputation as an isolated backwater, Maine was ahead of the curve when it came to superhighways. The Maine Turnpike, a four-lane divided highway from the New Hampshire state line to Augusta, 25 miles north of Lewiston, predated the Interstate Highway System.

On December 29, 1959, Governor Clauson came to Lewiston for a dinner at the DeWitt. Paragon Glass staged the event to thank the people of Lewiston (especially Sam) and other prominent Mainers for all the hospitality that they had shown during the company's move from New Jersey. By all accounts, Governor Clauson—a sixty-five-year-old former chiropractor from Waterville—was in high spirits at the Paragon dinner. Afterward he returned to the Blaine House, the governor's residence in Augusta—and died in his sleep.

Clauson's replacement, per the succession protocol, was Republican John Reed, president of the Maine Senate. The *Evening Journal* described Reed as "a well-to-do potato grower from Fort Fairfield," in rural Aroostook County.

Clauson's funeral was on January 2, 1960. That same day, Massachusetts senator John F. Kennedy announced his candidacy for president.

It's hard to imagine a better pairing of a presidential candidate and a community than JFK and Lewiston. The connection was as much spiritual as political. Kennedy was vying to become America's first Catholic president; Lewiston was an enclave of Franco-American Catholicism. Life in Little Canada centered around the Catholic church. The Church of Saints Peter and Paul at the corner of Ash and Bartlett, built at a cost of a million dollars during the Great Depression, was the dominant feature on Lewiston's skyline. It held 2,000 parishioners. And there were other, smaller Catholic churches sprinkled throughout Lewiston and Auburn. Here, religion wasn't a compartmentalized ritual reserved for Sundays—it was integral to daily life. Children attended parish schools. They wore uniforms and their teachers wore habits.

As Maine's second-largest city, after Portland, Lewiston had the power to turn a traditional Republican stronghold into a battleground state. Richard Nixon, the dour Quaker, remained the favorite to carry Maine. But with an overwhelming majority of Lewistonians supporting Kennedy, the outcome remained in doubt.

Underscoring Lewiston's importance to his campaign, Kennedy arranged to visit just two days before the election. Some 14,000 people crowded into City Park on Sunday evening, November 6, 1960, awaiting Kennedy's arrival. His speech was scheduled for 9:00 p.m. But, delayed at another rally in New Jersey, Kennedy didn't land at Auburn–Lewiston Airport until 11:30.*

Despite the delay, more than half the crowd remained. It felt like a holiday. And for the children of Lewiston, it was; while filibustering during the long wait, Senator Muskie had decreed that all the kids in the crowd could stay home from school the next day. Lewiston's mayor, a former motorcycle racer named Emile Jacques, felt pressured to make the proclamation official.

Sam Michael's ten-year-old son, John, was among those in the crowd. "It was cold," John recalled later, "and my dad's office was in the city building on the side facing the park. So we kept going up to the office to get warm and then running back down."

As the story later went, Kennedy said he had expected no more than a smattering of his supporters to remain at that late hour on such a cold night—and he expected those few to be angry with him. "So he's driving in from Auburn," John recalled, "and as he rounds the corner onto Lisbon Street, there's thousands of people just piled everywhere. I remember standing on the sidewalk, and when Kennedy went by in the limousine it almost looked like he was slumped down in the seat, trying to hide, because he was afraid he was about to get run out of town."

Instead, the crowd released five hours' worth of pent-up enthusiasm.

Kennedy climbed to the platform on the pagoda in the park. Mayor Jacques presented him with a key to the city. Kennedy smiled broadly.

Then he spoke: "Not only the key to the city, but the fact that so many of you were willing to wait so long warms my heart and will make me remember Lewiston."

The cheers grew louder.

In the gloom of a November midnight in the old mill town, Kennedy's words glimmered: "Maine and the country have a very clear choice on Tuesday. . . . Maine has a chance, and so does the country, to choose progress. . . . I believe this country has a great destiny in the

---

* Auburn police dispersed a small band of protesters with bad intent. After a vigorous pat-down from police sergeant John Jordan, the *Daily Sun* reported, a group of young boys "departed with eggs running down their legs."

sixties. I don't know any assignment it cannot meet, any responsibility it cannot bear. But it has to first recognize that it needs to move forward, that it needs action, that it needs direction, that it needs to finish the things that are still unfinished."

Three years later, Kennedy himself—the man in whom Lewiston had invested so much hope—was among the things that would remain forever unfinished.

CHAPTER FOUR

Goodbye JFK, Hello Cassius Clay

The winter of 1963–64 was like a prolonged eclipse in Lewiston. The enshrouding darkness arrived abruptly at midafternoon on Friday, November 22, with a bulletin out of Dallas. President Kennedy was dead.

As dusk settled, church bells throughout Lewiston tolled a requiem. The paralysis of grief took hold. "Everyone here is too stunned to work," an unnamed city secretary told the *Lewiston Daily Sun*. "We have no incentive to do anything."

The following Monday, the day of Kennedy's funeral, schools were closed and the entire city shut down so people could attend local services. Saints Peter and Paul was filled beyond capacity for the nine o'clock mass. It took four priests to accommodate communion. Smaller churches throughout the city were even more crowded. On Lisbon Street, the Holy Cross Church turned hundreds away. "We have never had such response before," said Monsignor Felix Martin.

Through the cheerless holidays and into the new year the penumbra lingered. The optimism of 1960 was a faint memory. JFK was gone.

And Raytheon was going. Undercut by an influx of cheap foreign transistors, the company announced that it was shutting down the Lewiston semiconductor plant.

It had all happened so fast. The ceremonial groundbreaking was in 1960; Senator Margaret Chase Smith was there for the photo op. Behind her Sam Michael stood before a sign that read 2000 MAINE PEOPLE WILL BUILD RAYTHEON TRANSISTORS HERE NEXT YEAR. The plant opened in June 1961 and during its brief peak employed 1,300 people. But in the end all Raytheon brought to Lewiston was another conspicuously empty building.

Sam's chronic optimism and bulldog assiduousness would be tested as never before.

Thanks to an accident of timing, something came along to help lighten those dark, deep-winter days. On the night of Tuesday, February 25, 1964, Sonny Liston, the fearsome heavyweight boxing champion, was fighting a brash young challenger named Cassius Clay in Miami Beach. Sam was involved, if only in an incidental way. He was working with Inter-Continental Promotions, which owned the overall rights to the fight, and Theatre Network Television, Inc., which had outbid seventeen other companies for the TV rights. TNT was showing the fight via closed-circuit broadcast at 271 locations in the U.S. and Canada, including two in Maine: Bangor Auditorium and the Portland Exposition Building. (In a new wrinkle, the fight would also be beamed to Europe on a slight delay via the Telstar satellite. The ground operation was at Maine's Andover Earth Station, about sixty-five miles northwest of Lewiston.)

Along with his brother, Joe Michael, Sam coordinated ticket sales for the Portland showing. Television, which had helped drive him out of boxing promotion when it was free, now drew him back in with a primitive version of pay-per-view. It was inevitable; the closed-circuit TV people needed knowledgeable locals to handle the logistics at all those arenas, theaters, amphitheaters, and halls the world over. In Maine, Sam was an obvious choice. "He had the connections and the opportunity," his son John said later. Sam's primary responsibility was to sell advance tickets in Lewiston, an easy 45-minute drive from Portland on the turnpike. Tickets were $5 in advance, $5.50 on fight night. Sam made these sales through the box office at Victor News, a longstanding local newsstand on Ash Street. It was an informal cultural center where Lewistonians gathered for gossip or to get a wider-angle view of the world through out-of-town papers like the *New York Times.*

Sam was not a young man. He'd turned fifty-eight that winter. But, as with his progressive approach as Lewiston's industrial development director, he had a younger man's vision when it came to boxing. The key to the sport's future—in fact, to the future of *all* professional sports—lay in broadcast rights.

This was not as obvious before the fact as it became in hindsight. When television first came along, the owners of many professional sports teams resisted it. Put your games on local TV for free, the thinking went, and you would undermine your own ticket sales. (Vestiges of that fear lingered until 2015 through the NFL's blackout rule, which required that every game be sold out seventy-two hours in advance to appear on local television.) This philosophy was rooted in blinkered parochialism, as well as an inability to grasp the scope of the prospective audience. Why, for example, would anyone outside the Chesapeake Bay region care about the Baltimore Colts?

It wasn't until the 1958 NFL Championship Game, a sudden-death overtime thriller between the Colts and the New York Giants at Yankee Stadium, that the true potential of broadcast rights became apparent. Although NBC's coverage was blacked out in New York, Yankee Stadium was still short of a sellout on that late-December Sunday afternoon.* By conventional logic, the broadcast should have been a bust in the heartland. Instead, the game drew a nationwide television audience estimated at forty-five million. And NBC had paid all of $200,000 for the rights.

Boxing, in large part because it wasn't tied to any particular city, was the first sport to fully leverage its broadcast rights. Back then the heavyweight championship transcended the sports pages, the way the Super Bowl does today. It didn't matter where it was; a title fight in

---

* One of those who had finagled his way into Yankee Stadium was an aspiring photographer named Neil Leifer, who had turned sixteen that day. Despite having limited equipment—a twin-lens-reflex Yashica Mat that had been donated to a local camera club he belonged to—and no photo credential, Leifer managed to secure a spot in the east end zone by helping disabled veterans into the stadium in their wheelchairs. Thus he was in perfect position to capture the decisive moment, as the Colts' Alan Ameche scored the winning touchdown against the moody backdrop of the Yankee Stadium lights. It was an arresting tableau that differed from a conventional close-up of the action. Leifer sold the image to *Sports Illustrated*, a four-year-old publication fighting to establish an identity. It was the first photograph he ever had published. Six-and-a-half years later, on assignment for SI in Lewiston, Leifer would again be in just the right spot, and he captured what might be the most famous sports photograph ever taken.

Chicago generated just as much interest in New York, Los Angeles, and everywhere in between. Heavyweight championship bouts already commanded the highest ticket prices in all of sports by a wide margin. Ringside seats for the Clay–Liston fight in Miami were $250—more than twenty times the cost of box seats for the 1964 World Series. And promoters could wring additional revenue from the bout through modestly priced tickets for closed-circuit TV broadcasts at movie theaters and sports arenas. (Except in a few isolated markets on the cutting edge of the cable-TV industry, the technology wasn't advanced enough to sell the fight to individual homes, as in today's pay-per-view broadcasts.) TV money increased boxing's revenue by almost tenfold in some cases.

That had another profound effect: For tax purposes, among other reasons, some popular fighters preferred to restrict themselves to one bout—and one huge payday—per calendar year. The rarity of the fights, subsequently, made the closed-circuit-TV model even more lucrative.

It also reduced the opportunities for prospective challengers.

The first closed-circuit broadcast that Sam Michael had helped promote was the Cassius Clay–Archie Moore bout in November 1962. That fight, in which Clay knocked out an over-the-hill Moore in round four, was a dog. It drew just a modest house at the Portland Exposition Building.

The Clay–Liston bout from Miami Beach appeared to hold even less promise. The main event wouldn't begin until 10:00 p.m., a late start on a winter weeknight in economically depressed Maine. And unlike many other closed-circuit locations, which were dedicated, comfortable movie theaters, the Portland Exposition Building was an aging, multipurpose hall. It had opened in 1915 with an agricultural fair. The fight would be shown on a temporary 300-square-foot screen that *Portland Press Herald* sports editor Roland Wirths complained was "much too small."

But the biggest problem was that the fight was perceived as a mismatch. Liston was a 7–1 favorite. He hadn't been seriously tested since suffering a broken jaw—and his only defeat—against Marty Marshall almost ten years earlier. Clay, on the other hand, had recently needed the full ten rounds to subdue Doug Jones, a 3–1 underdog, at Madison

Square Garden. Clay had trailed on all scorecards after seven rounds. When he rallied over the final three rounds to take a narrow decision, the crowd booed loudly and chanted "Fix! Fix! Fix!" and "Fake! Fake! Fake!" It wouldn't be the last time Clay heard that.

Before the Jones fight, Clay had originally declared—in an early poetry slam at the Bitter End in Greenwich Village—that he would dispose of Jones in six rounds. At the weigh-in he lowered that estimate to four rounds, although this time he did so silently, by holding up four fingers. His mouth had been taped shut on "orders" from his trainer, Angelo Dundee.

After the narrow decision Clay tried to stay in character with an improvised rhyme: "Jones came here fat as a hen, but he tricked me and lasted to ten." He then dropped the façade long enough to confess that Jones "was tougher than I figured and he tagged me."

At 188 pounds, Doug Jones was a heavyweight in name only. If *he* dished out all the punishment that Clay could handle, what would a 212-pound pile driver like Sonny Liston do?

The expectation that this would be a short fight was the dominant theme of the advance coverage. Associated Press reporter Will Grimsley noted that the record for the fastest KO in a heavyweight title fight was one minute, twenty-eight seconds (Tommy Burns over Jem Roche, March 17, 1908) "and many are convinced this old mark will be broken."

Grimsley's article, which described Liston as a "brooding destroyer," also noted that betting on the fight was almost nonexistent (an observation that would be conveniently forgotten in short order). Wrote Grimsley, "Most observers predict the lights will go out for [Clay] within minutes, perhaps seconds, after the scheduled 10 p.m. EST opening gong in Miami Beach's pink-and-blue Convention Hall."

Wrote Bud Collins in the *Boston Globe*, "Clay is expected to go down as fast as the evening's first martini."

The *New York Times* ran a story about ABC Radio's contingency plan to pad its broadcast in the event of an early knockout. Producer Maury Benkoil said the fallback was to interview assorted ringside celebrities. (With garrulous Howard Cosell holding the microphone, the questions alone would devour a substantial chunk of airtime.) Benkoil said that ABC would have a different problem if, by some miracle, Clay actually won: "We might have to stay on the air all night before he shuts up."

That one-liner revealed another challenge with this promotion. Neither fighter, as portrayed in the media, was remotely likeable. Liston was a thug. Clay was a loudmouth whose boasts were out of all proportion with his accomplishments. How was the ticket-buying public supposed to root for either of these jerks?

Never mind that these character sketches were shallow and lazy.

Take, for example, this account of a Liston press conference after a sparring session in Miami, by newspaper columnist Joe Williams:

> The sports writers seem uneasy and there are long pauses between their questions. The atmosphere is forbidding, almost malevolent. A Missouri writer turned and whispered: "I think the reason the guy crawls into his shell during these things is that they remind him too much of those third degrees our cops put him through back in his jail bird days."
>
> The Missourian would be more familiar with the champion's checkered past than most. Liston had done time twice out there.

In truth, *everyone* was familiar with Liston's checkered past because no one ever let him forget it. The press—and by extension the public—viewed his every move through the prism of his prison record.

Columnist Ray Haywood: "Sonny Liston [is] a sterling example of what can be accomplished through prison-taught trades. . . . When last seen he was mean, arrogant, cantankerous and unlettered, sullen, sarcastic and apparently indomitable."

Columnist Harold Scherwitz, noting that Liston's only loss had come against Marty Marshall: "Marty is the one gent who beat Sonny Liston in the ring. A few cops beat him outside of it but their names are not in the record book."

Columnist Red Smith, on a session in which people paid to have photos taken with Liston: "Across the bay there is a wax museum where tourists who want pictures with more animation can pose lighting John Dillinger's cigar."

Even those who tried to portray Liston in a more sympathetic light did so clumsily. Columnist Drew Pearson attributed this quote to Liston: "I first got into trouble by findin' things before they was lost." And this was how Robert J. Kaiser, Director of Kansas Penal Institutions, began a paper that was supposed to illustrate the value of a rehabilitative approach to incarceration: "Illiterate Sonny Liston learned to box in the Missouri State Penitentiary."

Liston's rap sheet had the same effect that the tattoo on Mike Tyson's face does today—you couldn't look at him without thinking about it. And Liston's awareness of this compounded the problem.

Sonny Liston had grown up on an Arkansas plantation, in almost inconceivably desperate circumstances. His mother, Helen Liston, produced either twelve kids or thirteen. (The precise number, like most details of Liston's childhood, is in dispute.) His father, Tobe Liston, may have produced as many as twenty-five. There wasn't enough of anything, from food to affection, to go around. Sonny's summary of those years: "The only thing my old man ever gave me was a beating."

Helen moved to St. Louis in 1946 and Sonny, uninvited and with no plan, eventually followed. Although in later years newsmen recorded ample evidence of his natural wit, Liston had no formal education. But he had an imposing physique: massive shoulders that suggested an unlimited reserve of latent power, and huge hands capable of concentrating that power to devastating effect. He also had an intimidating stare. Seemingly every writer described it with the same adjective, inspiring countless boxing fans to look up the word *baleful* in the dictionary.

The results were all but preordained. Take a poor, unschooled, physically imposing young black man and deposit him on the streets of a hardened Midwestern city in the late 1940s. Where would you think he'd end up? For Charles L. Liston—as Sonny was still known then—it was the state prison at Jefferson City. He was sentenced to five years for armed robbery in the spring of 1950—betrayed by his black-and-yellow flannel shirt.

Inmates at Jefferson City served the hardest of hard time. The foreboding gothic penitentiary was built in 1836, seemingly as a monument to human sorrow. It was at Jefferson City that Liston picked up his nickname—he never explained how—and began to box. The prison chaplain at that time, Reverend Edward B. Schlattmann, later claimed that he got Liston started. "After four weeks of fighting, nobody in the penitentiary would get into the ring with Sonny," Schlattmann told writer Nick Tosches.

Liston himself later credited Schlattmann's successor, Father Alois Stevens, with launching him as a boxer. And it indeed was Father Stevens who had the connections outside Jefferson City that led to Liston's early release, on October 30, 1952, and his one shot at a legitimate career.

Well, a *career*, anyway. Liston had the misfortune to enter boxing at a time when the sport was almost entirely under underworld control at its highest levels. Despite their good intentions, his benefactors had merely delivered Liston into the company of a higher class of criminal. And eventually his connection with organized crime, even if he had no realistic possibility of avoiding it, would brand him as guilty by association.[*]

As an amateur, Liston climbed to the top of the Golden Gloves ranks without effort, as if riding an elevator. On June 22, 1953, just eight months after getting out of prison, he claimed the Golden Gloves world title with a first-round knockout of Germany's Herman Schreibauer. Less than two months later he won his first professional fight—in thirty-three seconds.

Had Liston stayed out of trouble during his implacable march toward the heavyweight title, his reputation might have been different. Maybe the press would have settled on a redemptive story arc. *Kindly*

---

[*] In 1960, a subcommittee led by Tennessee senator Estes Kefauver launched an inquiry into the Mob's involvement with boxing. At one point a Kefauver investigator told Liston, "You see that briefcase over there? It's all Sonny Liston and it's all bad." But at least Liston actually answered the committee's questions. Most of his associates invoked the right to avoid self-incrimination. That led Liston to dub the Senate Office Building the Seagram building—because "everyone who goes in there takes the Fifth."

priest rescues lost soul in prison, turns him into heavyweight champ. But any hope of that vanished on May 5, 1956, when Liston was arrested for assaulting a police officer. The details—as always—were vague. The cop said that Liston disarmed him, threated to shoot him, and hit him over the left eye. The officer also suffered a leg injury. Liston claimed the cop provoked a physical altercation without any cause and that he had merely defended himself.

Regardless, he was convicted. And although his term lasted just seven months, Liston effectively received a life sentence. From then on the cops dogged him at every turn. The St. Louis police actually kicked him out of town (following an incident in which Liston supposedly deposited a cop in a trash can), just like in the movies. So he moved to Philadelphia.

His reputation got there first. Philadelphia patrolmen posted his photo in their squad cars. Liston later moved to Chicago and then to Denver and eventually to Las Vegas but could never fully escape scrutiny. Cops would harass him, he would act out, and that would give the cops all the justification they needed to haul him in again. Sometimes Liston was clearly in the wrong. Sometimes the cops were. But eventually the incidents all blended together into one long round of *Why were you running? Because you were chasing me!*

When he became heavyweight champion, Liston assumed that he would be accorded the same level of respect as other champions. When it didn't happen, his resentment deepened. He became even less inclined to cooperate with the press or the police or anyone else. That perpetuated the cycle of bad publicity and led most reporters to conclude that Liston was a hopeless recidivist. Their coverage reflected this. As a result Sonny Liston was perhaps the least-liked heavyweight champion ever.

At least until Cassius Clay came along.

CHAPTER FIVE

Float like a Butterfly, Sting like a Bee, Play 'im like a Fish

Cassius Clay took a different path to infamy. He *decided* to be a bad guy.

Based on his backstory alone, Clay should have been more popular than Liston. Liston became a boxer because he was a criminal. Clay became a boxer because he was a victim. He was twelve years old, living with his father (Cassius Clay Sr.), mother (Odessa), and younger brother (Rudy) in his native Louisville, Kentucky, when somebody stole his red-and-white Schwinn bicycle. Outraged, Clay reported the theft to the nearest cop, who happened to be Joe Martin, head of a local boxing program. When Clay vowed to beat up the perpetrator, Martin suggested that he come down to the gym and at least learn the basics of how to fight first.

Six years later, Clay won a gold medal at the Rome Olympics, fighting as a light heavyweight.

When he turned pro, Clay was backed by the Louisville Sponsoring Group, which consisted of eleven prominent Kentucky businessmen—none of whom had any known connection to the underworld. (When a *Sports Illustrated* writer did a piece on LSG, an unnamed member implored him to avoid using the word *syndicate* to describe them.)

But despite all that, Clay's effusive personality abraded a significant portion of boxing's followers. The press, a jaded bunch, bristled around him. They expected a certain decorum, even deference, from the boxers they covered—especially black boxers. Joe Louis had created the template of the Good Negro ("He's a credit to his race—the human race," columnist Jimmy Cannon once wrote). Floyd Patterson had adopted it for the early days of the civil rights movement. Patterson, like Liston, had spent some time on the streets (Brooklyn's streets, in his case) as a kid and got picked up by the police. He learned to box at the Wiltwyck School for Boys in upstate New York. "Some people would call it a reformatory," he wrote in his autobiography, *Victory over Myself.* "It reformed me, but I wouldn't put it in that class. . . . I saw the school first as a kid in trouble. I see it now as the place where I learned how to live. . . . For a boy like me, a Negro for whom there had been a growing awareness of what a difference in color meant, the interracial activities, whites being treated the same as the colored with no preference at all, this was a tremendous awakening."

Patterson's thoughtful prose exemplified the class expected of a champion. A world-class boxer wasn't supposed to predict his knockouts in verse and disrespect his opponents and declare himself the greatest—which Clay had been doing almost from the start. Throughout high school Clay had focused on boxing to the exclusion of almost everything else. He told anyone who would listen that he was destined to be the heavyweight champion. And a surprising number of people believed him. Among those who fell under young Clay's spell was Atwood Wilson, his high school principal. Wilson justified his decision to let Clay graduate from Louisville's Central High despite a shaky academic record (Clay had a D+ average and was 376th in a class of 391) by declaring, "Do you think I'm going to be the principal of a school that Cassius Clay didn't finish?"

So, as a teenager, Clay could hardly be blamed for concluding that his brashness worked for him.

As a pro, during his first trip to Las Vegas, Clay decided to double down on his showboating. He was in town for his first ten-round fight, with Duke Sabedong, a six-foot, six-inch Hawaiian who fought like a pro wrestler.* And during a promotional appearance on local radio, Clay

---

* In a 1959 bout, Sabedong used a takedown hold on Willie Richardson, then shoved aside the referee and hit Richardson while he was down; police escorted him from the ring in the second round. Against Clay, Sabedong would be penalized twice for hitting after the break and warned three other times.

was teamed with an actual pro wrestler: Gorgeous George, who was huckstering an upcoming bout with Classy Freddie Blassie.

Gorgeous George (real name: George Wagner) provided a graduate class in how to act like a heel. He was born in Nebraska and learned to wrestle in Houston, performing for years in relative obscurity. Then he hit upon the idea of parading into the ring like an eighteenth century French nobleman (picture John Belushi playing Louis XVI), to the strains of the *Pomp and Circumstance Marches*. During the 1950s, when pro wrestling became a hugely popular television spectacle, Gorgeous George was its best-known villain. He claimed to own a collection of more than a hundred florid robes, worth $100,000. TV announcers noted the particulars of each new robe, such as "gold brocade with a red velvet lining," or "flowing peacocks." His hair, which he described as a "Hellenic look, with a Grecian contour," was done by "Franklin and Joseph of Hollywood."

The ring announcer always offered some variation of the same introduction: "Here he is, the one and only, the toast of the coast, the human orchid, *Gorrrrgeous George!*" Then, as the TV play-by-play man solemnly intoned, "As is Gorgeous George's custom, he will not wrestle in any ring unless it has been perfumed and disinfected," a valet would brandish an elaborate atomizer and spritz the ring with Chanel No. 10. ("Why be half safe?" George said, explaining why he disdained mere Chanel No. 5.)

And then Gorgeous would make everyone *wait*. No one could hurry him. Not his opponent ("Don't touch my golden locks!"), not the referee ("Get your filthy hands off me!"), and certainly not the fans ("Quiet, you peasants!").

After appearing with Gorgeous George on the radio, Clay watched him perform at the Las Vegas Convention Center. The crowd was twice the size of the one that watched the Clay–Sabedong bout three days later. "A lot of people will pay to see someone shut your mouth," Gorgeous George told Clay after the wrestling match. "So keep on bragging, keep on sassing, and always be outrageous."

Clay's famous response: "This is a goooood idea!"

And it *was* a good idea, at the time. It was June 1961. Patterson was the reigning heavyweight champion. He had become the youngest heavyweight champ in history in 1956 by knocking out Archie Moore. He'd then lost the title to Sweden's Ingemar Johansson in 1959, regained it in a 1960 rematch, and defended it in yet another bout with Johansson in March of '61. In other words, in the past two years nobody but Patterson and Johansson had fought for the title. Fans were eager for a new rivalry. Given Patterson's large following, and the near-universal respect he received, the most compelling matchup would have been with an opponent that everyone despised. Sonny Liston, the ex-con who had joylessly destroyed everyone in his path, was the most logical choice. But Patterson's manager, Cus D'Amato, didn't like Floyd's chances against the much bigger and stronger Liston. So the Patterson camp ducked Liston. The Kefauver hearings into Liston's shady associates gave them a defensible pretext. Even when Liston switched managers, first jettisoning Pep Barone (suspected front man for mobster Blinky Palermo) for George Katz and then replacing Katz with Jack Nilon, D'Amato remained unswayed. "There's no change—whether it's Nilon, rayon, cotton, or silk," D'Amato said.

That's because Nilon, like Katz and Barone, was from Philadelphia—Palermo's territory. "This is a peculiar thing," D'Amato said. "Are there no other people? It could be Chicago, Los Angeles, New York. Why only Philadelphia people? As far as I am concerned, I see no change in the situation and see no reason to change my opposition to the fight." (Jack Nilon's response: "Hell, I don't blame Cus—he took a blown-up light heavyweight and made him a lot of money.")

All of which meant that, as of June 1961, there was no guarantee that Sonny Liston would ever get a shot at the heavyweight title. Liston had, however, decimated the field of prospective contenders. That left an opening for an up-and-comer like Cassius Clay. And if Clay could become an attractive box-office draw by turning up the contrast between himself and the ever-classy Patterson, why wouldn't he do that?

Patterson's class proved to be his undoing. His sense of fair play eventually compelled him to grant Liston a title shot, over D'Amato's objections. Liston obliterated Patterson in the first round at Chicago's Comiskey Park in September 1962 and repeated the performance the next summer in Las Vegas.

Patterson showed no self-confidence before either Liston bout. It's as if *he* were the convict—guilty of having deprived the rightful champ of the belt for too long. Patterson approached Liston with an air of resignation, as if ready to accept his penance. And Liston meted out the sentence with swift brutality, winning both Patterson bouts in a combined time of four minutes, sixteen seconds.

Thus the world now had a remorseless, cop-beating, Mob-connected reprobate for a heavyweight champion, and his next challenger was a snot-nosed bag of ego and entitlement who couldn't even lift Floyd Patterson's jock, let alone carry it.

In hindsight it's clear that the public was less gullible, or at least less cynical, than the boxing press was in 1964. Cassius Clay fascinated them. The Doug Jones fight was the first advance sellout in Madison Square Garden's thirty-eight-year history—an achievement attributable to "Clay's goofy glamour," United Press International noted. Scalpers commanded up to $100 for tickets with a $12 face value. At the weigh-in for a fight against Henry Cooper in London, Clay—having learned well the lessons of Gorgeous George—appeared in a crown and told the people of England, "You got a queen—you need a king!" Some 35,000 Englishmen turned out at Wembley, hoping to see Cooper shut Clay's mouth.

And although the Miami Beach Convention Hall was half empty for the Clay–Liston fight, ticket sales on the closed-circuit circuit boomed. Interest was particularly strong in America's primary cultural centers—Los Angeles, where the main event began at 7:00 p.m. local time; Chicago (a snowstorm held sales down somewhat), where the main event began at 9:00 p.m.; and New York, where the 10:00 p.m. start time was irrelevant because the city never slept. Those three markets accounted for more than thirty percent of the take, an indication that Clay had a solid following in urban areas.

If the press didn't appreciate Clay's sense of theater, plenty of other people did. Clay had just cut an album of seminal rap for Columbia Records called *I Am the Greatest.** It included a song titled "Will the Real Sonny Liston Please Fall Down." Sample rhyme:

I predict Mr. Liston's dismemberment
I'll hit him so hard
He'll wonder where October and November went

---

* Clay also cut a straightforward version of "Stand by Me" that peaked at No. 47 on the U.S. R&B charts.

Clay bought a used Flexible Visicoach to haul his growing entourage. This was not a luxury motor coach—it was a *bus*, the kind used at airports as a shuttle. And at times Clay drove it himself. The words "Cassius Clay Enterprises" were painted on the top, with "World's Most Colorful Fighter"—the letters of the word "Colorful" in a variety of hues—on the side. There was also a bold prediction, right there for all the world (or at least passing traffic) to see: "Liston Will Go in Eight."

Clay bought the bus in part because he was terrified of flying. (On his first ever flight, to Rome for the 1960 Olympics, he wore an army-surplus parachute.) But the bus also allowed him to stage some epic road trips. In the fall of 1963 (some eight months before Ken Kesey's Merry Pranksters set off on their legendary bus trip) Clay drove cross-country from Los Angeles to New York. The trip included a stop in Denver, Liston's newly adopted hometown, to sign the contract for the title fight. (Ben Bentley, Liston's PR man at the time, said Clay's arrival in Denver taught him the meaning of the word *incognito*: "It means putting on smoked glasses and traveling under an assumed name in a red-and-white bus with your real name painted all over it.") Clay got to the Denver Hilton, site of the press conference where the fight would be announced, a day early. The Hilton didn't have room for his entourage. So Clay checked into a different hotel. Then he drove his bus over to Liston's house, arriving sometime after midnight. (The time was variously reported as one, two, or three a.m.) Clay shined a spotlight in the windows and leaned on the horn while his entourage stood at the curb and called Liston out—literally. Clay challenged him to fight for the belt right then and there.

Clay called this "Bear Huntin'," a play on the nickname he had given Liston, "Big Bear"—or "Big *Ugly* Bear," as Clay invariably put it. A better term would have been Bear Baiting. It was all part of Clay's gamesmanship.

"In other houses, lights went on and windows went up," Clay later told Alex Haley in a *Playboy* interview. "You know how them white people felt about that black man just moved in there anyway, and we sure wasn't helping it none."

Liston appeared at the door. He was enraged but refused to engage. "Liston watched without any show of emotion," the Associated Press reported.

Clay remembered it differently: "You know that look of Liston's you hear so much about? Well, he sure had it on standing in that door that night. Man, he was tore up! He didn't know what to do. He wanted to come out there after me, but he was already in enough troubles with the police and everything."

Eventually, seven police cruisers arrived, including a K9 unit. "A big police dog was within inches of Clay as the No. 1 contender was told to 'move on right away or be taken in,'" the AP reported. For once, Sonny Liston didn't get the blame.

Liston tolerated Clay's nonsense up to a point because he knew it could result in a bigger payday. "Clay's the nicest thing to come along since Christmas," he said. He even played the PR game himself sometimes. At the fight's official announcement, at the Denver Hilton just a few hours after Clay's bit of street theater, Liston produced a pair of boxing gloves covered in rabbit fur. He told Clay he would wear them in the bout "so I won't hurt your pretty face." And, noting the way Clay dug into a plate of chicken, Liston said, "You eat like you headed to the electric chair."

Like most compelling performance art, Clay's best promotional work included an element of real danger. In the run-up to the second Liston–Patterson fight that summer, Clay had camped out in Las Vegas to harass Liston. One night in a casino he went too far, as he later recounted for *Playboy*. At first, said Clay, Liston took the badgering in good humor. "Maybe he was seeing me helping build up a gate for the fight we were about to sign for," Clay said. But Liston's patience wore thin, and abruptly ran out when Clay squirted him with a water pistol. "Very suddenly, Liston *froze* me with that look of his," Clay said. "He said real quiet, 'Let's go on over here.'"

In the private conversation that followed, Liston told Clay, "Get the hell out of here or I'll wipe you out." (According to other accounts, Liston actually slapped Clay across the face, declaring afterward that "I got the punk's heart now.")

"I ain't going to lie," Clay said. "This was the only time since I have known Sonny Liston that he really scared me. I just felt the power and the meanness of the man I was messing with. Anybody tell me about how he fought the cops and beat up tough thugs and all of that, I believe it. I saw that streak in him."

Clay pushed Liston close to the breaking point again when Liston flew into Miami on January 25. "They were making such a big thing out of his arriving, you would have thought the Cubans was landing," Clay said. "Well, I wasn't about to miss *that*!"

Decked out in a tuxedo, Clay yelled, "Fight me right now!" Liston and his party tried to make a quick getaway on an airport courtesy cart. Clay ran after them. Liston told the driver to stop, and he hopped off. "He was *mad*!" Clay said. "He hollered, 'Listen you little punk, I'll punch you in the mouth—this has gone too far!'"

According to Clay, Liston actually took a swing at him. "I ducked," Clay said. "He didn't know he'd had his preview of the fight right then."

The prefight "blowup" has become a trite ritual—so commonplace that Don King once recited a top-ten list of boxing press-conference brawls on *SportsCenter*. But Cassius Clay pioneered the art form in Miami in the winter of '64. And the boxing press, accustomed to the quiet dignity of Floyd Patterson and Joe Louis, fell for it. Said Clay, "Them newspaper people couldn't have been working no better for me if I had been paying them."

Liston fell for it, too. Joe Louis, brought in by the Liston camp to help soften the champion's public image, saw the danger signs. Liston, said Louis, "is an angry man and he can't afford to be angry fighting Clay. . . . Cassius is a master of psychological warfare. He irritates and disturbs, and whatever Sonny may think, maybe Clay bothers him. . . . [Liston's] title is a passport to respectability. He has got to hang on to it."

Clay brought his month-long campaign of psychological warfare to a spectacular conclusion the morning of the fight, during the weigh-in at the Cypress Room inside Miami Beach Convention Hall. At 10:30, Clay burst into the room accompanied by former welter- and middle-weight champion Sugar Ray Robinson and Clay's enigmatic sidekick Drew "Bundini" Brown, who wore a yellow plaid sport jacket. The *New York Times* identified Brown as "an assistant trainer and spiritual adviser" and described him as "a smiling, spaniel-eyed man." (Brown's own capsule bio: "Been round the world twenty-four times, in the Navy and Merchant Marine, getting wisdom.")

Clay ranted: "I'm ready to rumble! I'm the champ! I'm ready to rumble! You can tell Sonny I'm here with Sugar Ray! Liston is flat-footed, and Joe Louis is flat-footed, but me and Sugar Ray are two pretty dancers!"

The *Times* reported that Robinson seemed embarrassed. But not Brown. He egged Clay into a froth, and the two harmonized on what had become Clay's signature line in the build-up to the fight: "Float like a butterfly, sting like a bee!" (Brown later said he had learned the value of psychological warfare while fighting in the Pacific in World War II. "Gotta scream at people," he said. "Learned that from those Japs yelling 'Banzai!' Gets you in the mood and scares your opponent." Said trainer Angelo Dundee, "Bundini is crazy, but he's terrific. He's just what the doctor ordered. He keeps the champ in the right mood.")

After seven minutes of this, Clay and his entourage left. Clay returned in a terry-cloth robe at 11:09. When security men tried to prevent Robinson and Brown from joining him on the weighing platform, Clay objected: "Let 'em up! This is my show! This is my show!"

Security relented.

When Liston entered a few minutes later, Clay began heckling him: "You a chump! You a chump!"

Morris Klein, chairman of the Miami Beach Boxing Commission, made an announcement: "Clay is fined $2,500."

The boxing commission's physician, Dr. Alexander Robbins, recorded the fighters' heart-rate and blood-pressure readings along with their respective weights. Clay's pulse, fifty-four beats per minute at rest, was 120.

Clay's vital signs prompted a grave diagnosis from Dr. Robbins: "This fighter is scared to death. If his blood pressure is the same at fight time, it's all off."

Others wondered whether Clay would show up that night at all.

The press had never seen anything like it. TV and radio stations, along with evening papers across the country, duly reported this bizarre scene. In plenty of time for people to purchase tickets to see what would happen next.

CHAPTER SIX

Liston Gets a Lickin'

That Tuesday, as Sam Michael left for Portland in his Lincoln—white, with a light blue tinge—he could have been forgiven for a lack of enthusiasm. There just wasn't much to get excited about. It was cold—well below freezing all day, dipping down to the teens overnight. Snow banks from a recent nor'easter lined the streets. Beyond the dispiriting weather, promoting a fight that consisted of two apparitions sparring on a movie screen—absent the visceral sensation of seeing two men hit each other for real, up close—just wasn't the same. There was no way that driving to Portland for a closed-circuit broadcast could match the excitement Sam had felt fifteen years earlier, when he'd gone to meet Joe Louis at Union Station. Still, a trip to the Portland Exposition Building would give him a few hours' respite from the desolation of that Lewiston winter, and the pressure of the industrial development director's job. And despite the late start it would still be a fairly early night, to judge from the 7–1 odds in Liston's favor.

Having sat through the dated documentary *Monarchs of the Ring*, along with a short film about the latest advances in U.S. military technology, the 1,700 people gathered at the old brick exposition hall were ready for some real action by the 10:00 p.m. start time. Veteran announcer Steve Ellis worked the broadcast for Theater Network Television, with Joe Louis providing color commentary. (Another of Sam's old barnstorming acquaintances, Rocky Marciano, was doing color commentary on ABC Radio.)

Ring announcer Frank Freeman introduced assorted dignitaries and hangers-on. Then referee Barney Felix gave his instructions. TNT, in one of several innovative technical wrinkles, had wired Felix for sound.

"I want a clean bout, men," Felix said. "In the event of a knockdown, the man that is down must take an eight count. Man standing up will go to a neutral corner while I start counting. Do not resume boxing until I tell you to do so. Now I want a clean bout. When I order you to break, stop punching and step back. Good luck. Shake hands."

Boilerplate fight instructions. But the accompanying visual was arresting.

When covering the second Liston–Patterson fight, journalist Hunter S. Thompson had watched Liston work out several times at a distance before seeing him up close. Thompson was shocked to find that he was three inches taller than Liston. Such was Liston's intimidating presence in the ring that he boxed bigger than he actually was.

Viewers at the Portland Exposition Building now had an experience similar to Thompson's. "The audience buzzed," the *Biddeford-Saco Journal* reported the next day, "as Liston stared menacingly at Clay as the two pugilists met at the center of the ring just before the start of the bout."

Unlike Floyd Patterson, who had shrunk away in Liston's presence, exaggerating Liston's physical advantages, Clay stood tall—taller, in fact, than Liston. Just as important, all vestiges of Clay's clowning, and of the fear he had supposedly displayed at the weigh-in, were gone. When Liston fixed him with that menacing stare, Clay stared right back. He never flinched.

The fighters' contrasting styles were obvious even before the opening bell. As they stood in opposite corners, Clay danced lightly, a Ferrari revving at the starting line. Liston methodically shifted his weight from foot to foot, a truck releasing its air brakes.

Five seconds after the opening bell the truck and the Ferrari converged in the center of the ring. Liston fired his signature left jab and Clay snapped his head back, out of harm's way. It was a seemingly innocuous moment and yet it telegraphed the entire evening.

Clay circled clockwise. Liston threw a right and missed completely. It was not only short, but it was also wide. Clay had already danced away. Ellis: "Cassius Clay on the move, as we see, looking to get Sonny to lunge. [Clay is] carrying his left hand dangerously low."

Before Ellis had even finished this observation Liston had thrown another right and two more left jabs and come up empty three more times. At the twenty-seven-second mark, Liston completely straightened his left arm and just grazed Clay's chin as the challenger again pigeon-necked out of danger.

A moment later, as Clay covered up near the ropes, Liston finally connected with a solid right to Clay's ribcage, eliciting a "*Whoo!*" from Ellis. But Clay danced free, and fifteen seconds later Liston whiffed with a left-right combination. A few seconds after that he threw perhaps his hardest punch of the round, a rising left jab. This was the punch that had sometimes lifted opponents right off their feet. But this time it straightened just over Clay's ducking head.

A minute into the round Clay began to land his counterpunches, leading with his left. Ellis amended an earlier observation: "Clay's still in the danger zone in that he's keeping his hands low, but you'll notice one thing if you don't mind—he's at *long range* with the hands low." Ellis's tone reflected a rapidly growing respect for the challenger.

At the two-minute mark, Clay punctuated a flurry with a solid right hook to the head. Ellis: "The best punch of the night so far!"

Ellis's call just before the bell revealed the degree to which Clay's reputation had evolved in just three minutes. "We're down to the closing seconds of this first round," said Ellis. "And the long left lead is making the difference so far—by Mr. Clay!"

Mr. Clay. Not "Gaseous Cassius" or the "Louisville Lip" or any of the other derisive nicknames that the press had slapped on him.

This improbable turn roiled the crowd. Clay hadn't merely survived the first round—he had won it. The ovation was so loud that neither the fighters nor Barney Felix heard the bell. The round went on for four additional seconds and the bell rang two more times. And still the fight continued. Finally, after the fourth bell, Felix stepped in.

Before the fight Joe Louis had predicted that Clay would be an easy mark for Liston. He warned that if Clay tried pulling his head back, "Sonny will knock him through the front door."

But after round one, Louis said this to the TNT audience: "I think Clay completely outclassed Sonny Liston in this round."

Not that anybody in the Portland Exposition Building heard him. Like the fans in Miami Beach, they were cheering.

Although Liston rallied in round two, landing a hard left hook about twenty seconds in and a series of solid body shots, Clay continued to feint and block and minimize the damage. And he never stopped moving. Ellis: "This youngster has his own style and it's confusing for the champion to fathom this early in the fight." Later: "Liston wants to pump that jab to set up his other punches. He wants to use it as a left lead, to lead to other shots if he can get this kid to stand still."

Although Liston won the round, at no point did he seem close to scoring the early knockout that nearly everyone had predicted. After the bell, Louis surmised that Liston's trainer, Willie Reddish, was "telling Sonny to forget about Cassius Clay's head because he's pulling back too much and he's much too fast for that." The champion would have to try to accumulate damage with an onslaught of body shots. In other words, Liston's corner recognized that the fight was going to be one of attrition—an approach for which Liston was wholly unprepared. He hadn't fought into the third round in almost three years.

When a near-knockdown came in round three, it was Clay who delivered the blow. About thirty seconds in he concluded a flurry by squaring up a hard overhand right. "Wobbled!" Ellis bellowed. "Sonny wobbled! Cassius has him hurt!"

Clay's fusillade had opened a gash under Liston's left eye—the first time the champion had ever been cut in a fight. Liston was also bleeding from his nose.

But Liston had a keen survival instinct, and it kicked in near the end of the round. He concentrated his energy into a series of hops—the muscle memory of all those hours skipping rope to "Night Train"—launching his punches with everything he had left. With less than a minute to go in the round, he caught Clay with a left hook. Instead of drawing back, Clay's head snapped to the side. Ellis: "Hold the phone! Cassius is a bit hurt!"

But, like Liston, Clay regained his equilibrium by the time the bell sounded.

Round four was noteworthy mostly because of what happened in the corners before and after.

Before: Reddish and Joe Polino, Liston's cut man, closed around Liston like a Secret Service detail, working to stanch the bleeding from the gash on his left cheek. Back then cut men used assorted unguents and astringents, from Vaseline to wintergreen, as crude constrictors or coagulants. Polino apparently applied a copious amount of one or more of these to Liston's cheek. Some might have spilled onto Liston's gloves by accident. Or on purpose.

After: Clay, having landed enough punches during the round to puff up Liston's right eye as well as his left, retreated to his corner. His manner was casual. He slid his right glove along the top rope, still looking fresh as he turned and sat on his stool. Trainer Angelo Dundee wiped Clay's face with a towel, from the forehead down. Almost immediately Clay started blinking, which the TNT broadcast caught in a close-up. Lip readers in the Portland Exposition Building might have deciphered the anguished words that soon followed: "Cut the gloves off me!"

What transpired during those tense moments has long been the subject of conjecture. There's no question that something got in Clay's eyes. But exactly what it was or how it ended up there, no one can say. Did it come from Liston's gloves? Or was it something one of Clay's own cornermen had accidentally smeared on Dundee's towel?

In any case, Clay clearly overreacted when he felt the sting. It was an open secret by then that Clay was a close follower—if not an active member—of the Nation of Islam, or "Black Muslims," as the press labeled them. This was a radical movement, and one of its most vocal and controversial members, Malcolm X, had become close friends with Clay. Malcolm had spent much of February in Miami at Clay's invitation and was at ringside that night. Distrustful of the white people in Clay's camp—from the Louisville Sponsoring Group to Dundee—the Muslims had planted seeds of paranoia in Clay's mind. He wouldn't even let Dundee or Dr. Ferdie Pacheco, his physician, touch his water bottle before the fight for fear that someone would taint it. And so now, when he felt his eyes burn after Dundee wiped his face, he freaked.

Dundee quickly sponged clean water into Clay's eyes and tried to calm him down. Clay was in such anguish that he almost didn't answer the bell for round five. (The next day, Felix claimed that he had to bark at him, "Damn it, Clay, get out here!" He added: "If he hadn't moved in a split second—and I mean one second—he was all finished.")

If in his panic Clay overreacted, he nevertheless had good reason to be afraid. For all of his prefight taunting, he respected Liston as a boxer and genuinely feared his punching power. ("It frightened me, just knowing how hard he hit," Clay said later.) He spent all of round five in survival mode, keeping his distance and covering up as best he could.

Despite his growing fatigue, Liston went to work. Less than twenty seconds into the round, he closed in and unleashed his most sustained assault of the bout: eighteen straight body punches. Ellis: "Sonny's gonna try to pour it on!"

Given the way Liston suddenly let down his guard and began pounding away with impunity after having his face peppered for four rounds, it's tempting to conclude that something fishy was afoot. But Clay's distress, and his incessant blinking, was so obvious that even the most casual observer would have noticed. An experienced heavyweight like Liston certainly would have. And he would have tried to press his advantage.

Late in the round, Clay's eyes cleared enough for him to throw a few tentative counterpunches. By then Liston was exhausted from desperately pursuing what he must have known was his last chance. In the closing moments, as Clay face-washed him with his gloves, just keeping him at arm's length, Liston offered little resistance. As Clay later said, the aging champion was "snorting like a horse."

As with almost every other significant development in Sonny Liston's life, the truth regarding the events in Miami Beach Convention Hall that night was obscured by a veil. Obviously *something* ailed Liston—but what? The facts lay in shadow—indistinct and open to interpretation. Later it came out that Liston had had cortisone treatments for bursitis in both shoulders before the fight. (In an astounding conflict of interest, referee Barney Felix apparently knew about Liston's ailing shoulders. Felix, who was also a physiotherapist, had been giving Liston ultrasonic treatments at his Miami-based fitness center. "They said to keep it quiet," Felix later said.)

In any case, Liston clearly lacked command of his left hand by round six. In the fifth round, despite the opening Clay's temporary blindness had provided, Liston never tried a serious left jab; he relied almost entirely on left hooks. Now, in round six, his legs were gone, too. He shuffled to the center of the ring at the opening bell and planted himself there. Clay circled like a buzzard sensing a mortal wound.

Flat-footed from fatigue, and with a sagging left arm, Liston offered little resistance as Clay lit him up. Ellis sounded astonished: "Easy target! *Eeeasy!*"

Liston's left got worse as the round wore on. Near the end he wasn't so much punching Clay as backhanding him, as if trying to swat away a persistent insect.

At the end of round six Liston's cornermen had to perform triage. First they addressed the cut under his left eye. But they also had to apply ice to his right cheek and massage his left shoulder. All of this was captured on the TNT broadcast.

After that, viewers got a wide-angle shot of the ring. The TNT logo appeared on the screen, followed by the words ROUND 7. Although the audience at the Portland Exposition Building couldn't hear it, a whistle blew in Miami Beach Convention Hall—a signal for both fighters to get ready.

Later, Clay recounted the moment in a *Playboy* interview: "I happened to be looking right at Liston when that [whistle] sounded, and I didn't believe it when he spat out his mouthpiece. I just couldn't believe it—but there it was, laying there. And then something just told me he wasn't coming out! I give a whoop and come off that stool like it was red hot."

This was how that moment played out in the Portland Exposition Building, according to the *Biddeford-Saco Journal*: "The sudden ending of the battle caught the onlookers by surprise as they anticipated the beginning of round seven. The first inkling they had something was up was when the Louisville Bard began dancing in the center of the ring, and even then, some felt Cassius was putting on some of his usual antics."

On the TNT broadcast, Ellis made the call: "They may be stopping it! That might be all, ladies and gentlemen!"

Again, no one in the Exposition Building could hear. "A roar went up when Clay's hands were raised in victory," the *Biddeford-Saco Journal* reported, "but it was not until several minutes later that the throng learned the reason the champion did not come out for the seventh round."

Officially, Liston retired because of an injury to his left shoulder. But a glimpse on the TNT broadcast of Liston's face told the real story. The fleeting image was shot from in close, at ringside, fifteen seconds after what turned out to be the final bell. Liston's face was framed by the ropes and his cornermen's arms. Both cheeks were swollen and his eyes were half shut. He looked like he had blundered into a hornets' nest.

Float like a butterfly, sting like a bee.

After boasting for months of what he would do, Cassius Clay had gone out and done it.

Sam Michael had been around boxing long enough to appreciate the historical significance of what had just happened down in Miami Beach. And he felt fortunate to be among the handful of Mainers who saw it unfold in real time. That night he practically floated home from the Exposition Building, all the pressures of his day job consigned to the backseat of his Lincoln.

"Boy!" Sam told his wife Doris back at the house on Summer Street. "I wish you could've seen it. Clay gave Liston a lickin'!"

The wheels were already starting to turn.

CHAPTER SEVEN

(Grandma) Moses and Muhammad

The excitement over Clay's historic upset didn't spread beyond people like Sam Michael, who actually saw the fight. Everyone else could only go by what they read in the papers. And what they read in the papers was the same sort of cynical, dismissive coverage they'd read before the fight. Despite what they had just witnessed, many on the boxing beat still didn't believe that Cassius Clay could beat Sonny Liston. They concluded, therefore, that the fight must have been a sham. The AP's Will Grimsley offered this cryptic description of the post-fight atmosphere in Miami Beach: "Seasoned boxing writers, accustomed to all sorts of weird occurrences in this sometimes sordid sport, were seeking answers to questions which they said left them befuddled."

A headline in the *Boston Globe* put it more bluntly:

LISTON'S INJURY EXCUSE HARD TO BELIEVE

The Miami Beach Boxing Commission contributed to the air of suspicion by withholding the purse, pending Liston's exam at St. Francis Hospital. Within hours a team of eight doctors determined that Liston's shoulder injury was genuine. Said Dr. Alexander Robbins, the commission's chief physician, "There is no doubt in my mind that the fight should have been stopped."

Of course, this was the same doctor who had been so suckered by Clay's performance at the weigh-in that he had pronounced him "scared to death." So maybe his credibility was in question.

In any case, the commission had set a tone, which was reflected in the coverage across the country the next day. An AP brief on the front page of the *Lewiston Evening Journal* noted that Florida state attorney Richard Gerstein had requested copies of Liston's medical records. "He declined to elaborate," the item noted, leaving readers to jump to their own sinister conclusions.

Soon enough came revelations about those bursitis treatments that Liston had received on his shoulders. Reporters saw this as evidence not of his vulnerability but of his deceitfulness. An explanation from Jack Nilon, Liston's de facto manager, did Liston no favors: "We thought we could get away with it."

What Nilon meant, no doubt, was that they thought Liston could get by with some minor soreness—not that the Liston camp had tried to hide something. But the damage from those poorly chosen words lingered. It didn't matter that Liston's primary doctor, Robert C. Bennett, later said that the bursitis "wasn't anything too big."

Added Bennett: "We made X-rays of both shoulders the night he got hurt. There was no evidence of the bone degeneration that is present in very severe cases of bursitis. I think Liston's problem in the fight was that he swung and missed, severely stretching or rupturing his arm four or five inches below the shoulder. In our post-fight examination, we could see the swelling and the blood."

Liston himself had said essentially the same thing: "I made a mistake in the first round. Wild punching. I felt [something] pop."

In other words, it was Clay's elusiveness that had done Liston in—not a pre-existing shoulder injury.

But again, that didn't seem to matter to the press. This was Sonny Liston, after all. He had to be guilty of *something*. As Norman Thomas put it in the *Lewiston Evening Journal*, "Liston and Nilon ought to be jailed for keeping a secret or for a more deliberate sellout."

Politicians weighed in, too. In what had become standard operating procedure in big-time boxing, a congressman demanded an investigation. This time it was Senator Philip A. Hart, a Michigan Democrat, who had replaced the late Senator Estes Kefauver as head of the Senate's busybody subcommittee.

The investigation proved only that whatever Liston's backers lacked in experience they made up for in candor.

Inter-Continental Promotions was an offshoot of Nilon Brothers, Inc., a group of Pennsylvania-based "catering engineers." The Nilon brothers, who had parlayed a construction-site sandwich stand into a lucrative concessions business, were new to the boxing game. Sonny Liston was the first fighter they had ever worked with. Before that, their only boxing experience had been as childhood neighbors of a Damon Runyon character named Baron Jimmy Dougherty (he had refereed the Jack Dempsey–Tommy Gibbons fight at Shelby, Montana, in 1923), and as concessionaires for occasional bouts at Philadelphia Municipal Stadium.

There were four Nilon brothers: Joe was two years older than Bob, who was seven years older than Jack, who was three years older than Jim. Growing up in Ridley Park, Pennsylvania, the Nilon brothers had been gifted schoolboy athletes.

Bob, whose game was hockey, was the best. In December 1933, as a key member of an Amateur Athletic Union team, he sailed from Boston to Liverpool, England, aboard the steamship *Laconia* for a tour of Europe. His coach was Walter Brown, who later founded the Boston Celtics and was president of Boston Garden and the Boston Bruins.

During that European tour, Brown's AAU team won the silver medal at the world championships in Milan, Italy. Bob Nilon scored the only goal in a 1–0 victory over Czechoslovakia in the tournament opener and added another goal in a 3–0 win over Germany in the semifinal.* The tour also included exhibition games in London, France, Switzerland, Czechoslovakia, Austria, and Germany—where, according to a later story in the Nilons' hometown paper, Bob received a handshake and a medal from Adolf Hitler.

---

* "My father was not a boastful man," Bob's son Terry later recalled, "but he believed with all his heart that had the war not intervened he would have been in the National Hockey League." Bob Nilon almost certainly would have made the 1940 Olympic team had the Games not been canceled due to the outbreak of World War II. Nilon, who received an early iteration of the Hobey Baker Award, played three years at Clarkson, and then with the minor-league Minneapolis Millers, a Chicago Blackhawks affiliate, before joining the Army. Five-and-a-half years of military service (and the chronic bronchitis that he brought home with him) ended his hockey career.

The Nilons had a jock-y directness that served them well in business. When they started, in 1946, they had practically nothing. "It seemed like every night was New Year's Eve for Irishmen while we were in the service," Bob said later, "and we all came home broke. So we put our money together, a sum of $100, and opened a hot dog stand at a construction job. We grossed $185 the first day and . . . well, it's developed."

As the business rapidly expanded beyond that original stand into sports concessions, the Nilons set their sights on the plumpest local plum: the annual Army–Navy football game at Philadelphia Municipal Stadium, which drew a crowd of 105,000. They figured that account would put them on a par with any concessionaire in America.

So in 1948 Bob Nilon simply drove to West Point and asked for it. "They were extremely courteous," he later recalled, "but I could see I wasn't getting through to them."

Undeterred, he drove to Annapolis the following year and met with Captain Morris D. Gilmore, aka Mr. Army–Navy. "I talked without stopping for about two hours," Bob later said. "When I finished, Captain Gilmore stood up, walked around his desk, and stuck out his hand. 'Young man,' he said, 'you've got yourself a job.'"

Nilon Brothers then added golf tournaments to their repertoire, starting with the 1950 National Open at Merion, Pennsylvania. Bob saw vast room for improvement in golf concessions. "They were conducted like a third-rate bazaar," he said. "We felt that we could not only help the tournaments make more money but could add to the picturesqueness with custom-made tents and stainless-steel equipment." Thus the Nilons were pioneers in the modern concept of "corporate hospitality" at sporting events.

Jack, an avid golfer, became the Nilons' primary representative at tournaments. In 1955, when Sam Snead's partner failed to show for a pro-am, Jack took his place; he and Snead tied for first. And in June 1960 at the US Open at Cherry Hills Country Club in Denver, Jack met Father Edward Murphy, a Jesuit priest from the local St. Ignatius Loyola Church. Joe Nilon, who had left the concessions business in 1957 to join the Jesuits, made the introduction.

At the same time, Father Murphy was developing a close relationship with Sonny Liston, who was in Denver to train for a bout with

Zora Folley that July. "I feel I have found a true friend for the first time," Liston said.

Father Murphy turned out to be the contact the Nilons needed to realize their latest ambition. They wanted to make the transition from merely running concessions at sporting events to owning a piece of the action. They wanted a team in either the NFL or Major League Baseball—or a piece of a heavyweight contender. "My dad always felt that that was the greatest belt that an athlete could hold," Bob Nilon's son Terry later recalled. "That's why they were all so fascinated by having Sonny Liston. They felt like if they could get this guy under contract he would become champion. He was just the *man*."

And in 1960, the man lived in Philadelphia, not far from the Nilons.

The stars seemed to be aligning. Employing the same approach that had landed the Army–Navy game, Bob Nilon drove to Liston's house in the summer of '61 and knocked on the door. He pitched Sonny on Nilon Brothers promoting a Liston–Ingemar Johansson bout. Nothing came of that proposal, but with Father Murphy's blessing ("Father Murphy was at our house many times," Terry Nilon recalled), the idea of an alliance between Sonny Liston and Nilon Brothers gathered momentum. "Liston and Father Murphy came to me," Jack Nilon told *Sports Illustrated* in 1963. "I didn't go to them. I said, 'I'll think about it,' and the more I thought, the more I liked the idea."

The deal became official on March 1, 1962, when Jack Nilon signed a management agreement with Liston—although Nilon preferred the term "adviser" to manager. Jack served in this capacity for Liston's two Patterson fights, as Liston slowly extricated himself from underworld influence.

Along the way, Inter-Continental Promotions was born.

The new corporation's inexperience showed from the start. To begin with, their timeline was overly ambitious. With Clay–Liston in line to be their first fight, Inter-Continental hoped to hold the bout practically in the Nilons' backyard, Philadelphia Municipal Stadium, on September 30, 1963. That was just ten weeks after Liston had defended his title against Patterson in Las Vegas. Jack Nilon estimated that a Philly fight would draw 70,000 fans. That would have given the Nilons not only huge gate receipts but also significant revenue from parking and concessions, which Nilon Brothers operated.

This was to be the Nilons' big payoff in big-time pro sports. And so, basically, Inter-Continental was structured with this singular proposal in mind. Liston was named president and given 47.5 percent of the stock (a setup designed to reduce his tax bite). Bob Nilon was named executive vice president and split 47.5 percent with his brother Jim. A law firm got the remaining five percent.

Jack Nilon got nothing. "I have no equity," he'd told *Sports Illustrated* earlier that year. "In the state of Pennsylvania a boxer can be a promoter. The manager cannot be. It's all been checked out legally."

But the Nilons' due diligence wasn't as diligent as they thought. On July 31, Pennsylvania attorney general Walter E. Alessandroni advised the state's athletic commission to reject Inter-Continental's application for a promoter's license, citing a 1955 Pennsylvania law stipulating that "no officer, director, stockholder, or employee of a licensed promoter shall have any interest in any professional boxer . . . or professional contest . . . except as a matchmaker."

There are several ways that a boxer who controls the rights to his fights, and who has a financial interest in his opponent, could abuse this arrangement. The most obvious is to insist on a return clause—meaning that if the boxer/promoter loses, his opponent has to fight him again in his next bout. Imagine a heavyweight champion drafting a contract (with a return clause) to fight a heavy underdog—say, 7–1. The champ could then bet against himself, throw the fight, and collect a huge illicit payoff in addition to his legitimate take as a fighter. Then, invoking the return clause, he could fight for real the next time, destroy the unsuspecting upstart, and reclaim the title. Which isn't to say that's what Sonny Liston had in mind going into the first Clay fight in Miami. But when he quit on his stool and surrendered the heavyweight championship to a 7–1 underdog, he played into a jaded public's worst suspicions.

And he made Pennsylvania's attorney general look prescient.

It was awkward for Inter-Continental Promotions to stage a fight in Florida with a financial structure that had been tailored (albeit incorrectly) for Pennsylvania. A company called Delaware Advertising and

Management Agency, an offshoot of Inter-Continental, itself an off-shoot of Nilon Brothers, had been set up to handle the ancillary rights. Jack Nilon owned eighty percent of that.

Tension grew between Sonny Liston and Jack Nilon. "He didn't know anything about fighting before and he don't know nothing now," Liston said after losing in Miami. "He's only a hot dog salesman."

The straight-talking style that had served Jack and Bob Nilon so well in business meetings and on golf courses didn't play as well in public forums. After the Hart committee's disclosure that Liston had transferred more than half his shares in Inter-Continental Promotions to Sam Margolis, a Philadelphia vending-machine company operator who reportedly had ties to the Mafia, Jack Nilon expressed neither surprise nor outrage. Margolis claimed that Liston was simply repaying him for his support earlier in Liston's career, when Sonny was broke. Nilon accepted that explanation at face value, stating, "Anyone who can put up with [Liston's] antics as long as Mr. Margolis has—if he got the whole [purse], he'd be underpaid."

In another embarrassing revelation, Bob Nilon said it was news to him that Jack had received fifty percent of Liston's purse from the Clay fight. "The first time I knew that was when [Jack] testified here," Bob told the committee. He displayed similar naiveté regarding the disclosure that Inter-Continental had paid Clay $50,000 before the Liston fight for the right to promote Clay's first title defense in the event of an upset. Bob said that he thought Clay had about as much chance against Liston as "Grandma Moses." So he never even considered "as a remote possibility" that Clay would win the title—and what an unseemly conflict of interest that would create for Inter-Continental.

Meanwhile, medical records in hand, Florida state attorney Richard E. Gerstein led a separate probe. His month-long investigation turned up no evidence of a fix. Still, that didn't stop Gerstein from insinuating that he'd smelled enough smoke to conclude that there must have been a fire. Said Gerstein, "A well-known gambler and bookmaker enjoyed the full run of Liston's training camp, and was present in Liston's dressing room prior to the fight."

This was hardly a bombshell. The "well-known gambler" was Irving "Ash" Resnick. He and Liston became friends before the second

Patterson fight. Resnick served as "athletic director" of the Thunderbird Hotel, the Las Vegas resort casino where Liston had trained. In fact, Liston's cornermen had worn shirts advertising the Thunderbird Hotel *during* the Clay fight. So it's not as if Liston made any attempt to hide the association.*

Against this tattered backdrop of innuendo, Liston got arrested again. Two weeks after the fight, Denver police charged him with driving seventy-six miles per hour in a thirty-mile-per-hour zone, driving without a valid license, and carrying a concealed weapon (a .22-caliber revolver). Further, Liston admitted that he had consumed half a bottle of vodka. But he refused to take a Breathalyzer test—and the arresting officer, James Snider, didn't push it because "he thought Liston would have passed the test easily," according to United Press International.

That might have been the only time that a cop gave Sonny Liston the benefit of the doubt.

As for the new champion: He might have won the public over, and created better financial opportunities for himself, by recasting his image. But that wasn't his style. And if Cassius Clay hadn't planned to use the role of heavyweight champ as a bully pulpit, nor did he shy away when the opportunity arose.

It didn't take long. At a press gathering two days after the fight, a reporter asked Clay point blank if he were a member of the Black Muslims. Clay didn't recoil from the question, just as he hadn't blinked when Sonny Liston tried to stare him down.

First, he rebuked the reporter for his choice of words.

---

* Nothing speaks more clearly to Liston's can't-win-for-losing reputation than this: More than fifty years later, two damning—though contradictory—rumors about that Miami Beach fight persist. One rumor, supported by declassified FBI files, holds that Liston threw the '64 Clay fight in a fix that Ash Resnick engineered. (Even though there was no evidence of any unusual betting pattern—or of much betting action at all—before the fight.) The other rumor, supported by cut man Joe Polino's "confession" to writer Jack McKinney, holds that Polino deliberately juiced Liston's gloves (on Liston's orders) before round four, leading to Clay's temporary blindness. Combine the two rumors, and Sonny Liston stands accused of cheating to try to win a fight that he intended to throw.

"You call it Black Muslims," Clay said. "I don't. The real name is Islam. That means peace. Yet people brand us as a hate group. They say we want to take over the country. They say we're Communists. That is not true. Followers of Allah are the sweetest people in the world. They don't carry knives. They don't tote weapons. They pray five times a day."

The words were hardly inflammatory. Clay's most controversial statement was that he and other followers of Islam believed in segregation. "We don't think one people should force its culture upon another," he said. "I don't like hot Mexican food and I would be unhappy if somebody made me eat it. At the same time, you may not like what I like—turnip greens and hominy grits, or country music. If you don't like it, you shouldn't have to accept it."

At the time many white Americans also believed in a "separate but equal" doctrine—and some weren't even willing to concede the "equal" part. But when the sentiment came from a prominent young black man it was interpreted as divisive.

A widespread perception was that Clay had joined the Nation of Islam for reasons other than his religious convictions. As an unnamed ad executive, commenting on Clay's dim endorsement prospects, told the *New York Times*, "Clay would be controversial because of his alleged political beliefs."

Not religious beliefs—political beliefs. *Alleged* political beliefs at that.

Clay's popularity declined further in early March, when Nation of Islam leader Elijah Muhammad granted him a new name: Muhammad Ali. The press responded with editorial eye rolling. From small-town papers in Maine (the *Biddeford-Saco Journal* later referred to the champion as "Ali Babba, or whatever he is calling himself today") to the wire services (an AP story identified him as "Cassius 'Call me Muhammad Ali' Clay"), newsmen sneered. The general public was even more hostile: When Ali asked to be addressed by his new name during an appearance at Madison Square Garden for the Luis Rodriguez–Holly Mims fight, the crowd booed. (Ali's reaction: "If I changed my name to Jimmy Jones or Calvin Washington nobody would say nothing.")

Ali's reputation suffered further damage over a development beyond his control. In accordance with the Selective Service Act of 1948, Ali—still known as Cassius Clay—had registered for the draft at Local Board

No. 47 in Louisville back in 1960, when he'd turned eighteen. But twice he failed to pass the military's entrance exams (the results of the first attempt were labeled "inconclusive").

At first, the press treated Clay's draft status lightly—a good way to end a sportscast with a chuckle. When Clay had reported for his first test (along with eighty-nine other inductees) at Coral Gables, Florida, a month before the Liston fight, the UPI brief was heavy on cornball humor. Clay joked that he was "getting the Army more publicity than anybody since Elvis," whose 1958 induction was grade-A gossip fodder.

Added the UPI account: "An Army spokesman reported that the only autograph Cassius gave out was the one on the bottom of the test form."

At the time, the presumption was that Clay's days as a celebrity were numbered. Once Sonny Liston disposed of him, "Gaseous Cassius" would be shipped off to Uncle Sam and never heard from again.

But in short order Clay won the heavyweight title, announced his conversion to Islam, and changed his name. When the press learned that he had failed his second entrance exam, the stories on his military status took on a different tenor. So many reporters wondered aloud whether Clay had failed his exams on purpose that the Army felt compelled to issue a statement refuting that possibility: "Interviews conducted by experts in the field of testing and analysis of results of the two tests indicate that Clay put forth his best efforts on both occasions." (Jack Raymond noted in the *New York Times* that the communiqué had come straight from the Pentagon, "cleared through command channels with the care normally attached to the status of missile scientists.")

When it came out that Ali had failed the math portion of the exam, politicians and journalists ridiculed him. "Had I flunked math," said Ohio congressman William H. Ayers, "I still could have peeled potatoes for the first two months of my Army service—which I did."

One story reported that Ali had scored 78 on an IQ test at a Louisville junior high in 1957. The headline of an AP story read:

MATCH WITS WITH CASSIUS, TRY THESE MATH QUERIES

"Are you smarter than the heavyweight boxing champion of the world, Cassius Clay?" the story began. "Try these little problems on for size."

This was a sample question:

Q. A man works from 6 in the morning to 3 in the afternoon with one hour for lunch. How many hours did he work? A–7, B–8, C–9, D–10.

Two years later, with the Vietnam War escalating, the US Army would broaden its entrance standards and Ali would be reclassified as draft-eligible. His refusal to be inducted on religious grounds, and his subsequent legal battle and effective banishment from boxing, would become a complex, nuanced story that played out during a time when public support for the Vietnam War was eroding. But when Ali failed his military entrance exams in 1964, the press painted him with the broadest possible brush. He was either a moron or a malingerer. Either way, it angered people that the Army had exempted him from service. Syndicated columnist Robert Ruark's take was typical:

The Army has chickened out on Cassius Clay, Allah's gift to the world. It was clearly the Army's duty to draft Cassius, or Muhammad Ali X, as an object lesson to the world that you can make a silk purse into a sow's ear. . . . Some morals are involved here. I do not refer to his title. He won nothing important from a cheap hoodlum, [Sonny] Liston, under what certainly must have been false pretenses even in the rottenest racket in the world. But the Army needs Clay like the jailhouse wants Liston as a permanent occupant. . . . The reputation of all our military force is at stake. Is Cassius Clay, Allah's newest recruit in the Black Muslims, bigger than the defense department?

Even within boxing circles few people publicly supported Ali. On March 22 World Boxing Association president Ed Lassman declared Ali "a detriment to the boxing world" and asked that the WBA's executive committee vote to strip him of his title. Lassman never cited Ali's conversion to Islam as the reason. (In fact, he later offered an explicit denial.) Still, anyone perusing the sports pages could be forgiven for connecting those dots based on the way the story was reported. This was the AP's summary: "Clay won the title in Miami Beach with a seventh-round technical knockout over Liston when the defending champion injured a shoulder. A short time later, Clay acknowledged that he was a member of the Black Muslims, a Negro supremacy group. Clay said last week he would be known in the future as Muhammad Ali, and if he were ever introduced in the ring as Cassius Clay, he would not answer the bell."

This paragraph was followed immediately by a Lassman quote: "Clay has proven himself by his personal action as a detriment to the boxing world and has set a poor example for the youth of the world."

Ali's reaction: "I'm a beautiful model for youth. I don't drink. I don't smoke. I've never been caught stealing. I don't run around with women and carry pistols. I'm am Olympic gold medal winner for this country. And I won the heavyweight title fair and clean.

"Honestly, I'm so clean and peaceful. I've never been in any kind of trouble. Lassman's thinking of Sonny Liston."

Knee-jerk needling aside, Ali respected Liston. He made that apparent in an interview with Robert Lipsyte of the *New York Times*. It took place in a Harlem hotel room a month after the Miami Beach title bout. Said Ali, "I feel sorry for Liston. The championship meant so much to him. But don't you think he would train real hard for the next fight? That he'd be hungry?"

Good questions.

From an objective perspective—which was hard to find at that point—there was little doubt that Ali and Liston should meet again. On paper, the first fight was closer than people realized. It was 3–3 on the judges' scorecards when Liston retired. So if he could rehab his shoulder and rebuild his stamina, Liston would be more deserving than any other prospective heavyweight contender. Plus, return bouts had become a boxing tradition—even though the WBA was trying to legislate against them because of the inherent opportunities for corruption.

To lessen the appearance of a conflict of interest, Liston sold his shares in Inter-Continental Promotions to a Denver attorney. But the damage had already been done. With a return bout in the works, the WBA, the press, and the public still thought the whole arrangement had a decidedly low-tide odor.

All of which meant that no city was clamoring to host the fight. Who wanted to be associated with another installment of the washed-up jailbird versus the loudmouthed quasi-Arab draft evader in what felt like a pro-wrestling-style setup? When Inter-Continental officially announced the return bout on July 27, they did so without knowing exactly where or when it would take place. "Our target date actually is Monday, September 28," Jack Nilon said. "We hope to hold the bout before the World Series, which begins the first week of October, and the Olympics, which start October 10 in Japan."

Inter-Continental looked at three prospective host cities: Baltimore, Las Vegas, and Ali's hometown, Louisville. Jack Nilon, demonstrating that his experience before the Hart committee had taught him nothing about the finer points of public relations, made his feelings plain. "I'd love to have the fight [in Louisville]," he told the press. He added that he was reluctant to choose Baltimore because it would require a closed-circuit blackout in a major market, and "Las Vegas does not have enough seating capacity."

Two days later, Nevada boxing commissioner Art Lurie made the question of Vegas's viability moot. "Las Vegas does not want the fight," he said.

When even Sin City thinks it's too good for you, you know you're in trouble.

By mid-August, Inter-Continental had scrubbed Jack Nilon's target date of September 28. Baltimore fell out of the running to host the bout, and by September 1 so had Louisville. Kentucky boxing commissioner Bob Evans made the announcement after a WBA gathering in late August, when the association formally voted "to suspend indefinitely any and all persons, including the referee, who might have anything to do with a Clay–Liston return bout."

In fact, not only would Kentucky's boxing commissioner refuse to sanction the bout in his state—he wouldn't even allow it to be shown on closed-circuit TV. (Exactly how Evans planned to enforce a ban on closed-circuit coverage in Kentucky wasn't clear.) For all that, Evans tried to handle the status of Kentucky's homegrown heavyweight champion diplomatically. "We have no quarrel with Clay," Evans told the *Louisville Courier-Journal.* "All he has to do is sit out the December 1 expiration of the [return] contract with Jack Nilon and then fight any recognized contender before the end of his first year as champion. That will keep him on top, clean as a hound's tooth."

Given that Inter-Continental spokesman Harold Conrad had already announced that the fight would be held "somewhere in the United States in November," the Evans proposal seemed disingenuous—nothing more than an attempt to placate Ali's remaining fan base in Louisville.

Almost immediately, rumors sprouted that a new city was in the running for the fight: Boston.

Inter-Continental had a solid connection in the city. Bob Nilon's old AAU hockey coach, Walter Brown, was president of Boston Garden, as well as both the Celtics and Bruins. Even before the Clay–Liston fight in Miami, Nilon had floated the idea of a Boston bout. "If [Brown] wants to promote a heavyweight championship, Liston will fight for him in Boston one of these days," Nilon had said in February.

He added: "Walter Brown bought me my first good pair of shoes, Church brand, in Piccadilly. He was always doing things like that for kids on the team."

But there were limits to Brown's largesse. Buying a needy kid some shoes during the depths of the Depression was one thing. Ponying up to promote a heavyweight title fight was another. And Brown had already experienced buyer's remorse over boxing years earlier, declaring that "I simply can't make any money with it."

In light of the huge losses that promoter Bill MacDonald had suffered on the Clay–Liston bout in Miami (he had fallen far short of the sellout he had needed to secure a profit) it seemed unlikely that Brown would have had a change of heart.

So the Boston rumors appeared to have no more substance than any of the others that had bubbled to the surface and then burst in the past six months. The Massachusetts Boxing Commission, which had just voted in lockstep with WBA members not to recognize a return bout, tried to quash the rumors quickly and completely. "We think Clay and Liston should fight somewhere else," MBC chairman Herman Greenberg said on September 3. "They definitely will not fight in Boston. Our commission will abide by the rules."

Ten days after those words appeared in the *Boston Globe*, Greenberg posed for a photo with Sonny Liston and Muhammad Ali at a hotel near Logan Airport. The two fighters were shaking hands for the cameras, symbolic of their agreement to stage a return bout at Boston Garden on November 16.

CHAPTER EIGHT

Meet the *Other* Sam

T he climate in Boston had changed abruptly. On September 7, Walter Brown died of a heart attack. Inter-Continental Promotions' best Boston connection was gone, just like that. (Bob Nilon attended Brown's funeral.)

Three days after Brown died, in a stunning political upset, Massachusetts lieutenant governor Francis X. Bellotti defeated incumbent governor Endicott "Chub" Peabody in the Democratic primary.

The bad news for Governor Peabody was that his re-election campaign was over before it began. The good news was that he could do what he wanted during the last four months of his term without worrying about the political fallout.

Peabody and Bob Nilon had some talks. It's easy to imagine them hitting it off. Peabody was a former Harvard football star and a World War II vet. Ex-Navy man. He liked the policy aspects of politics but hated the PR part. "No candidate was ever more thoroughly destroyed by television than Endicott Peabody," wrote *Boston Globe* political editor Robert Healy.

Privately, Peabody and Nilon discussed the ways that a heavyweight title fight in Boston could benefit them both. For Nilon the advantages were obvious: He needed a place to hold the fight, and he needed it as soon as possible.

Peabody's motives were more difficult to pinpoint. One possibility: Having served just a two-year term, Peabody hadn't had time to do much. One of his accomplishments, however, was to create a new Division of Economic Development. Anything that Peabody could do to goose the Massachusetts economy in the waning days of his administration might burnish his legacy. A title fight at the Garden could have seemed like a good start. As many as 14,000 people could shell out as much as fifty bucks a pop for tickets, with six percent of that money going to the Commonwealth.

Whatever his reasons, Governor Peabody successfully pressured the Massachusetts Boxing Commission to reverse its stance and approve the fight—although the MBC denied that that's what happened. "The governor didn't pressure us," said commission member Edward Urbec. "He just let us know he thought this fight would be a good idea for Boston."

Not that there was any genuine outrage over the MBC's going rogue; the WBA was generally seen as self-righteous and hypocritical, with no real authority. (Syndicated columnist Red Smith dismissed them as "a band of delicatessen owners, haberdashers, and morticians.") And although the WBA planned to hold a tournament to replace Ali as heavyweight champ, Urbec guessed (correctly) that it would be a flop.* "I can't visualize the public not accepting Clay as the champion," he said. "Titles are won or lost in the ring."

In any case, for the first time since 1940 Boston had a heavyweight title fight—even if the gathering for the official confirmation had all the joy of a shotgun wedding. The press conference started an hour and twenty minutes late because the parties were still sorting out the fine print. The exchanges were stilted. Chub Peabody, the outgoing governor who was not the outgoing type, made the formal announcement. (Bud Collins described Peabody's demeanor as "lame duck-ish" and likened it to that of Johnny Pesky, embattled manager of the eighth-place Red Sox.)

As for the Massachusetts Boxing Commission's abrupt about-face—welcoming the bout after voting not to recognize it at the World Boxing Association convention—Urbec offered a creative rationalization: "We

---

* On March 6, 1965, Ernie Terrell beat Eddie Machen for the vacant WBA crown at the International Amphitheatre in Chicago—"an arena built for livestock exhibitions," Robert Lipsyte noted in a *New York Times* account that carried the subhead "How to Become Champion of Part of the World Without Really Trying." The fight was both a financial and esthetic disaster. Terrell grossed just $28,200—and had to give $20,000 of it to Machen. Terrell spent much of the fifteen-round fight leaning on his shorter opponent, "enveloping him," Lipsyte wrote, "dancing with him, hugging him—a man drowning in his lack of talent dragging another talentless man down with him."

shouldn't have been allowed to vote in the last WBA meeting anyway. We didn't pay our dues last year or this year because of our financial condition."

Ali, combatting a bad cold, failed to provide the usual levity. His exchanges with Liston lacked the sizzle of the Miami build-up. Even when Liston mocked his Muslim name ("I ain't fighting no Allah Molly. I met him as Cassius Clay and that's the way I'm gonna leave him") the champion failed to take the bait. "He just don't understand," said Ali, who at one point in the press conference pretended to fall asleep.

But there, amid the awkward atmosphere of the Envoy Room at the Logan Hotel, alongside those reticent fighters and cynical writers, stood the happiest man in Boston. His name was Sam Silverman.

Like Sam Michael, his friend and counterpart in Lewiston, Sam Silverman had knocked around the New England fight scene for decades. In fact, his first experience in boxing had been in Maine (Bath, to be exact), in 1930. Silverman, a student at Boston's Cambridge Latin High School at the time, had coerced a classmate to sneak up north and enter the bout. Silverman served as his manager. "He got his jaw broke," Silverman recalled. "We both were suspended from school but they finally let us graduate."

Unlike Sam Michael, who had backed away from small-time fight promotions when times got tough, Sam Silverman was in it for the duration. "The small clubs are the incubators of boxing," he once said.

It was in such incubators that Silverman honed his survival instincts. Once, during a card at the Rollaway Arena in Revere Beach, north of Boston, a portion of the floor caved in. Silverman had the ushers escort jittery spectators from the collapsed section of the building to a more stable area. "No refunds," he said. "We can't stop the fights just because the joint falls down."

Silverman's wife Helen and their daughter Elaine learned where they stood in Sam's pecking order in 1953, the day that Helen had a miscarriage. "Sam comes into the hospital room," Helen recalled years later, "and the first thing he says is, 'Helen, suppose we match Tommy Collins and Jimmy Carter? What do you think they'll draw?' Not 'How are you?' or 'It's awful about the baby.'"

"It's a funny story now," Helen added. "It wasn't funny then. But it wasn't lousy, either. I mean, it was Silverman. Elaine and I learned something then: Boxing was more important to Sam than anything. Sacred."

Silverman almost paid for that devotion with his life. Boston's postwar boxing scene had a seamy underside, and Silverman had his share of misunderstandings. In 1948 he was beaten with brass knuckles. One of his associates was later bludgeoned into a coma with a lead pipe. In 1951 someone put a bullet through his living-room window, narrowly missing Helen. No one had heard any shots, leading police to conclude that the gunman had used a silencer.

Silverman took his rivals' best shot in June 1954, when an explosion rocked his house in Chelsea, Massachusetts. No one was hurt; Sam, Helen, and Elaine were away that day. Displaying a peculiar code of honor that treated a terrorist bombing as an in-house problem, Silverman refused to press the issue with police. Although investigators found primer cord and traces of either cordite or dynamite at the scene, Silverman claimed that the blast was caused by "a defective refrigerator."

"Who the hell knows who did it?" he later told *Sports Illustrated*. "In this business you're always in a jam with somebody."

In the early '50s Silverman had begun promoting nationally televised fights from Boston Garden. This didn't go over well with the International Boxing Club of New York, which promoted its own nationally televised fights at Madison Square Garden. The IBC, which essentially had a monopoly on the heavyweight title, froze Silverman out. In 1956, IBC executive director Harry Markson declared, "Silverman will promote no title fights."

Added Markson, "We can't make Silverman a big league promoter. . . . It's as simple as that."

Even in his own playpen Silverman had trouble playing nice. He once had a fistfight with an unhappy boxing manager at Boston Garden; the manager vowed afterward that his fighter would never participate in another Silverman promotion. In 1963, after Silverman had announced a bout without first notifying the Massachusetts Boxing Commission, MBC commissioner Thomas Rawson drily noted, "Only last week we laid down the law to Silverman. That must have been for the fiftieth time."

But through all the setbacks, letdowns, and laying-downs-of-the-law, "Unsinkable Sam" (he was also known as "Suitcase Sam" for his fly-by-night ways) persevered—convinced that his big break was coming. Recently he had helped put together a surprisingly successful series of bouts for former middleweight champion Sugar Ray Robinson, who was still fighting regularly in his early forties. Earlier that year Sugar Ray had fought at the Portland Exposition Building and Wahconah Park, an aging minor league baseball stadium in Pittsfield, Massachusetts. The year before, Silverman had even taken Sugar Ray into territory that Sam Michael had ceded. That bout, with a one-fight wonder named Billy Thornton, drew 4,000 fans at the Lewiston Armory.

By the following year the crowd had swelled to 6,000 in Silverman's telling. Whatever; it was a lot of people. "In *Lewiston*," Silverman marveled to the *Boston Globe*. "A cemetery."

Apparently it never occurred to him that some of the living dead in that cemetery might read the *Boston Globe*.

That was the other big difference between the two Sams. Sam Michael was generally polished and well spoken. He chose his words as if selecting glassware. Sam Silverman was a bullshitter let loose in the china shop of public relations. Once, when a journalist asked his opinion of the fabled Harvard–Yale Regatta, Silverman said, "I hope they all drown. What are you sportswriters doing writing about them guys paddling backwards when you should be writing about boxing?"

Another time, while on a fight tour in France, he referred to the *Notre Dame de Paris* as "the joint where that hunchback hangs out." And according to Bud Collins, Silverman checked out of "the stylish Meurice by pushing a mound of US currency about the size of a basketball at the cashier, saying 'I ain't got time to count it, but there's more than enough. Keep the change.'"

To Sam Silverman, life was strictly a cash business.

And now, after thirty-four years of hard knocks and haymakers, he had realized his implausible dream. He was promoting a world heavyweight championship fight at Boston Garden.

Or co-promoting it, anyway.

According to Silverman, bringing the fight to Boston was *his* idea. "When it became apparent that Liston and Clay were outcasts, about four months ago," Silverman told the *Boston Globe*, "I went to Bob

Nilon, who's in charge of the promotion, and told him I thought I could get it in Boston. I went to work."

No doubt there was some truth to that. But it's likely that Silverman really became a front-runner for the deal only after Walter Brown died. At that point, with no further hope of finding a Bill MacDonald-style sugar daddy to buy the rights for the live gate, Inter-Continental Promotions decided instead to rent Boston Garden and promote the fight themselves. What they needed was a local guy with connections. Just as important, they needed someone with a Massachusetts promoter's license. Inter-Continental didn't have one. But Sam Silverman did.

And that's how he found himself at Logan Airport on Sunday, September 13, the night before the official announcement, waiting with a crowd of reporters to meet the heavyweight champ's plane.

The champion, in a churlish mood, greeted the Boston press corps like this: "Let's get this understood right now. My name is Muhammad Ali. M-U-H-A-M-M-A-D. It's not Cassius."

He took a few questions. Someone asked about the possibility of a Floyd Patterson bout in the future. Ali's eyes flashed anger. He said that he hoped to fight Floyd Patterson after the Liston rematch because Patterson had disparaged his religion and refused to call him by his Muslim name. "I hate him so much I'd kill him," Ali said. "I'd kill him."

An awkward silence followed. Sam Silverman stepped in to save the day. "I guess that's all for now, Cassius," he said.

The champ glared. *"Muhammad Ali."*

That moveable object, the Ali–Liston fight, was about to meet an irresistible farce.

CHAPTER NINE

Sonny Spars while Muhammad Speaks

How different it all might have been.

Over the summer and fall of '64, as the press remained focused on the superficial and the inconsequential, Sonny Liston and Muhammad Ali charted a course for a fascinating return bout.

Their roles had reversed. Liston was now the one who had something to prove. He had bottomed out in March, with his latest arrest, and his weight ballooned to 235 pounds. And then he got serious. Aside from a sixteen-dollar speeding ticket in June, Liston remained in seclusion and largely out of the news.* He ditched many of the hangers-on from the Miami fight—or they ditched him. "One day you are the king," Liston said later. "Your friends—or the guys you think are your friends—are all around you. They give you, 'Yes, champ. No, champ. You got no worries, champ. No one in this whole world can beat you, champ.' Then all of a sudden you're not the champ and all of a sudden you are alone. The guys with the big mouths are out talking about you, not to you, and what they say ain't what they said the day before. It's a big price to pay."

And so Liston bid good riddance to all those who had contributed to his false sense of security in Miami. One of the few who remained was his trainer, Willie Reddish. But their relationship had changed. Because so many people—including Liston himself—had blamed a lack

---

* In May Liston paid a $600 fine for the earlier charges of reckless driving and carrying a concealed weapon, and in June a judge dismissed a $1.3 million breach-of-contract suit brought against him by former manager George Katz.

of conditioning for his Miami defeat, Reddish became defensive. When *Sports Illustrated*'s Mark Kram asked if Liston had been out of shape in his last fight, Reddish snapped, "What you tryin' to do, put me on the spot with that question? Forget about the last fight. Right now only counts."

Reddish was no longer Liston's only trainer—or even his primary one. That role now fell to an unpaid volunteer, forty-one-year-old Stanley Zimmering, who had a second-degree black belt in judo. He and Liston worked out at Zimmering's studio, the Amid Karate & Judo Club, in south Denver. Zimmering focused on rehabbing Liston's injured left shoulder. "I've been working with him on a certain exercise for three months," Zimmering told Kram, "and [his shoulder is] as good as ever."

Liston also did extensive roadwork, running five-and-a-half miles a day in the high altitude of the Rocky Mountains. And there was greater specificity to his sparring sessions than in the past. One partner, Foneda Cox, did nothing but provide a target for Liston's left jab, as the former champ tried to restore the weapons-grade punch that had defined him as a fighter for so long. Another partner, Leroy Green, mimicked Clay's shiftiness. "I'm kinda special," Green said. "Ain't nobody hits me."

Amos "Big Train" Lincoln had the worst assignment. He had to absorb Liston's best body shots. "I wouldn't wanna be Clay," Lincoln said after taking another of his many poundings.

Liston kept up this regimen until late October, when it was time to decamp. By then his weight had melted to 214 pounds. And he wasn't finished yet. As he relocated to the White Cliffs Hotel in Plymouth, Massachusetts, overlooking Cape Cod Bay, for the final weeks of training before the November 16 rematch, he intended to go harder still. Said Reddish, still stung by the blame heaped upon him in Miami, "We gonna take 'im in at 210 or 212."

Said Liston, stung by *everything* that had happened in Miami, "Ain't no playin' this time."

He didn't like how it felt to be a former heavyweight champion. "That title—*my* title—is there and I'm going to get it and I'm going to keep it a long time," he said.

Ali was now the one who was distracted and out of shape. By the time of the Logan Airport announcement he was at least twenty pounds overweight. Muslims, he explained, "don't smoke or drink or run around, [but] you got to have pleasure, and food is something to do."

Ali had spent much of his energy that year sorting out his new Muslim identity. He took a tour of Africa. The tour, which Ali claimed was supposed to last four months, began on May 16, when he flew to Ghana. Thousands of people greeted him, chanting his name. Having come from the United States, where he had been the object of relentless ridicule—much of it with a not-so-subtle racial undertone—the young Muhammad Ali had trouble keeping his ego in check in the face of such sudden adulation. The ironic result was that Ali acted, at times, like the ugliest of ugly Americans.

It started on his first full day in Africa, at the Hotel Ambassador in Accra, Ghana's capital. Ali had a chance meeting with his old friend Malcolm X, who had just completed a *hajj*, or pilgrimage to Mecca. The brief encounter illustrated how much the two men's lives had changed since the title fight, not even three months earlier. That night in Miami Malcolm had celebrated with Cassius Clay. Now everything was different—even their names. They were no longer Malcolm X and Cassius Clay; they were El Hajj Malik el Shabazz (Malcolm's newly adopted Sunni name) and Muhammad Ali. And the differences in their perspectives at that specific moment could not have been more pronounced.

Malcolm X had left the Nation of Islam in March. His departure was inevitable. Born Malcolm Little in North Omaha, Nebraska, in 1925, he had joined the Nation of Islam while at Massachusetts' Charlestown State Prison in 1948. As the NOI became more visible during the volatile 1960s, Malcolm posed a threat to Elijah Muhammad, who had led the Nation since 1934. Malcolm, who was twenty-seven years younger than Elijah Muhammad, had more energy and greater personal magnetism. He had launched the NOI's influential newspaper, *Muhammad Speaks*. And as minister of New York's prominent Mosque No. 7, he had become the Nation's most effective recruiter and charismatic spokesman. All of which served Elijah Muhammad well—as long as Malcolm stuck to the script.

But Malcolm had his own opinions about world affairs, which he often expressed in public—too often for Elijah Muhammad's taste. After the Kennedy assassination, Muhammad gave explicit instructions to all NOI ministers not to comment. But during a speech at the Manhattan Center, Malcolm drew a parallel between the Kennedy killing and the assassination of South Vietnamese president Ngo Dinh Diem just twenty days earlier. Malcolm contended that Kennedy had been "twiddling his thumbs" during the planned military coup that resulted in Diem's death. Kennedy, he said, "never foresaw that the chickens would come home to roost so soon." He added: "Being an old farm boy myself, chickens coming home to roost never did make me sad; they've always made me glad."

Although Malcolm later claimed that the latter remark was taken out of context, the backlash was severe. Elijah Muhammad barred Malcolm X from public speaking for ninety days.

It was during this probationary period that Malcolm X visited Miami for the title fight. By then Elijah Muhammad—who had once condemned boxing—saw how useful Cassius Clay could be to the Nation of Islam. But only if Clay won the heavyweight title. A loser wouldn't help the Nation's image.

After Clay beat Liston, Elijah Muhammad moved swiftly. He as much as claimed credit for Clay's success. "They said that Sonny Liston would tear up that pretty face of yours," said Muhammad. "But Allah and myself said, 'No, no.'"

And he gave the new champion the name Muhammad (*worthy of praise*) Ali (*highest*). It was an extraordinary honor for such a young and inexperienced NOI member.* Whether he liked it or not, whether he even realized it or not, Ali had become a pawn in the Nation's internal power struggle.

---

* "My father called me on the phone about changing Cassius Clay's name to Muhammad Ali," Elijah Muhammad's son, Herbert Muhammad, said later. "This name would connect him with five billion Muslims all around the world, and they would rally behind him and he would become like a Statue of Liberty in the harbor of New York—that everyone would want to see him and that everyone would want his autograph."

Malcolm X certainly realized it. Two days later he announced that he was leaving the Nation of Islam. He formed a new group called the Muslim Mosque, Incorporated.

Malcolm had made his pilgrimage to help resolve his crisis of faith. The *hajj* was a privilege rarely granted Nation of Islam members—with good reason. Upon his arrival in Saudi Arabia, Malcolm was chagrined to discover that he was ignorant of Islamic prayers or native rituals. As Walter Dean Myers wrote in *Malcolm X: By Any Means Necessary*, "He was a Muslim minister in the United States, without knowing any of the fundamentals of his own religion."

So he vowed to learn them.

The six-day pilgrimage to Mecca was spiritually and physically demanding. Men had to refrain from shaving and were required to wear the *ihram*, which consisted of two pieces of plain white cloth, and sandals. The intent of this simple, uniform appearance was to eliminate all outward signs of status and put everyone on an equal plane. This had a profound effect on Malcolm X. As he wrote in a "Letter from Mecca":

> There were tens of thousands of pilgrims, from all over the world. They were of all colors, from blue-eyed blondes to black-skinned Africans. But we were all participating in the same ritual, displaying a spirit of unity and brotherhood that my experiences in America had led me to believe never could exist between the white and the non-white. America needs to understand Islam, because this is the one religion that erases from its society the race problem. . . . You may be shocked by these words coming from me. But on this pilgrimage, what I have seen, and experienced, has forced me to rearrange much of my thought patterns previously held, and to toss aside some of my previous conclusions. . . . Each hour here in the Holy Land enables me to have greater spiritual insights into what is happening in America between black and white. The American Negro never can be blamed for his racial animosities—he is only reacting to four hundred years of the conscious racism of the American whites. But as racism leads America up the suicide path, I do believe, from the experiences that I have had with them, that the whites of the younger generation, in the colleges and universities, will see the handwriting on the walls and

many of them will turn to the spiritual path of truth—the only way left to America to ward off the disaster that racism inevitably must lead to.

In the Nation of Islam, Muslim principles were interlaced with a doctrine of black separatism. Malcolm now saw this as a mistake. In anticipation of Ali's arrival in Africa, Malcolm had sent him a telegram, imploring Ali to put aside the NOI's petty internal politics and be a role model for Muslims the world over:

> Because a billion of our people in Africa, Arabia, and Asia love you blindly, you must now be forever aware of your tremendous responsibilities to them. You must never say or do anything that will permit your enemies to distort the beautiful image you have here among our people.

It was in this spirit that Malcolm—bearded, carrying a walking stick and still wearing his simple white robes—greeted Ali at the hotel in Accra.

Ali's response? "You left the honorable Elijah Muhammad," Ali said. "That was the wrong thing to do, Brother Malcolm."

End of discussion.

As for Malcolm's assertion that Ali carried "tremendous responsibilities," Ali was equally dismissive. "He didn't seem very responsible to me," Ali said, referring to Malcolm. "Man, did you get a look at him? Dressed in that funny white robe and wearing a beard and walking with that cane that looked like a prophet's stick? Man, he's gone. He's gone so far out he's out completely."

The break was clean, if painful. While Malcolm X had been transformed by his visit to Mecca, the birthplace of the Prophet Muhammad, Muhammad Ali was still following the Las Vegas teachings of Gorgeous George. Having dispensed with his old friend, Ali declared that his first order of business would be to dig up some diamonds. Literally. "Hey, Herbert," he said to Herbert Muhammad, Elijah's son. "When's the man coming to take us diamond hunting?"

"What man?" Herbert said.

"That man we met last night who told us about the diamond mines here. I heard they got a lake somewhere so full of diamonds you just wade in and feel around."

When one of the locals told him there was no such place, Ali looked disappointed. Then he brightened. When he got to Egypt, he said, he would find four wives to take home with him and live in the $100,000 house he planned to build. "It'll be like a castle and I'll have a throne room for my heavyweight crown."

The four Egyptian beauties would be named Abigail, Susie, Cecilia, and Peaches. ("I don't know yet what she'll do," he said of Peaches. "Sing or play music, maybe.") From there Ali went to the hotel balcony, where he quickly attracted an admiring crowd. "Who's the king?" he yelled.

"You are! You are!"

"Louder! Now, who's the greatest?"

"You are!"

He turned away. "OK, let's go to the beach."

And with that he was whisked away in a white convertible.

And so it went for the entire tour. Based on dispatches reaching the States, it was hard to tell whether Ali was in Africa on a spiritual journey or on an extended spring break. From Ghana he traveled to Nigeria. There he sparked a minor international incident when he announced that he was cutting his visit short. He had to get to Cairo, he said.

His hosts, who included Walter K. Scott, deputy chief of mission at the US embassy, and Hogan "Kid" Bassey, former Nigerian featherweight champion, took umbrage. A surreal exchange followed:

Ali: "They've got big things lined up for me in Cairo. [Egyptian president Gamal Abdel] Nasser wants to see me and they planned big doings for me two months ago. It's more important than Nigeria."

Bassey: "Cairo is not more important than Nigeria! Nigeria is the biggest country in Africa!"

Scott: "One out of every five people in Africa lives in Nigeria."

Ali: "Well, isn't Egypt the powerfulest country, with all them rockets and their big army and their dams?"

Bassey: "Mr. Muhammad, you are a champion. You are supposed to keep your promises. We scheduled an exhibition in Ibadan. Thousands have bought tickets to see you. We organized a soccer game specially in your honor. We invited important officials to banquets. You were picked to judge the Miss Nigeria contest Saturday. If you leave us now you'll mess everything up."

Ali: "Now, look. I don't appreciate anybody telling me to do this or that. Nobody tells me what to do or when to do it but me."

It didn't help when, after departing the tense meeting, Ali made an unscheduled stop "to get me a record player."

"That clown," Bassey fumed. "He wants to go shopping? He calls himself a champion? When's he going to realize he's over twenty-one and start acting like it?"

Egypt produced more photo ops and sound bites. Ali rode a camel on a tour of the pyramids. When the camel acted up, its nervous owner tried to step in. Ali objected. "I'm the champ," he said. "I can tame a camel just like I handled Sonny Liston."

In Port Said, Ali said that if Egypt had another showdown with Israel, similar to the 1956 Suez crisis, "I should be pleased to fight on your side and under your flag."

This did not endear him to Americans—particularly Jewish Americans—still resentful of his exemption from military service.

Ali returned to New York on June 23. According to the *New York Times*, he said he had cut his trip short because he was "too tired."

"People have been mobbing me," Ali said. "They've been killing me. Women and children were jumping off roofs, and people were coming straight out of the mountains to see me. I was treated like a politician."

More and more, he acted like one. On June 28, he attended a Nation of Islam rally at the 369th Regiment Armory in Harlem, in support of Elijah Muhammad. In the wake of Malcolm X's defection, Elijah recognized the importance of shoring up support for the Nation in New York, Malcolm's home base.

The atmosphere was charged. The pro-Elijah Muhammad crowd, jittery over rumors of an assassination attempt, attacked a suspected Malcolm X loyalist, shouting, "Kill him! Kill him now!" The man, who was actually an Elijah Muhammad supporter, was beaten before police could intervene.

Elijah Muhammad, who had to fly to Chicago immediately after the rally, addressed the crowd. Then it was Ali's turn. He was immaculately dressed in a dark suit, white shirt, and tie. And he now gave a different reason for cutting his Africa trip short. "Brothers and sisters," he began. "I don't want to take up too much time today because our leader and teacher must get to the airport. I would like to say that we just came off of a scheduled four-month tour, but we heard that our leader and teacher would be here so we had to cut short our trip in Cairo and take the next jet back to New York."

The crowd interrupted with applause.

Ali continued: "A lot of people listen to our leader talk and they say, 'Well, he's just another man with some program for Negroes.' But if you could travel around the world like I have, if you could go to Nigeria, Ghana, Cairo, Egypt, and talk to rulers of the world—as soon as I talked to President Nasser, for example, the first thing he said was, 'How's the honorable Elijah Muhammad?'"

More applause.

Ali concluded his brief remarks by presenting Elijah Muhammad with a miniature gold mosque from the Supreme Council of Islamic Affairs in Cairo. After accepting the gift, Elijah Muhammad thanked Ali, thanked the crowd, and said he hoped to return to New York soon. Hearing that, Ali applauded harder than anyone—concussive claps delivered with the force of the heavyweight champion of the world.

There could be no doubt as to where Ali stood in the power struggle between Elijah Muhammad and Malcolm X.

Less than a week after the Harlem rally, Ali met Sonji Roi, a part-time model and aspiring singer who worked at *Muhammad Speaks*. (Herbert Muhammad introduced them.) She was a couple of years older than Ali, with a son from a previous marriage and considerably more experience than Ali in male-female relationships.* She was not a Muslim nor was she particularly interested in becoming one.

Six weeks later they were married. Sonji took the last name *Clay*.

The champ's new bride created tension among the many Muslim hangers-on and advisers in Ali's camp. (This was to say nothing of the tensions between the Muslims and the Louisville Sponsoring Group, which still held Ali's contract.) Meanwhile, Sonny Liston remained in seclusion in Denver, continuing his single-minded preparation for the return bout.

All of which explained why, at the press conference in Boston that September, Liston looked fit and relaxed. Ali looked bloated, sick, and agitated. The fight was just two months away. Ali needed to get to work. Could he regain his edge? Could Liston retain his edge?

The clock was ticking.

And then, just before zero hour, it stopped.

---

* When Sonji died on October 11, 2005, her obituary listed her age as fifty-nine. That would have made her just eighteen in 1964, which seems unlikely. A January 7, 1966, UPI story about the couple's divorce said she was twenty-six, which would have meant she was born in either 1939 or 1940. Regardless of her chronological age, she was mature beyond her years, having lost both parents during her childhood and entered the workforce while in her teens. Still, she resented implications in later years that she was a predatory gold digger. "I know how I met [Ali], why I married him, and why we broke up," she told *Jet* magazine in September 1976. "There was nothing whorish or horrible about our relationship." Sonji was so put off by this characterization, in fact, that she refused to sign a release for an impending biopic, *The Greatest*, starring Ali himself. "When it comes to that part of his life with me," she told *Jet*, "they can write in 'intermission' so the people can go out and buy some popcorn and soda. When they come back after intermission, the script can pick up with Ali's life after our divorce."

CHAPTER TEN

An Ill-Timed
Bout of Illness

I n November, three days before the scheduled fight, Ali was in his
suite on the sixth floor of Boston's Sherry Biltmore Hotel, with
his entourage of about fifteen people. It was early evening. Friday
the thirteenth. Ali & Co. were watching a rented movie, *Little Caesar*
(which, in 1964, required the use of a projector).

Ali had indeed regained his edge. He had dropped his weight to
215. He had trained hard.

Probably too hard, it turned out.

In that day's *New York Times*, Robert Lipsyte had described Ali as
"bigger and seemingly faster than he was in Miami Beach earlier this
year. . . . In two rounds with Harvey (Cody) Jones, a vintage sparmate,
Clay moved with speed and assurance, rocking the 215-pound Detroit
boxer with quick combinations to the head, dancing lightly away from
his jabs and spinning off the ropes with an apparently careless attitude
toward protecting his stomach."

That workout had been on Thursday. On Friday Ali did five miles
of roadwork in the morning, then skipped a planned afternoon workout. He shopped for a suit instead.

Before the evening movie Ali ate a steak dinner. It didn't stay with
him long. "He got violently sick and started to throw up," the ever-
present Bundini Brown said later. "His stomach swelled up the size of a
football. I wanted to call a doctor but he said, 'No, get me to a hospital
quick. I'm in bad pain.'"

"The bellyache felt all round the world," the *Boston Globe*'s John
Ahern called it the next day.

Ali ended up at Boston City Hospital. Diagnosis: an incarcerated inguinal hernia. An inguinal hernia is a weakness in the abdominal wall. Ali later said that he had felt "something slipping, a funny sensation" in that area before, but it had never caused any problems. That evening, however, the weakness gave way and a loop of Ali's intestine became trapped in the opening. (That was the *incarcerated* part.) The result was an obstructed bowel. If the hernia had progressed from incarcerated to strangulated, it would have cut off the blood supply to the intestine—a life-threatening condition.

Dr. Thomas G. O'Brien, senior chief resident at Boston City Hospital, was the first to examine Ali. Dr. O'Brien called in Dr. William McDermott, head of the surgical team. Dr. McDermott was a Harvard man, and one of the best surgeons in Boston.

Dr. Nathan Shapiro, the Massachusetts Boxing Commission's designated physician, also weighed in. He had examined Ali on Monday and found nothing—because, he said, there was nothing to find. "This came on very suddenly," said Dr. Shapiro. "There was no sign of a hernia Monday."*

Dr. O'Brien concurred: "There was a small defect which suddenly gave way," he said. "There had been a weakness in that area for some time."

Most likely the weak spot was congenital, and "excessive physical conditioning and training" had caused it to give way, said Dr. Shapiro.

Bundini Brown blamed himself. "I had him wearin' real heavy shoes to train in," he said. "Could that give him a hernia?"

Dr. Shapiro: "I don't think his roadwork did it."

Regardless of the cause, the effect was clear. Dr. Shapiro, acting on behalf of the Massachusetts Boxing Commission, made the obvious

---

* Not that Ali hadn't *tried* to give himself a hernia on Monday. Just before visiting the doctor, he had reprised his "bear huntin'" shtick. As Bundini Brown spread puddles of honey, Ali lugged an enormous bear trap down Babcock Street, dodging streetcars and shouting: "Have you seen that bear? There's a bear loose and I gotta catch him." This time even Liston—stranded in the resulting traffic jam with Boston commuters—eventually cracked a smile. Not so Inter-Continental president Bob Nilon. "Five million dollars all tied up and he's running behind trolley cars," Nilon said. "Get him the hell off that street."

recommendation. His patient consented. "Doc," Ali said, "go ahead and fix it."

Dr. Shapiro left the actual operation to Dr. McDermott. The *Boston Globe*'s Bud Collins said that having a surgeon of Dr. McDermott's stature perform a hernia repair was like having Picasso paint his wife's fingernails.

The procedure took 100 minutes. Afterward the surgical team told the press that the patient was "in excellent condition."

Ali might have been in excellent condition for a hernia patient—but not for a boxer. There would be no heavyweight title fight in Boston on Monday night, or any night soon. Probably not until the spring of '65 at the earliest.

Because it was Friday evening when the incarceration occurred, most of those connected with the fight had dispersed throughout the city. They heard the news at different times and in different ways, but their reactions were all basically the same. "I never saw anything like it in my life," said veteran trainer Al Lacey. "People were stunned. It came like a clap of thunder. . . . Even Silverman was speechless."

It was a loud commentary on the state of boxing in November 1964 that almost no one accepted the news at face value. Said Angelo Dundee, who was at McHugh Forum on the Boston College campus, watching his hometown Miami Hurricanes beat up on the BC Eagles in a closed-circuit football telecast, "I thought somebody was getting funny, but I rushed over [to the hospital] anyway."

Bill Faversham of the Louisville Sponsoring Group had just talked to Ali at 6:30 that evening before leaving for Boston Garden to watch the Celtics–Lakers game. His reaction when he heard a short time later that Ali was en route to the hospital: "What funny thing is he up to now?" Others veered down a darker road, speculating that someone—the Mob? Operatives from Malcolm X's Muslim Mosque, Incorporated?—had poisoned Ali. But the conspiracy theorists had confused cause and effect—the hernia had induced vomiting, not the other way around.

The initial shock of the news quickly gave way to a feeling of depression. "Two days!" Brown sobbed. "Just two days to go, and he was so pretty! He was gettin' evil, too, good and evil like he had to be for this. All this work—it's like milkin' a cow and having him kick it over."

But of course no one was more devastated than Sonny Liston.

L iston had just returned to the White Cliffs Hotel from an after-dinner walk when Willie Reddish broke the news. Liston had the universal reaction: "I don't believe it. It's another one of his tricks."

Soon enough Liston received confirmation that it was not a practical joke, not a psychological ploy to pierce his iron resolve. Ali's hernia was legitimate. The fight was off.

In some accounts Liston tried to brush the news aside with his underrated wit. "It might have been worse," he said. "It might have happened to me." Mostly, though, he was forthright in expressing the depth of his disappointment. "What a letdown," he said. "I build up to this—and then *this*."

The timing, in particular, was cruel. "I feel very bad," Liston said the next day. "I was ready to go. If it had to happen, I wish it happened earlier instead of waiting until the hard work was over."

His words echoed Bundini Brown's milk-cow analogy. But there was a huge difference in the outlook between the two fighters' camps. Beyond the immediate disappointment, the delay meant little to Ali; in the spring he would simply be six months deeper into his prime. Liston would be six months further away from his. When it came to borrowed time, his interest already exceeded his principal.

In his buildup to November, Liston had squandered much of his remaining vitality. This was his one opportunity to regain the thing in life that had meant the most—the heavyweight championship. And with the belt back in hand, he could have assured a few more big paydays, which could have secured a future beyond boxing—a future that he must have seen all too vividly by then. He could have fought a few more times against the likes of Ernie Terrell and Eddie Machen and then retired with his dignity and his bank balance intact.

Newspaper reports about the financial implications of the postponement provided an insight into each boxer's perspective. For Ali, the delay amounted to a windfall of sorts. "He's just discovered that this will be a big year for him as far as taxes are concerned," said PR flack Harold Conrad. "It will cost close to $75,000 in training expenses, and for the first time he's got a loss to deduct. That pleases him." (Ali even caught a financial break on his surgery. According to the Associated Press, Dr. McDermott would not bill Ali because Boston City Hospital didn't charge for emergency services. "I was called in by the resident surgeon, and I was glad to be of service," Dr. McDermott said. "The patient did not ask for me." Ali would, however, be billed for his room—at $45 or $46 a day.)

Liston also joked about his losses. But there was a glumness to his humor, which hinted at the grim premonition he must have had of life after boxing. "Well," he said, pondering the tab he had run up at White Cliffs, "let's all put on our aprons and go to work to pay the bills."

CHAPTER ELEVEN

Meanwhile, Back in Lewiston. . . .

I t wasn't just the fighters who felt the financial pinch. Harold Conrad estimated that Inter-Continental Promotions took a $50,000 loss. SportsVision, Inc., the company that had won the bid for the closed-circuit rights, got hit even harder. "I'd say $250,000 plus would be a good guess," said Fred Brooks, SportsVision's twenty-nine-year-old president.

All those losses trickled down to the individual distributors—including Sam Michael, up in Lewiston. This time Sam had planned to show the fight at Portland City Auditorium, which had a smaller capacity (1,900) than the Exposition Building but more traditional theater seating. He would have to eat the cost of incidental expenses such as advertising. (An ad for the Portland closed-circuit showing appeared in Saturday's *Lewiston Daily Sun*, on the same page as a story about the postponement.)

But those were two-bit problems compared to what Sam was dealing with down at Lewiston City Hall. He was finishing up his eighth year as industrial development director. Working on an annual contract was getting old. Every year he had to tap-dance for the city's five-member Finance Board, trying to justify every penny of his budget. ("For office equipment, Michael is requesting four office chairs at $40 each," the *Daily Sun* duly reported in its exhaustively itemized report of his 1964 budget request.)

The Finance Board had been born of corruption in 1939. In Lewiston, it seemed, the best way to get by during the Great Depression was to get elected. A group calling itself *Les Vigilants* began investigating alleged improprieties down at city hall. The *Portland Sunday Telegram* screamed the results:

LEWISTON CITY GOVERNMENT SCANDAL
NEVER EQUALLED IN STATE'S HISTORY

As the charges piled up, a parade of aldermen and other officials ended up in jail or fleeing to Canada, accused of everything from larceny to embezzlement to malfeasance of office. A doctor in the city's health department had paid a bribe to land the job. So had a school janitor—and people at every level in between. And if people didn't have money to pay officials off—well, there was always the barter system. In exchange for fixing a dairy contract, some officials got free milk deliveries. Another official appropriated twenty-six tubs of butter from a federal welfare program.

And that's to say nothing of all the cronyism. Municipal offices were larded with phantom positions like Assistant Tax Collector Without Portfolio. And on and on it went, prompting one citizen to ask, in a plaintive letter to the editor, "Aren't there ten righteous men left who have some interest in our city besides looting it?"

So the Finance Board was a well-intentioned effort to bring accountability to the city's accounting practices. But over twenty-five years the law of unintended consequences had taken hold. For some Finance Board members, it was no longer enough to ensure that appropriations weren't misappropriated. They now took it upon themselves to determine which programs would be funded and how much each city official would be paid—or even if they would be paid at all. The Finance Board could eliminate a legitimate job with the slash of a red pen. And because the Finance Board members were appointed, not elected, they answered to no one. Not to the voters, not to the aldermen, not even to the mayor who appointed them. (The mayor's term was just one year; each Finance Board member's term was five years.) Some took perverse pleasure in making their political enemies grovel for every nickel. City officials often felt like kids pleading for their allowance.

Sam Michael, perhaps because of his background as a fight promoter, was a polarizing figure. A year earlier, a member of the Finance

Board had proposed slashing Sam's $12,500 annual salary. (That would be equivalent to about $96,000 today. "I think there was some jealousy there," Sam's son John recalled, "because they were paying him a pretty good sum.") The implications were obvious. "There has been some talk about cutting Michael's salary, as a means of forcing him out of the job," the *Daily Sun* reported. After much wrangling, his contract was renewed by a vote of three to two.

Fiscal year 1965 brought more of the same. The negotiations began with Finance Board member Jules Goudreau proposing that Sam take a $5,000 pay cut.

This time, as he fought for his job, Sam acquired an unlikely ally. A new mayor took office that January, Robert Couturier. He was, at twenty-four, the youngest mayor in America.* Couturier was a Lewiston native. He had graduated from St. Dominic's High School and majored in government at Bates College. In high school he had contributed to *Le Messager*. He now hosted a French-language radio show. He taught at St. Peter's Grammar School. He had a fierce civic pride. He was precocious and earnest. He dressed impeccably.

The one boxing match he attended had sickened him.

But Lewiston's twenty-four-year-old mayor and its fifty-nine-year-old fight-promoter-turned-industrial-development-director were alike in a lot of ways. Couturier, like Sam Michael, had a grander vision of Lewiston than most other Lewistonians did. He wanted to pursue federal funding for urban renewal, for instance. A study claimed that of the $2,789,609 required to modernize the downtown area, Lewiston would be required to pay just $136,278. The feds would pay the rest.

Couturier anticipated a battle in trying to get even that much money. He had reached the same conclusion before his first day at city hall that Sam Michael had after eight years. The hidebound Finance Board was holding the city back. As long as the Board controlled the

---

* It wasn't long before the first *Aw, isn't that cute—the mayor's just a kid!* story hit the wire services. "I looked around for a good candidate I could support for mayor, and I couldn't find one who was willing to run," Couturier told the Associated Press. "I had to run for the office or shut up."

budget, it would be almost impossible to make anything of note happen in Lewiston, Maine.

Couturier's inauguration was on Monday evening, January 4, 1965. An estimated 3,000 people jammed City Hall Auditorium. This was not a fight crowd. The men all wore suits. The women wore dresses and hats. Nuns in full habit were scattered among the pewlike benches, making it look like a church service. Right Reverend Msgr. Felix Martin of Holy Cross Church delivered an opening prayer. The Lewiston High School band opened the ceremonies with the national anthem, accompanied by *Les Petits Chanteurs* ("the little singers") of St. Peter's.

Governor John Reed was there. He said he was "pleased to see a young citizen seizing the opportunity to actively participate in government."

City clerk Lucien Lebel administered the oath of office. And then the young mayor spoke.

Anyone expecting a gust of gee-whiz platitudes received a rude shock.

After thanking Governor Reed and the citizens of Lewiston, Couturier launched a full-scale attack on the Finance Board. "Excessive checks on the power of any official will only slow down the wheels of government," Couturier said. "It might even bring those wheels to a standstill, creating a situation where progress is no longer possible or feasible. There is no doubt in my mind that the charter under which the City of Lewiston functions today is not the same New Charter of 1939. . . . Where power was formerly balanced, it has been funneled—due to loopholes— into the hands of one single appointed body: the Board of Finance."

After enumerating the many difficulties the Board had imposed upon the city, Couturier concluded: "I know that come the day of decision, you will gladly rid our city of its octopus and replace it with a free, modern, democratic form of government where the people not only pay the taxes, but through their *elected*"—he hit that word hard— "representatives decide what government shall accomplish. In the near future I will name an official committee to look into this matter."

He concluded by channeling members of the original Tea Party: "I believe that you agree with me when I say that taxation without proper elected representation is nothing less than tyranny."

City Hall Auditorium swelled with applause.

Couturier didn't mention any current city officials in his speech, with one exception: Sam Michael.

"I have heard executives and people in the industrial development field praise the director," Couturier said. "I have listened to citizens tear him to shreds. Even if one does not think that Mr. Sam Michael was ideally suited for the position when he was appointed eight years ago, the fact remains that we have spent a considerable amount of money in training him."

And, concluded the mayor: "We have paid for contacts that could pay off very shortly."

The next day the Finance Board voted four to one to retain Sam at the same salary. The lone negative vote was from Jules Goudreau, the man who had pushed for a pay cut. But it was too late. As Robert Couturier made his noisy entrance into Lewiston's city government, Sam Michael was quietly planning his exit strategy.

The timing at the end—as was often the case with Sam—was unfortunate. By April Robert Couturier and Jules Goudreau were at war. Goudreau joined a petition drive to oppose the mayor's urban renewal project. (Sam Michael's old nemesis, Ernest Malenfant, also came out against urban renewal, calling it a "Communist-inspired plan originating in Russia.") Then Goudreau leaked the "news" that the city was in near rebellion over this new whippersnapper-in-chief, with eleven prominent officials on the verge of resigning.

Couturier's response: "It is true that resignations are expected in Lewiston city government. I have requested the resignation of certain officials because of incompetence, nonfeasance, or misfeasance. . . . It is most surprising that certain members of this government would not know where the city is going, what we are striving for."

Sam resigned that same week—even though his resignation was not among those that Couturier had requested (a point that Couturier confirmed with a statement the next day). And despite the mudslinging, Sam emerged with his reputation intact. "Mr. Michael has had to work under severe handicaps," the *Daily Sun* wrote in an editorial. "His office has been a political football and city officials have relished in hamstringing him by restrictions rather than providing the whole-hearted cooperation which could have produced even more results. . . .

"It is true that Mr. Michael did not perform miracles. But no one can reasonably expect them in the highly competitive field of industrial development."

Within days came the news that Sam Michael had accepted the newly created job of industrial development director in Oxford County, just west of Lewiston. On the surface it seemed like a strange choice. True, Sam was getting a twenty-percent salary bump, to $15,000. But beyond that, it seemed like a lateral move at best—and a big step down at worst. The entire county had a population of 44,345—just a few thousand more than Lewiston, divided among thirty-nine communities. And those thirty-nine communities were spread over 2,175 square miles, stretching all the way to the Quebec border.

But where a lot of people would have seen empty fields, Sam Michael saw a blank canvas. All those square miles of open space in Oxford County inspired greater optimism than all those square feet of vacant factory floors in Lewiston.

According to the terms of his four-year contract, Sam would be Oxford County's recreational director as well as its industrial director. His recent return to boxing, even if it was only through closed-circuit broadcasts, had renewed his interest in entertainment promotion. He called closed-circuit TV "the salvation of boxing," because revenue was no longer restricted to the live gate. Further, because most of the money now came from TV rights, major venues like Madison Square Garden had lost their stranglehold on title fights. Sam had told a reporter a few years earlier that he thought Maine now had as much chance as anywhere else to host a big-time bout.

Yes, in Sam's mind, Oxford County had all kinds of potential. It was a popular camping destination. Who knew? Maybe there was a way to combine camping and show business—to put Oxford County in the same league as the Catskills. Also, Oxford County had an auto-racing track. Maybe that could be a draw.* Without the restrictions of

* Within two years, NASCAR stars Bobby Allison and Richard Petty would win races at Oxford Plains Speedway.

the Finance Board, Sam felt liberated. "If I can't do anything for Oxford County in two years," he declared, "I won't stay."

And the best part about the new job was that he didn't have to move.

That was the thing that all of his detractors had missed. He hadn't taken the industrial development director's job as a steppingstone. It was never his plan to milk the city for contacts and experience and then bolt for a better offer outside Maine. Yes, he had established connections all over the country—but he had put down roots in Lewiston/Auburn. And he still loved it, despite his ill feelings toward a handful of Lewiston's political figures.

Anyway, Sam wasn't the type to burn bridges. He gave a full month's notice, to make the transition easier. He appeared before the Finance Board to recommend that they use some of his unpaid salary to update a brochure he had prepared touting all the benefits Lewiston offered. "I'm sorry I have to throw this in your lap," he said.

Sam's last day on the job in Lewiston was supposed to be Friday, May 21. His first day on the job in Oxford County was supposed to be Monday, May 24.

But that schedule had to be adjusted.

Something came up.

PART TWO

CHAPTER TWELVE

A Public Nuisance

The rumblings were faint at first, like the precursory tremors of a volcano. In Massachusetts, people of influence were taking a closer look at the Ali–Liston return bout, rescheduled for Tuesday, May 25, 1965, at Boston Garden. A story in the April 8 *Boston Globe* carried the headline:

D.A. BYRNE PROBES LISTON'S ANTICS

According to the story, Suffolk County district attorney Garrett Byrne had "ordered one of his assistants to meet with the state boxing commission at 2 p.m. today to discuss the championship bout between Cassius Clay and Sonny Liston. . . . The talks will focus particular attention on Liston, his background, his behavior, and whether he should be allowed to compete in Massachusetts. . . . Why the former champion's status suddenly becomes important enough to be brought up at an executive session with an assistant district attorney wasn't divulged."

But it was easy to guess. The political climate had changed dramatically since November. Endicott Peabody, the Democratic governor who had championed the championship fight, had left office in January. His replacement was Republican John Volpe. And it was becoming apparent that opposition to the fight was bipartisan. In fact, it was possible that D.A. Byrne had received his mysterious directive not from the Republican governor but from a Democratic senator, Edward Kennedy.

The first family of Massachusetts politics were no fans of Sonny Liston. Before the first Liston–Patterson fight, President John F. Kennedy had told Patterson to "make sure you keep that championship" because JFK hated the thought of the title falling into Liston's hands.

And when Liston associates Frankie Carbo and Blinky Palermo were convicted of conspiracy and extortion after attempting to strong-arm two Los Angeles men who managed welterweight champ Don Jordan, Attorney General Robert Kennedy said, "This verdict will be a great aid and assistance to the Department of Justice and local authorities in taking further action against the attempts of racketeers to control boxing and other sports."

Given the Kennedys' obvious enmity toward Liston, why hadn't Ted Kennedy stepped in back in September, before the fight was first announced? For one thing, Kennedy wasn't able to step anywhere at that point; he was laid up with a broken back, suffered in a June '64 plane crash. He had called Peabody that fall to express his displeasure, but that was as far as it went.

But in the spring of '65 Kennedy was back on his feet. And he no longer had to worry about the political awkwardness of opposing a Democratic governor.

Still, just because the Massachusetts political machine might have decided that they didn't want the fight in their own backyard, they had no legal right to prevent it.

Or did they?

As D.A. Byrne pointed out, state law empowered the Massachusetts Boxing Commission to "revoke any license when in the judgment of the commission the licensee has been guilty of an act or offense detrimental to the public interest. . . . Sonny Liston has a criminal record dating back to June 1, 1950, including such crimes as assault with intent to kill, first-degree robbery, and larceny. Is it in the public interest to have a man with this background licensed as a boxer in Massachusetts?"

Byrne declared the fight "a public nuisance."

The fight's promotional team, a combination of inexperienced out-of-towners and a local hustler whose fly-by-night ways had earned him the nickname "Suitcase Sam," made it comedically easy for Byrne to build his case. For instance, it soon came to light that Sam Silverman's license had expired on April 1.

April Fool's Day. Of course.

Silverman easily remedied the license problem. But there wasn't much he could do against a bipartisan political alliance that seemed determined to run the fight out of town. And given the TV people's reluctance to postpone the bout a second time ("We'll hold this heavyweight title fight May 25 if we have to hold it on a barge in a Florida swamp," SportsVision's Fred Brooks said), Byrne didn't even have the burden of proving anything in court. All he had to do was schedule additional hearings, ask for more documents, etc.—all perfectly reasonable requests—and let the plodding pace of bureaucracy force the promoters' hand. "Even if we do beat this injunction," an unnamed Inter-Continental spokesman told the *Globe*, "how do we know that Gary Byrne won't come up with some other harassment just before the fight? He's got us jumpy."

Any additional delay would compel Inter-Continental to cancel the fight. Or take it elsewhere.

Public opinion was not on the promoters' side, either. It had been a tumultuous winter, with each new development casting Ali and Liston in less favorable light than ever:

- Liston got arrested for DUI on Christmas Day. It took ten Denver cops to get him into the paddy wagon. That same day, former Ali associate Leon Ameer—who had defected from the Nation of Islam in support of Malcolm X—was severely beaten. Four members of Boston's NOI temple were charged with assault. "If my life is worth three cents," Malcolm X said later, "then his is worth two cents." Three months later Ameer was found dead.

- On January 19, Clay was behind the wheel of his bus, Big Red, on the way to the Monticello, New York, training camp of George Chuvalo, in advance of the Chuvalo–Floyd Patterson fight, when he went off the road into a ditch. Writers on the bus had to escape through the emergency exit.

- On January 22, the *Boston Globe's* Bud Collins noted that Liston faced jail time on the DUI charge, and his possible sentence could put the rescheduled return bout in jeopardy. Wrote Collins: "Liston drunk would be more rational than Cassius Clay sober, but I don't suppose that is admissible as a defense in Colorado." (Liston was acquitted on January 30.)

- On February 1 Patterson beat Chuvalo. But even a victory for boxing's "good guy" resulted in another black eye for the sport. Patterson revealed afterward that he had fought with an undisclosed injury to his left hand. The New York State Athletic Commission launched yet another investigation.

- On February 17 a UPI report referred to Ali as "the defrocked world champion" because the World Boxing Association had formally stripped him of the title. The story also reported that Ali had been granted a license to fight an exhibition bout in Chicago to benefit the Black Muslims.

But the most malevolent development occurred on February 21, when Malcolm X was shot to death while speaking at the Audubon Ballroom in Washington Heights, New York. Multiple gunmen were involved, but only one, NOI member Talmadge X Hayer, a.k.a. Thomas Hagan, was apprehended at the scene—because he had been wounded in the leg by return fire from one of Malcolm X's bodyguards. Police estimated that more than thirty shots were fired in the ballroom.

The assassination had a chilling effect on the American public. It had been just fifteen months since President Kennedy had been gunned down on a Dallas street. The idea of public figures being murdered in public places did not seem farfetched. And the heavyweight champion was linked to a couple of extremist groups who were prepared to settle their differences with guns in crowded halls, bystanders be damned.

Almost immediately, speculation flowed that Malcolm's followers would seek revenge—possibly by targeting Ali for a hit. "I believe somebody important will have to pay when Malcolm X's followers or the others angered by his murder reciprocate against the Muslims," said Aubrey Barnette, a former member of the Nation of Islam. "They will try to get back at the Muslims in some way to make a big impression, with someone the equal of Malcolm in national stature. Clay has that stature. But I think he is in danger from the Muslims, too, because he was a friend of Malcolm's. Malcolm brought him into the movement, and anyone who was ever friendly to Malcolm is in danger."

The assassination and its aftermath added a dose of real-world menace to the prefight coverage. The weekend after Malcolm X's killing, security was heavy at the Nation of Islam convention at Chicago Coliseum. Nevertheless, Ali went ahead with his advertised exhibition bouts, against his brother, Rahaman Ali. "There was this nagging danger in the Coliseum," columnist Jimmy Breslin wrote. "Some of Malcolm X's followers had said during the week, 'Why not? Why shouldn't we shoot him?' Saturday, there was this small chance, in the middle of this rickety afternoon, that somebody would shoot Clay in the back."

Despite all the negative press and prophecies of doom, preparations for the fight proceeded as normal through the end of April. On Saturday, May 1, Sonny Liston flew from Denver to Boston, accompanied by his wife, Geraldine; his accountant, Archie Parolli; and his father-in-law, Dusty Crawford. Asked about the D.A. office's investigation, Liston was dismissive. "I don't know nothin' about contracts," he said. "What contracts? You mean on the fight, the promoters, and that stuff? I don't know nothin'."

At the same time, Ali was stranded en route from Miami to Massachusetts aboard his bus, Big Red. He had invited several writers, including Bud Collins, to ride along with him. For Collins, it was a welcome respite from reporting on the dreary legal proceedings connected with the fight. And unlike many other writers, Collins enjoyed Ali's company—even if he did describe the trip as "three days in an echo chamber on wheels."

"Fasten your seatbelts," Ali announced upon departure. "We gonna take off and there may be some turbulence."

Turbulence, indeed. On May Day Collins sent a mayday. MAROONED WITH CASSIUS CLAY IN CUMBERLAND COUNTY, NORTH CAROLINA, read the *Globe* dateline. Big Red had come to a smoky halt along a rural road sixteen miles outside Fayetteville when a bad wheel bearing caused the rear axle to catch fire. "This bus is all gas and no grease," Bundini Brown complained.

The heavyweight champion of the world and his entourage were stranded for nine hours. "Food ran out," Collins wrote, "and also money." He reported that by trip's end Ali would be "into the accompanying correspondents for $300."

Even so, Ali eventually came up with a rescue plan. With virtually no money down, he chartered a Trailways bus to take over for Big Red. But what the balance of the trip offered in comfort and security, it lacked in color. "The Trailways people are sissies," Collins wrote. "They have tires with treads. . . . They don't honk the horn at chicks in small towns. . . . And the Trailways driver wouldn't even let Clay near the wheel to show them how he steered with his knees."

With his keen sense of the absurd, Collins made the debacle sound like a freewheeling good time. And in the process he might have given Boston's fight fans a false sense of optimism. Despite all the obstacles in their respective paths, both Ali and Liston had made it back to Massachusetts, ready to begin final training. Maybe all the D.A.'s tough talk was just that—talk. Maybe he just wanted to be sure that everyone connected with the fight knew he was watching them. Maybe, in the end, his legal posturing was just another hurdle to clear, like a DUI arrest or a burnt wheel bearing.

Maybe the fight would still happen at Boston Garden as scheduled.

Watching all this from up in Lewiston, Sam Michael knew better. He understood how challenging it was to promote a boxing match. He also knew how hard it was to fight city hall. Trying to do both at the same time would be futile. He had conveyed that message to Inter-Continental Promotions the previous summer, when the Nilon brothers were having trouble finding a major city to host the return bout. Sam had called Inter-Continental and offered up Lewiston as an alternative. With his connections in Maine boxing as well as with the state's department of economic development, he was in a better position to secure the fight than a promoter who had to deal with an adverse big-city bureaucracy.

In the summer of '64, Inter-Continental didn't take his proposal seriously.

But Sam Michael didn't give up easily. With the Boston Garden date in jeopardy and time running out, he picked up the phone again.

But this time instead of calling Inter-Continental directly, he made his pitch to his old friend Sam Silverman. "Why don't you bring that Clay–Liston fight to Maine?" Michael told Silverman. "We'll give you all the help you need. There are two or three places it could be held, and all your worries will be over."

"Thanks, but I'm in no mood for joking," Silverman said. "This thing has me bugged."

"Who's joking?" Michael said. "You don't care too much about the live gate. You've just got to have a ring to fight in, and it looks as though the Massachusetts lawyers are going to drive you out of the state."

He ended with this: "When that time comes, don't forget about this phone call."

CHAPTER THIRTEEN

"Guess What? My Dad's Gonna Bring the Fight Here."

If not for the vagaries of the major league baseball schedule, the second Ali–Liston fight might have been at the Astrodome. Houston's space-age indoor stadium had just opened in April 1965. It drew breathless reviews (evangelist Billy Graham called it "the Eighth Wonder of the World") and bedazzled crowds. The Astrodome was such an enchanting novelty that it transformed the dreadful Houston Colt .45s into a popular attraction. The Colt .45s finished next-to-last in the National League standings in 1964 and dead last in attendance. Rechristened the Astros, the team would finish next-to-last again in 1965. But home attendance would nearly triple, to more than two million, thanks to its wondrous new park.

The Astrodome's futuristic magnetism could have served as an antidote to the Ali–Liston fight's atavistic negativity. Given a clear path, Inter-Continental Promotions would have moved the fight there without hesitation. Unfortunately for Inter-Continental, the Astros finished the month of May with a sixteen-game home stand, including a date with the Cincinnati Reds the night of May 25. Because the fight date was inflexible, the Astrodome was quickly ruled out as an alternative site.

So Inter-Continental kept looking. Publicly, they remained committed to Boston. But behind the scenes they investigated other options with growing urgency, spooked by D.A. Byrne's obstructionist tactics. If they got a firm offer elsewhere—and it could be just about anywhere—they would bail out of Boston Garden.

Meanwhile, the two fighters went about their business. Each had set up camp in an unusual location. Sonny Liston's entourage had a half-dozen forty-five-dollar-a-day suites at the Towers Motor Inn in Dedham, Massachusetts. It was at the Route One interchange, among the burgeoning high-tech firms on suburban Boston's Route 128. Liston's training facility was on the second floor of an unfinished office building. Ali had set up at the Schine Inn in Chicopee, eighty-five miles west of Boston along the Massachusetts Turnpike. He would spar in a room above a bowling alley next door.

Each fighter immediately assumed a familiar role—unwittingly, in Liston's case. As was the custom, Liston's camp charged spectators a dollar to watch Liston work out. Or at least they did until Walter H. Carroll, Dedham's chief of police, told them to cease and desist. Turned out that they were violating an obscure statute that no one had ever bothered to enforce until Sonny Liston came along.

The police were watching Ali, too, but for a different reason. Rumors continued to circulate that Malcolm X loyalists had marked him for death. Nevertheless, Ali remained open and accessible. And the Schine Inn did the Chicopee police no favors by printing Ali's itinerary on a hand-out card:

6:00 A.M. – Early Rise
6:30 A.M.– Road Work (5 Miles Daily)
7:30 A.M. – Hearty Breakfast
8:30 A.M. – Workout (Closed to Public)
12:00 P.M. – Training Lunch
12:45 P.M. – Press Conference
1:00 P.M. – Workout (Open to Public) Drills, Jump rope, etc.
2:00 P.M. – Sparring
3:00 P.M. – Workout– Drills, Jump rope, etc.

Gawkers grabbed the cards and thrust them at Ali for his autograph. Although he usually obliged, not everyone was happy with the results. "What good is this?" one schoolgirl complained after noticing the "Muhammad Ali" signature she'd received. "I wanted him to sign 'Cassius Clay.' Now nobody will ever believe I met the heavyweight champion."

On Thursday, May 6, Ali took the day off. Or part of the day, anyway. Things were coming to a head in Boston. Ali and Liston had been ordered to appear before Equity Court judge Felix Forte on Friday, for reasons unclear. There was no sense in either fighter continuing to train until they were sure that the fight was actually going to happen. Friday would be D-Day, one way or another.

On Thursday Ali spent a long while listening to his ever-growing record collection. His favorite recordings were those of Sam Cooke, whom he had befriended before the singer's death at age thirty-three in a bizarre shooting at a Los Angeles motel five months earlier.

After this contemplative time Ali grew restless. He wanted to take a walk. Bundini Brown implored him to stay put: "Just take it easy and relax. There'll be plenty of work yet before the fight."

Ali insisted on going out. But he never made it past the lobby. A group of airmen from nearby Westover Field spotted him.

Champ! Hey, Champ!

Halfway through his day off, Ali was back on.

That same day, some 200 miles to the northeast, Sam Michael was feeling a little out of sorts himself. Having made his pitch to bring the fight to Maine, all he could do was wait. Probably nothing would come of it. Inter-Continental had told him that the possibility was remote.

He had plenty to keep his mind occupied. Although he was still the industrial development director in Lewiston, he had begun preparing for the transition to his new job in Oxford County. That afternoon he had to give a speech at a Kiwanis Club luncheon in Norway, a town of about 5,000 people on Lake Pennessewassee.

Meanwhile, the principals at Inter-Continental Promotions felt a rising sense of panic. The fight's hard-and-fast date was less than three weeks away. Things looked bleak in Boston and Inter-Continental was running out of alternatives. Atlantic City, Baltimore, Chicago, Detroit, Houston, Indianapolis, Las Vegas, Pittsburgh, Seattle—none of them had panned out. On Wednesday, in an act of irrational optimism, a contingent from Inter-Continental had flown to Cleveland along with SportsVision's Fred Brooks. They met with longtime local boxing promoter Larry Atkins about trying to move the fight to Cleveland Arena. Atkins said that he was "fairly confident" he could get it done—even though Dave Ott of Cleveland's boxing commission threatened to resign if the fight came to town.

It all sounded too familiar. Inter-Continental wanted assurances from Cleveland mayor Ralph Locher that there would be no political resistance. Locher had little tolerance for public discord; the year before he had banned rock concerts in the city following rowdy performances by both the Beatles and the Rolling Stones, declaring that "such groups do not add to the community's culture or entertainment."

Atkins tried to set up a meeting between the mayor and the Inter-Continental contingent for Thursday morning. The mayor refused to take it. "There is no need for me to step in," Locher said. "I am not opposed to boxing, but Dave Ott felt this particular [fight] would not be good for the city. I concur with him in this."

Suddenly the remote possibility of holding the fight in Maine appeared to be the only possibility of holding the fight at all. The Inter-Continental folks called Sam Michael's house on Summer Street in Auburn. Sam's wife Doris answered. She told them that Sam was giving a speech, and gave them the name of the church where the Kiwanis Club luncheon was.

The church didn't have a phone. "So we called the state police," Inter-Continental's vice president, Sam Margolis, said a couple of days later, "and they delivered a message to him at the speaker's table."

After getting through what was probably the most distracted public speaking performance of his career, Sam Michael returned the call from Cleveland. Immediately after that, the Inter-Continental representatives flew to Logan Airport in Boston. They rented a car and headed north. Sam Michael jumped in his Lincoln and headed south. They met on Thursday night in Kittery, on the Maine–New Hampshire border.

The next morning, Sam Michael's fourteen-year-old son John had a scoop for his classmates at Webster Junior High School. "Guess what," he told them. "My dad's gonna bring the Clay–Liston fight here."

His friends all offered a variation of the same response: "You're crazy."

Said John, who had inherited some of his father's opportunism, "Wanna bet?"

By the end of the school day, he was about fifty dollars richer.

The buzz, much of it spoken in French, swirled about Lewiston's cafes and lunch counters as noon approached. Over their twenty-five-cent creton sandwiches—cold pork pate—the locals chewed on the outlandish rumor. And then someone spotted Robert Croteau, the superintendent at the Central Maine Youth Center, an arena on Birch Street used primarily for high school hockey. He ought to know what was going on. *Hey, Croteau, tell us about the big fight!*

"I didn't know as much as the people knew," Croteau said later. "But I would not lie to my friends."

So he told them what he knew: "I got a call from the good Fathers and they told me some gentlemen would look at the building. The gentlemen came and they were in a hurry. I could tell that they were not interested in the seating capacity. They talked mostly about where to put the big cameras. They stayed a while and left for Augusta. They said they had to see Governor Reed."

The official announcement came Friday afternoon in the Executive Council's chambers at the State House. "I'm very pleased that Inter-Continental has made the decision to come to Maine for this spectacular international event," said Governor John Reed.

Barely twenty-four hours had elapsed since Sam Michael returned the distress call from Cleveland.

Governor Reed said that the fight would be held as scheduled, Tuesday, May 25, at the Central Maine Youth Center in Lewiston. He added that Maine attorney general Richard F. Dubord has "assured me that he anticipates no legal problems."

Ali and Liston never did appear before Judge Forte in Boston. And although D.A. Byrne vowed to continue his investigation—some might call it a vendetta—few people saw the point. Attorneys for both sides agreed to a stipulation that the fight would not take place at Boston Garden, and that was pretty much the end of that.*

---

* A wire-service story on July 23 said that the D.A. office's entire case was based on suspicions that Sonny Liston had concealed a shoulder injury before the Miami fight. Sol Silverman, chairman of the California Committee on Boxing Safeguards, told UPI, "Boston District Attorney Garrett Byrne told me evidence gathered by his office showed that Liston wasn't fit to fight Clay in their first bout at Miami."

Also on hand for the announcement were Fred Brooks, Sam Margolis, PR man Harold Conrad, Inter-Continental president Bob Nilon, and Inter-Continental attorney Garland Cherry. They crowded around the governor for a press photo.

Margolis noticed that someone was missing. "I had to go and hunt for Sam Michael in order to get him into the picture," Margolis said later.

That was fitting. Until the last minute, Sam Michael and Lewiston—or "Lewistown," as the *New York Times* had it in one story—were completely out of frame. No one in the media had seen this twist coming. Even the Lewiston papers had no inkling. Norman Thomas had been sports editor of the *Lewiston Evening Journal* since 1919; when the biggest local story of his career broke, he had the day off.

But that disappointment was small Maine potatoes compared to what Sam Silverman felt.

There was a thin silver lining for Silverman. The change of venue, it turned out, would actually result in a financial windfall. Silverman secured the closed-circuit rights at Boston Garden, Boston Arena, and several other theaters around New England, which were no longer subject to blackout. His take from the ticket sales would exceed the $15,000, plus $5,000 in expenses, he was to have received for co-promoting the fight at the Garden. (In typical Silverman fashion, he immediately gave some back by scheduling a live boxing card to precede the telecast at Boston Garden, featuring promising local welterweight Ted Whitfield versus eighth-ranked Gaspar Ortega. "It's costing me money," Silverman said, "but I'm doing it to give Whitfield exposure. Whitfield is the best fighter we've had around here in forty years. He has the fastest hands and feet in the country—faster than Clay's, who may be the best heavyweight we've ever had.")

But no amount of money could have saved the sting of losing out on his lifelong dream. "Not every guy gets to promote a heavyweight championship fight," Suitcase Sam said.

He attributed the loss to "a lot of legal technicalities and foolishness," but claimed he wasn't bitter. For one thing, D.A. Byrne, a fight fan, was a friend of his. "Gary told me that I was the last person in the world he would want to hurt," Silverman said.

Nor did he see any point in dwelling on what might have been. "What the hell, it's all over and you can't make money being bitter," Silverman said. "So I'm going ahead and making more money than I could have before. But it's not like being the top man of the actual promotion.

"One thing—I'm glad they moved the fight to Lewiston, kept it in New England. And I'm glad for my friend Sam Michael. . . . He's a great worker and deserves the break."

CHAPTER FOURTEEN

Characters and Hoopla

For the newly formed promotional alliance, optimism burned through the fog of fatigue. "The reception we've received here has been tremendous," Inter-Continental president Bob Nilon said the next day. "Out of this world. Everyone has treated us royally. They've made us feel welcome.

"I can't say the same for some of the other cities we've looked at."

Said Sam Margolis, "We have received enthusiastic support and cooperation, from waitresses in restaurants all the way up to the governor's office. And believe me, we really appreciate it."

Said Sam Michael, "This championship fight will mean more than a million dollars in publicity for Lewiston–Auburn and the State of Maine. They couldn't buy this publicity for all the money in the DED [Department of Economic Development] budget."

That was a nice little parting shot at the tightwads on Lewiston's Board of Finance. On Friday Sam had informed them that, due to the demands on his time in promoting the fight, he was ending his lame-duck tenure as the city's industrial development director, effective immediately.

Nilon said it could be the beginning of a long-term relationship. "If this show sells out as quickly as it appears," he said, "and all other things go well, I'm sure Inter-Continental would consider Lewiston as the center spot for its future shows that will be featured nationwide on closed circuit TV."

Sam's response: "That'd be just great for Maine, for Lewiston—and for Sam Michael."

But there was dissonance between the way things looked on the ground in Lewiston and how they looked from just about everywhere else. Johnny Carson joked about the change of venue in his *Tonight*

Show monologue: "They moved the fight out of Boston because they don't allow dancing after eight o'clock."

In the *New York Times*, Arthur Daley summed up the general sentiment across the nation: "The fight game has gone tank town like a struggling road show."

Even some Mainers were appalled. An unidentified professor at Bates College opined to the Associated Press that it was "pathetic to be picking up the bedraggled, ragged end of a discredited sport."

The fighters didn't say much one way or the other.

Ali: "I don't care if they stage the fight in a phone booth."

Liston: "I don't care where I fight him, even if it's Vietnam, as long as I get to fight him."

The negative coverage didn't faze Inter-Continental's press flack, Harold Conrad. In a warped way, he welcomed it. "What would the scoffers do without the fight racket?" he once said. "The fight racket has got characters and hoopla."

One of those characters was Conrad himself—and he was a genius at generating hoopla. Conrad didn't believe that a publicist should lurk. He stood out. He was tall and dapper and charismatic. He wore expensive suits and ascot ties. "I'm around to give you bums some class," he once told Jack Nilon. (On another occasion he told his wife Mara why he gravitated toward the fight racket in the first place: "I would rather spend the evening with a shit-heel who is interesting than with some scoutmaster who is a bore.")

Conrad had one foot in the 1960s counterculture. He preferred pot to booze. He did the dark-glasses-and-cigarette-holder thing before Hunter S. Thompson did.[*]

---

[*] Although Thompson was an obscure reporter at that point, he and Conrad already knew each other. Thirteen years later, Conrad got Thompson the access he needed to write "Last Tango in Vegas," a lengthy profile of Muhammad Ali for *Rolling Stone*. "The interview with Muhammad was one of the best I've seen," Conrad wrote in a letter to the magazine afterward, "and overall I thought 'Last Tango in Vegas' was brilliant—even though [Thompson] did call me a pig fucker."

Conrad had developed an affection for boxing during his teens, when he covered fights for the *Brooklyn Eagle*. During World War II he was assigned to Army intelligence. Later he churned out *Joe Palooka* radio scripts. He wrote a million-selling novelization of the movie *The Battle at Apache Pass*. He enjoyed abstract painting and restoring furniture.

But mostly Conrad excelled at social networking, long before anybody called it that. He was a man both of the world and about town. The first time he got stoned, he was with Louis Armstrong. He'd been Hemingway's drinking buddy in Havana. He knew the Duke of Windsor and King Farouk. He was pals with Casey Stengel and Milton Berle and Damon Runyon. He was the inspiration for the character Eddie Willis, played by Humphrey Bogart in the 1947 movie *The Harder They Fall*. (Said sportswriter Budd Schulberg, who wrote the novel on which the film was based and who later wrote the screenplay for *On the Waterfront*, "Close your eyes, and the legendary Bogie sounds like our very own Hal Conrad.")

Conrad understood that you couldn't sell a fight to the general public solely through standard tale-of-the-tape coverage. People wanted storylines. And Conrad had a knack for advancing—if not actually inventing—the kinds of storylines that sold tickets. For example, when the Beatles first came to the U.S. in February 1964, they happened to be in Miami just before the Clay–Liston fight. Conrad: "It doesn't take any genius to figure out that putting the Beatles together with Cassius Clay would make a picture that would be irresistible to most editors around the world."

Maybe not—but no one else in the fight game would have made the considerable effort it took to actually do it. Conrad did.

Just as many veteran sportswriters failed to recognize Clay's brilliance in 1964, most American critics dismissed the Beatles as no-talent louts. Not Conrad. "The older folks seem to be resisting it," he said of the Beatles' music, "but I find it getting to me." He was fifty-three years old.

In a letter to reporter Bob Musel, later published in the book *Dear Muffo*, Conrad described that photo op in Miami: "As they pose for the photographers, I watch this Summit meeting—the Beatles and Cassius

Clay—the two hottest names in the news, worldwide. They are all about the same age. I wonder how posterity will treat them."

Conrad's instincts for a good story made him a favorite source among reporters. "And once the sportswriters rely on you," Conrad said, "you can get away with a lot of things. Not lies—but you can broaden things."

Conrad also made sure to court the literati as well as the sporting press—guys like Norman Mailer and James Baldwin—at a time when novelists were true celebrities. "You don't see these guys at a World Series, a pro football playoff, or the Stanley Cup," Conrad said. "But at a big fight, you do."

Often because Harold Conrad made sure they got there.

But Conrad's most significant contribution might have been that he understood the importance of rhythm and pacing when promoting a heavyweight title fight. "You have to plan it so you'll reach your peak a week before the fight," he said. "Then all the writers come in and take over.... You've created this hysteria."

No fight ever had a greater atmosphere of hysteria than Ali–Liston II, which was partly a testament to Conrad's dark genius. Other publicists might have shrunk from the challenge in despair. How do you sell a bout between two immensely unpopular boxers, fighting under circumstances widely believed to be corrupt, at a hockey rink in a rinky-dink Maine mill town, amid threats of violence?

Maybe by leading people to believe that one of those unpopular fighters might actually be *assassinated in the ring*.

While Harold Conrad tried to convince the likes of Norman Mailer to come to Lewiston—and also kept every member of the press apprised of the latest rumors regarding the revenge plot against Muhammad Ali—the rest of the promotional team began sorting through the hundreds of mundane tasks that made a televised boxing match happen. "We are doing a job in two weeks that usually takes about four months," Sam Margolis said.

The work began immediately. Well, almost immediately. On Saturday the fight promoters had to wait for a bunch of teenagers to clear out of the Central Maine Youth Center before they could get down to

business. The kids were having a party, rocking and roller-skating to
the latest hits from bands like Freddie and the Dreamers. (Bringing the
world's heavyweight championship to the arena, said building superintendent Robert Croteau, "creates problems. We have to suspend the
children's roller skating for two days before the fight.")

The promoters could have picked a couple of other Maine venues
but ruled them out for various reasons. With its bench-style seats, the
Portland Exposition Building wasn't conducive to scaled ticket prices.
Bangor Auditorium had a larger seating capacity—about 8,000—but it
was too far from Boston to make it practical.[*]

As soon as the roller-skating party ended, Sam Michael comman-
deered the arena. Along with Bob Nilon and Garland Cherry, he started
work in the most basic way possible, using a tape measure and a scratch
pad. In short order they had worked out the ticket plan. There were
2,803 permanent seats, arranged in eleven rows at each end of the arena
and rows of ten along the sides. The floor was 200 feet by eighty-five,
which would increase the capacity to around 5,400, with about 4,000
saleable seats and another 1,400 or so comps for members of the press
and assorted dignitaries. Based on these numbers, Inter-Continental
scaled the seats at $25, $50, and $100.

Bob Nilon tried to put a positive spin on the cozy dimensions.
"There isn't a bad seat in the house," he said. "The farthest seat is
130 feet away from ringside. In Boston, our ringside reserved section
extended more than 100 feet away from the ring center."

He continued to sing Maine's praises. "The arena is perfect," Nilon
said, "expenses are low, and running a fight here you have every major
U.S. city wide open for the closed circuit TV."

---

[*] This led to an awkward moment during the press conference in Augusta,
when Norbert X. Dowd, executive secretary of the Bangor Chamber of Com-
merce, interrupted the proceedings to dispute the contention that Bangor was
too far away. And years later, Sam Michael's son John offered an alternative reason that the fight ended up at the Central Maine Youth Center: "The fight was
in Lewiston because my dad didn't want to travel back and forth to Portland
every day to work on it. He wanted it to be right up the street."

Maybe he sounded like a Pollyanna. But if anyone could have envisioned great things from the floor of a small-town hockey arena, it was
Bob Nilon. The path that had led him to Lewiston on that Saturday
morning in May 1965 stretched back to the polished ice of the Ridley
Park Lake in the late 1920s. Nilon's success in youth hockey had a lot to
do with his becoming a successful sports concessionaire and promoter.
And it had given him connections to people like the late Walter Brown,
who had brought him to Boston Garden and, indirectly, to Lewiston.

Also, like Sam Michael, Bob Nilon was no graying sentimentalist.
He had little patience for those who lamented the good ol' days, when
a heavyweight title fight had to be held in a place like Yankee Stadium
to be profitable. Pay TV was the future. You could whine about it—or
you could be a part of it, if you hustled.

Still, Nilon agreed to make one significant change in the Lewiston promotion, strictly for perception's sake. The suggestion came from
Lewiston's feisty young mayor, Robert Couturier, who stopped by the
Central Maine Youth Center to introduce himself. Couturier, who was
deeply invested in preserving Lewiston's Franco-American heritage, saw
an opportunity to push a favorite cause: changing the building's name
to St. Dominic's Arena. That was the name of an earlier structure on the
same site, where St. Dominic High School fielded Maine's predominant
hockey team. When the original St. Dom's Arena burned down during
a snowstorm in 1956, Lewistonians were devastated. The Dominican
Fathers who had operated the arena appealed to parishioners for dona-
tions to rebuild. Simultaneously, other civic groups brought in outside
fund-raisers who boasted that they could secure $1 million. The catch:
The new arena had to be nondenominational, to broaden the prospective donor base. (This new consortium also wanted an arena that would
be available to everybody, and that could easily be converted for uses
other than hockey. Boxing, for instance.)

Although the Dominican Fathers got much better results than the
professional fund-raisers, they were bound by that awkward compro-
mise. That's how the new arena—a public/private hybrid that opened in
January 1959—ended up with a clumsy, bureaucratic name suggestive
of a reform school: the Central Maine Youth Center.

Mayor Couturier saw a perfect opportunity to resurrect the old name. "We've talked about it many times," he said. "Maybe the time is ripe to do it."

Nilon was immediately sold. "That's not a bad idea," he said. "I like the name—St. Dom's Arena. Sort of gives the building a blessed atmosphere, like St. Nicholas Arena in New York."

And, he said, "'St. Dom's Arena' would make better sports copy than 'Central Maine Youth Center.'"

It would also overcome an obvious image problem, which an unidentified "sports fan" had pinpointed in the *Portland Press Herald*: "Who ever heard of staging a world heavyweight championship fight in a youth center—a kiddie place? This is ridiculous!"

That was that. On the spur of the moment, Nilon decided to disregard the building's official name and print "St. Dominic's Arena" on the tickets instead.

And so, with the first items on his lengthy to-do list completed, Nilon hustled out of the newly rechristened arena. He had to get an order in to the National Ticket Company in Pennsylvania. Phone calls were already coming in, and he had nothing to sell.

Nilon's decision to have the tickets printed in Pennsylvania illustrated the sometimes awkward nature of the alliance between Inter-Continental Promotions and Sam Michael. As the co-promoter, Sam received a flat fee of $15,000 (equivalent to about $115,000 today). He supplied the necessary Maine license and the local contacts. But when it came to people and equipment, Inter-Continental relied heavily on its own network of vendors and contacts. This produced mixed results.

It turned out to be a great help in securing the most basic requirement for a heavyweight title fight—or any fight, for that matter: a ring for the boxers to box in. Although Sam had kept a foot in the fight game through closed-circuit broadcasts, he hadn't promoted a live bout in years. Finding a suitable ring proved to be more troublesome than he could have anticipated. The first one he brought in, from the nearby Brunswick Naval Air Station, was too small, just sixteen by sixteen. The contract called for a twenty-by-twenty ring—and Ali's trainer, Angelo Dundee, wasn't going to bend. "The smaller the ring, the more it favors Liston," Dundee said. "My man likes plenty of room to maneuver."

In addition, Dundee had set Ali up with a twenty-by-twenty ring at his training site in Chicopee, and "I don't want him expecting ropes where there ain't gonna be ropes in the fight."

Liston, on the other hand, trained in a ring that was just fifteen-by-fifteen. And while that made it easier for him to keep his sparring partners within range, it did little to prepare him to chase the fleet-footed Ali around a ring that would be larger by 175 square feet.

After Dundee rejected the first ring, Sam brought in a second ring, from Portland. It was supposed to be twenty-by-twenty but was actually just nineteen feet, four inches on each side. It was also embarrassingly threadbare.

With time growing short, Bob Nilon stepped in. Nilon Brothers had the concessions contract at the Baltimore Civic Arena, and Nilon arranged to borrow the arena's twenty-by-twenty ring and have it trucked up to Lewiston. Harold Conrad, as always, found a way to spin a silk purse from this sow's ear of a story. It involved the "Sarong Queen," actress Dorothy Lamour, who had starred with Bob Hope and Bing Crosby in a series of "road" movies in the 1940s. With a straight face, Conrad told the Associated Press that "Miss Lamour saved the fight. She lives in Baltimore now and is on the Civic Committee, whose approval we needed to borrow the ring. Her vote swung the deal for us."

Sonny Liston had the heavyweight title for just seventeen months. It had now been almost that long since he had lost it. Having to defer to Ali on the size of the ring was just one more reminder of his diminished stature. There would be plenty of others throughout the month of May.

Some were small. Ali chose white trunks, for instance, while Liston reluctantly agreed to wear black. "That guy'll blow his guts [otherwise]," Liston told his camp director, Al Braverman. "We might as well give him what he wants."

Other concessions were big. The promoters wanted both fighters to come to Maine as soon as possible. Having everyone in the same location would make it easier to arrange press conferences and other events.

Sam Michael had already done the legwork and found two prospective fight camps. One was the brand-new Holiday Inn, which had just opened off the Maine Turnpike in Auburn. It was on par with the accommodations that each fighter had in Massachusetts.

The other prospect was the Poland Spring Resort, about twelve miles from Lewiston. If it wasn't in the middle of nowhere, it was within walking distance of it.

Poland Spring had sprung up in the nineteenth century, at a time when wealthy travelers regarded mineral waters as a miracle elixir. ("Cures dyspepsia," proclaimed an 1859 advertisement for the waters at the Poland Spring Resort. "Cures liver complaint of long standing. Cures kidney complaint. Cures gravel. Drives out all humors and purifies the blood.")

Which fighter would go where?

For Ali the point was moot, at least in the short term. He flatly refused to leave Chicopee until he had finished his training. That wouldn't be until Friday, May 21, just four days before the fight. "There's no sense in moving from where we are now," said Angelo Dundee. "The champion likes this place and we intend to stay right here and complete our training."

Not even Harold Conrad could muster the English to put a positive spin on that. "He's the champion," Conrad said. "And you just don't go around telling the No. One man what to do."

But when you were No. Two you often got treated like number two. Word filtered down to Liston's camp: They *must* be in Maine by the end of the week. "The message says we have to fly there," said Babe Wood, who oversaw Liston's sparring partners. "Not ride by car or by bus. Fly. That's the order."

Liston's response when told he would have to transfer to Maine? "Why me? Why not Big Mouth?"

He already knew the answer.

For eight-year-old Mike Feldman, the Poland Spring Resort was an enormous playhouse. His grandfather, Saul Feldman, had taken over in 1962 and made the resort a renovation project for the whole family. "Basically as a kid my job was to stay away from my mother and father," Mike recalled later. "I thought they would keep me from doing the things I wanted to do, which was climb into the towers, play on the roofs, drive the elevator in place of the elevator operator—who, by the way, used to let me knock on his wooden leg when people came in.

"So I either hung out outside or in my grandfather's office, which was a safe zone. And I was sitting in his lap one time and there were eight people in the room having what to me began as a boring discussion. But then it turned out that these were the people who were trying to make the deal to bring the fight to Maine after it was banned in Boston. I remember Sam Michael was there, and I'm not sure who else. And I remember my grandfather saying, 'You know, this is a great choice you've given me. You've got Sonny Liston, who's supposedly owned by the Mob, and nobody's sure why he didn't come out for the seventh round in his last fight. And on the other hand you've got Cassius Clay/Muhammad Ali, who's aligned with Elijah Muhammad, whose people are accused of assassinating Malcolm X, and now Malcolm X's supporters want to assassinate him. These are the two choices you give me.'

"And then someone—I think it was Sam Michael, but it might have been someone else—looked at me, and then he looked back at my grandfather and he said, 'Look, I will tell you one fact that might affect your decision. Whatever else his problems are, Sonny Liston *loves* kids. He will be wonderful with your grandson, and he'll be wonderful with all the other young people here.'

"That's why Sonny Liston—and not Muhammad Ali—stayed at our hotel."

CHAPTER FIFTEEN

Maine Awaits

With St. Dom's closed on Sunday, per orders from the Dominican Fathers, Mainers who were curious about the fight preparations reflexively drove instead to Poland Spring—even though there was nothing to see. Liston wouldn't arrive for another six days. "I don't know what made them feel Sonny was here," Saul Feldman said. "But the traffic here is typical of the enthusiasm that the fight is causing."

The flood of phone calls seeking reservations, some from as far away as South America, was another indication. For Mike Feldman, this was a wonderful new game. He sat at the hotel switchboard, asking his grandfather, "Where do you think the next call will come from?"

The resort complex consisted of a golf course and edifices of different sizes, in varying degrees of splendiferousness and dilapidation. One structure, the Maine State Building, was a vestige of the 1893 World's Columbian Exposition in Chicago. After the Exposition, the Ricker family—which had founded Poland Spring—dismantled the building and had it transported by ox cart and train to the resort, where it was meticulously reassembled.

The Feldmans reserved a building called the Mansion House for Liston's use. The footprint dated to 1794; the original structure, called the Wentworth Ricker Inn, served as a way station along the road from Portland to Montreal. Later, when Poland Spring became a health spa, the Ricker family added a second large inn, called the Poland Spring House. They rebuilt the Wentworth Ricker Inn and changed the name to the Mansion House. They expanded the Mansion House again in 1898, and by 1906 had fully modernized it—for the time—with electric lights. The Rickers also added a new dining hall, which a 1913 brochure called "a great room of golden buff and ivory, enclosed on three sides by large plate glass windows. It covers nearly five thousand square feet of floor space, and is entirely free from obstructing supports of any kind." A crosshatch of heavy beams lined the ceiling, forming rectangles around the chandeliers. Stained glass topped the windows. Steam radiators lined the walls. "Its westward outlook is over a great broad veranda which mellows the summer sun," the brochure effused, "and in winter, being enclosed and heated, resembles a bower in some great conservatory."

The dining hall still looked like that half a century later. Time had dulled its cutting edge to the bluntness of a butter knife. But it was in this hall, in this incongruous setting, that Liston would conduct sparring sessions for public view, at a dollar a head. In the midst of training for the fight that would determine how history would remember him, he would decamp from a modern hotel on "America's Technology Highway" and resettle in a place whose best days predated paved roads.

The disruption of Liston's regimen would give Ali another psychological advantage—and Ali knew it. In many ways, he understood Liston better than Liston understood himself. "He's older," Ali told syndicated columnist Milton Richman, "and things like this shake him up more."

Ali had a growing conviction that this fight would be easier than the first. "I made [Liston] quit the last time because he was whipped," Ali said. "He was tired and exhausted and he knew he had no chance. Next time it will be worse. I know when the fight's going to end. If I knew how long it would take the referee to get to him and start counting I could tell you the second it will end."

While Maine waited for the two world-famous fighters to arrive, news continued to flash:

MONDAY

- Maine Boxing Commission chairman George Russo took all of his accrued vacation time from his full-time job at B.D. Stearns, a Portland meat wholesaler, to focus on the fight. (Columnist Red Smith, employing the subtle condescension that characterized much of the national media coverage, identified Russo as "the meat salesman who heads up the State Boxing Commission.") Russo said that the fight judges would be from Maine, but that the referee would be from elsewhere. The referee would be chosen from a list of nine candidates submitted to each camp. The list reportedly included Barney Felix, who had refereed the Miami Beach fight, and former heavyweight champions Joe Louis, Jim Braddock, Jack Sharkey, and Jersey Joe Walcott.

TUESDAY

• Massachusetts state representative Richard S. Landry called for a probe into "the circumstances behind the transfer of the Cassius Clay–Sonny Liston heavyweight championship fight from Boston to Lewiston." His goal, he said, was "to clear up the biggest mystery in Boston in some time." He wanted, in other words, to investigate the investigation.

• Sam Michael, Sam Margolis, and attorneys Laurier Raymond (representing the promoters) and William Rocheleau (representing the Dominican Fathers) met in a fifth-floor office of First Manufacturers Bank in Lewiston to sign the lease agreement at St. Dom's, which allowed the promoters to use the facility from May 20 to May 26, except Sunday. (Earlier reports, which were never corrected, said the promoters were paying the Dominican Fathers $2,500 for the "one-day use" of the facility, ten times the going rate. This was typical of the lazy reporting on the fight. Obviously the logistics of a heavyweight title fight required leasing the building for more than one day.)

Later that day, Sam Michael learned that his sister Annie had died. On Thursday, in the midst of the most hectic week of his life, he would travel to his hometown of Lowell for the funeral.

WEDNESDAY

• Representatives from various police agencies met to begin coordinating their security efforts. Maine State Police offered the Lewiston

Police Department assistance. ("All I have to do is ask," said Lewiston police chief Joseph Farrand.) The Androscoggin County Sheriff's office, Androscoggin County Civil Defense, and even agents from the Maine State Liquor Commission would be mobilized. "At least 168 men will be involved in law enforcement throughout the city at the peak of the crowd influx," the *Lewiston Evening Journal* reported.

- Sam Michael's old nemesis, Ernest Malenfant, resurfaced in the news, objecting to reports that Governor Reed's executive council had authorized the Maine Department of Economic Development to spend "up to $10,000 to entertain the world's press when it arrives in Maine." "Those people are well paid, and they've got a big expense account besides that," Malenfant complained. "And I would like to know who is going to control the $10,000, and if they are going to spend it all."

THURSDAY

- The *Portland Press Herald* secured the award for "Best Achievement in Ironic Foreshadowing" with this headline:

LISTON WARNS MAINE FANS:
'DON'T BLINK OR YOU'LL MISS THE KAYO'

- The *Press Herald* also noted that the mood at Ali's camp in Chicopee was "unusually glum" due to the death of Sonny Banks, who had lapsed into a coma on Monday night after being knocked out by Leotis Martin in Philadelphia. Banks died Thursday without regaining consciousness. "Banks was a close friend of Solomon McTier, Clay's assistant trainer," the paper reported. Banks, who had knocked Ali down in a 1962 bout, "had been invited to become one of the champion's sparring partners but decided to keep his job in a Detroit automobile assembly plant." The *Press Herald* added that "Hollywood personality Stepin Fetchit went out of his way in a pre-workout monologue to relieve the melancholy."

- Also from the *Press Herald*: "Clay is a general favorite here [in Chicopee], especially with the teenagers. His hi-fi can be heard almost any hour of the day or night . . . . He knows all the latest dance steps and frequently gives an exhibition in the lobby of the swank Schine Inn."

- The Boston *Globe* reported that Liston had become friends with a group of kids in Dedham. Together they had afternoon visits with Betsy, a young Morgan horse that the *Globe* called "the pet of the entire neighborhood." Said Liston's wife, Geraldine, "He loves children, young animals, and everybody who's nice to us. It won't be easy leaving. He's been so happy with the kids. But he knows he has to go. There's important things ahead—getting that championship back. He's lonely and hurt without it. Little kids and those small animals help him get by."

FRIDAY

- At noon, the ticket office officially opened at 32 Ash Street in Lewiston. Moments later Norman Roy of 485 Main Street became the first Maine resident to buy a ticket. An unnamed Inter-Continental official told the *Portland Press Herald* that, because so many out-of-state residents had reserved tickets by phone, "there have been resentful murmurs since we arrived here that Lewiston people weren't given a fair shot at the lower-priced seats. So today the bosses decided to cut 500 of the $50 seats to $25 and put them on sale immediately."

- The *Lewiston Daily Sun* conducted a straw poll that ran 3–2 in favor of Ali. Said Ward Four alderman Nicholas Punteri, "I say Clay is going to win, but I would rather see Liston win. I don't like Clay. I just don't like his actions in public." Fire chief Roland Dumais had the same sentiments. This prompted police chief Joseph Farrand to pick Liston for balance. Postmaster Roger Albert also picked Liston, but had no plans to attend the fight: "I like to bowl," he said. "It's more fun than watching boxing at $100 a throw."

- The *Daily Sun* also printed a letter from former Lewiston resident Rossiter J. Drake, who now lived in Westport, Connecticut. "It galls me to think that anyone could possibly think that a fight between two lackluster heavyweights could reflect much credit on the State of Maine," Drake wrote. "In my youth there were better fights between the French and the Irish than anything that will be seen at the Lewiston Youth Center. Those fights were free of charge too."

- Having visited each fighter's camp, *Portland Evening Express* sports editor Blaine Davis wrote an incisive analysis that rivaled anything the guys from the big-city dailies or national magazines came up with. "It's the consensus of most veteran observers who have seen both men at their training sessions that Liston won't be able to catch the champion," Davis wrote. "Clay is fast and nifty as a lightweight and in comparison Liston seems to plod as he pursues his sparring partners. In the twenty-foot ring in Lewiston, he'll likely be as many as three moves behind Clay. . . . In his workouts Clay resembles a feeding swallow. He dips and darts and swoops around his spar mate, the long left jab flashing in and out with amazing speed. There must be some power in it, too, for when it lands the charging boxer stops as though he'd run into a wall. . . . Old-timers who've seen the heavyweight champs all the way back to Jack Johnson claim Clay is the quickest of them all. He even, they say, could out-speed Gene Tunney, whose feet kept him out of harm's way except for one brief flurry of punches in two bouts with Jack Dempsey. Yesterday Clay boxed five rounds with a fast light heavyweight [James Ellis] who managed to land only two punches, and the champion took one of those going away. Moreover, no sparring partner has been able to crowd Clay into a corner. And Liston will have to corner Clay to beat him." And finally: "Clay gave newsmen yesterday what he called a 'financial tip.' 'Hock your houses,' he said, 'and bet on me.' He couldn't understand why Liston is favored at 7–5. Neither can most of those who've seen the two at work. . . . It's our guess that Clay will win by a knockout."

SATURDAY

- The time had come for Liston to leave Dedham and head for Maine, where that day's *Lewiston Daily Sun* contained reports of a moose on the loose near Sabattus Street, and of a sixteen-year-old girl being placed in her grandparents' custody "after being found guilty of behaving in an incorrigible manner with danger of falling into vice."

- The *New York Times* reported that Liston tried to keep the mood light as he broke camp by using one of his favorite practical jokes— a fake box of chocolates that gave the victim an electric shock, like a joy buzzer. Asked how he thought the move to Maine would affect his training, he said, "How should I know? I'm not there yet."

CHAPTER SIXTEEN

"What Would Toots Shor Do in Poland Spring?"

Liston landed at Auburn–Lewiston Municipal Airport at 6:05 Saturday evening. There to greet him was Auburn mayor Harry Woodard, with his wife and two sons. A reporter asked Liston for his first impression of the area as he'd come in on the plane, an Eastern Airlines DC-3. "All I saw was dust," Liston said.

Sam Margolis had a car waiting. The police provided an escort for the short drive to Poland Spring. Within half an hour Liston was whisked to a press conference at the Mansion House. Gawkers peered through the windows. The *Portland Press Herald* described Liston's demeanor as "anything but jovial." He had been up since five a.m. and had put in a full day of training. He was hungry. It was ninety minutes past his dinnertime. Like Ali said—he didn't handle changes in his routine well.

Jim Braddock and Jersey Joe Walcott also arrived at Poland Spring that day. "I like this Liston in about nine rounds," Braddock said. "He's in great shape. He went with three sparring partners yesterday and wasn't even breathing hard at the end."

Harold Conrad stood outside the Mansion House, smoking a cigar in the evening sun. He told the milling onlookers that this was just a hint of what they could expect. He estimated that 600 reporters from around the world would be on hand by fight night.

After enduring the press conference with a stone face and clenched teeth, Liston dropped his defenses. When introduced to Tudi Feldman—Saul's daughter-in-law and Mike's mother—he pulled the "shock box" trick. Her startled reaction induced a guffaw.

It was the start of a warm, if brief, relationship between the Listons and the Feldmans.

Not on hand for Liston's arrival at Poland Spring was Sam Michael. It wasn't a snub; Sam had a previous engagement. He and his brother Joe were at the Knights of Columbus Hall down in South Portland, for the Old Time Boxers Banquet. It was a night of mingled emotions. Maine's boxing establishment took time away from the biggest bout in the state's history to remember those who had slugged it out in obscurity at places like Mechanics Hall in Rumford and Pastime Arena in Biddeford. (Jack Dempsey sent a check to cover the expenses of five former boxers who couldn't afford to be there.) Also on hand was Francis McDonough, a longtime fight timer who worked as a pressman for the *Press Herald*. He had cut short a Florida vacation to be there. And although he didn't work many fights anymore, he would agree to serve as the knockdown timer at the Ali–Liston fight, a decision he would deeply regret.

Many of Sam's boxing buddies hadn't seen him since the big news broke. They stopped to offer congratulations on the coup—along with condolences on the loss of his sister Annie.

Lefty LaChance, the kid who had almost brought Sam a featherweight title during his days as a manager, back in WWII, was there, too. But he wasn't a kid anymore. He was, at forty-three, a grandfather. He worked at Maine Electronics in Lisbon. His wife, Jeanne, ran a beauty salon, and their daughter, Doris, helped out. Doris was married now, and a mom herself.

How quickly the generations turned. Doris was a newborn back in September of '43 when Lefty beat Phil Terranova, the NBA featherweight champ. But to Lefty, that night was still so vivid, still a large part of what made him who he was. When he'd started out, he wasn't even the most talented featherweight on the card at the old Punchbowl in Lewiston. But from there he had fought his way all the way to the top of his weight class. For one night, at least, he was the best in the world at what he did.

Not bad for a skinny Frenchman from Maine.

Harold Conrad wasn't kidding about the coming media onslaught. "I never knew up to that point what an attraction a heavyweight title fight was," Fred Gage, a reporter for the local ABC Radio affiliate,

WLAM, said later. Once Liston got to town, calls poured into the radio station from scoop-hungry reporters all over the US.

Gage also got a call from Howard Cosell, a fellow ABC reporter. Cosell was a rising media star. In Lewiston he would provide ringside color commentary on the Mutual Broadcasting Network radio coverage and would later anchor ABC-TV's Lewiston fight package on *Wide World of Sports.* (Cosell would eventually develop an ongoing shtick with Ali during their frequent appearances on *Wide World.*) He requested help from WLAM in securing an "engineer"—although what he really wanted was someone to run interference for him. "I want to go right up into the ring the minute the fight's over," Cosell said.

"I've got an engineer that's pretty nimble," Gage told him. "He'll take care of you."

Cosell had another request. "I'm looking for a good place to eat," he said. "I heard about a place that has baked Alaska. . . ."

"Yeah, I know a place that has baked Alaska, right here in Lewiston," Gage told him. "Steckino's."

"Can you get me in there?" Cosell said.

"You don't need *me* to get you into Steckino's," Gage said. "You just go."

Gage's attitude—friendly, accommodating, toggling between amused and bemused by all the fuss—typified Lewiston's reaction to becoming the unwitting center of the sports universe. "A community simultaneously exhilarated and uneasy," syndicated columnist Jim Murray wrote. "It never had a heavyweight championship before. And it may never want one again."

Newspaper surveys of Lewiston high school students yielded a variety of reactions:

"I don't think much of boxing but it might help the city in many ways."

"Good for millionaires—that's all."

"I am sure it will go well unless the wrong type of people come."

"I hope it doesn't give the boys ideas."

One girl had to think before coming up with anything to compare the fight to: "We had the Ice Capades here a few years ago." (That was, incidentally, another Sam Michael production.)

A gas-station attendant said, "I'd throw both those bums out of the state."

Said a female mill worker: "You don't go to see fights on what they pay you here."

A UPI reporter happened upon "an intense young man in a business suit" playing pinball in the back room of the Bill Davis Smoke Shop ("Pipes of distinction"). "Clay's going to win," the man declared. "I think he's too fast for [Liston]."

The reporter asked the man what he did for a living.

"I'm a minister," he said, adding that his congregation was mostly "Liston people."

Mary E. Bennett, head librarian of the Alvan Bolster Ricker Memorial Library in Poland, was a Liston person, too, "mainly because of Clay's association with the Black Muslims, a group I am fearful of." Bennett reported keen interest in the fight among library patrons, including a girl who came in with "a pair of gloves hanging round her neck."

Another Poland resident, Bob Wilson, a native of Ireland who had done some boxing in Boston, encouraged visitors to come to his B&B. "The price won't change," he declared. "It's $3.50 a day including breakfast."

Wilson wasn't alone in trying to cash in on the fight. A sign at US Cleaners and Launderers ("We're the greatest") on Birch Street in Lewiston boasted:

WE HAVE BEEN SELECTED TO WASH THE
RING CANVAS FOR THE CLAY–LISTON FIGHT

Oakdale Auto on Lisbon Street promised "Champion Deals from the Champion Dealer." Advance Auto Sales of Auburn offered "Fight Day Specials," including a 1960 Rambler for $495. And a collection of businesses pooled their money to buy a full-page "Welcome to Maine" ad in the *Lewiston Daily Sun*. The message captured the town's naiveté: "Perhaps the main event will be of such short duration that some of you will not have time to discover the wonderful points of this great Vacationland—or the warmth of our people! Therefore [we] hope you will find the opportunity to come back again for that 'longer look' that builds a real and lasting friendship!'"

Despite numerous rumors of celebrity sightings all over town, legitimately famous people proved as elusive as blue lobsters. Louis Armstrong, Jackie Gleason, VIP host Toots Shor, and VP Hubert Humphrey were among those reputed to be in town or en route. One story had Elizabeth Taylor shopping at Peck's, a longtime Lewiston department store. Another story had her at a discount outlet called The Mart. "I'd like to see Elizabeth Taylor," said Mrs. Doris Labrie of the Stardust Motel in Lewiston. "They say she's the most beautiful woman in the world." Instead, the Stardust was filled with shoe salesmen making their usual rounds.

Frank Sinatra was also the subject of persistent rumors. "Sinatra is in town—on film, anyway, starring in *None But the Brave* at the Empire on Main Street," the *New York Times* reported. "That was as close as he was expected to get."

Jim Braddock explained why this bout lacked the usual influx of high-rollers and hangers-on. "The fight crowd is used to good accommodations and night-club action," the Cinderella Man said. "What would Toots Shor do in Poland Spring?"

Braddock did his part to carry the celebrity mantle. The former heavyweight champion was a ubiquitous presence during fight week. He presented an award at Lisbon High School's annual sports banquet. He threw out the first pitch at the Auburn Little League opener. He appeared at a Layman's League meeting at St. Joseph's School cafeteria in Lewiston. He attended a state-sponsored clambake at Reid State Park (thanks to that ten grand the state had authorized to wine and dine the press). Braddock also endorsed St. Dom's as a worthy site for a world heavyweight boxing championship—sort of. Said Braddock, "You could run a title fight today in a big garage."

Geraldine Liston was another familiar figure about town. "I know my way fairly well around Lewiston now," she said toward the end of fight week. "I've been over in Lewiston all afternoon, doing my wash at a laundromat over there. I didn't intend to go to Lewiston, but the laundromat [in Poland] was closed."

She stopped at a deli while she was out. "I got bologna sandwiches in there," she said. "I get so tired of restaurant food and eating out, and I love bologna."

Geraldine also visited a Lewiston astrologist, Marie de St. Pierre, who predicted a Liston victory. "Liston just can't lose; every sign is good," St. Pierre declared. Of course, she was basing her prediction on the dubious birthdate that Geraldine supplied for her husband: May 8, 1934.

In addition to her astrology practice, St. Pierre also worked at a Lewiston nursing home. She told Geraldine about Willie Maxwell, a young man who was in the nursing home because of severe cerebral palsy. "If I could meet Sonny Liston," Maxwell had told her, "I'd remember it all the rest of my days."

Sonny didn't get out as often as Geraldine did. In his first venture outside Poland Spring, on Sunday night, he ended up at the Androscoggin County Jail. But for once his visit to a local lockup was perfectly innocent. As part of a coordinated security force, Androscoggin County Sheriff's deputies had shadowed Liston all day. That evening Liston asked if he could see where they worked. During his visit to department headquarters he posed for pictures, and he signed autographs for the inmates over in the jail.

As Liston departed the antiquated cellblock, which had iron bars from floor to ceiling, one inmate yelled, "Good luck, Sonny!"

Liston spent much of his time at Poland Spring in a prison of his own making. He and his entourage had the Mansion House to themselves. The press corps and an eclectic assortment of guests—ranging from 108 clergymen on a retreat, to a drum-and-bugle corps called the Pine Tree Warriors, to a convention of New England trial justices (including Felix Forte, who had presided over the D.A. Byrnes proceedings), to the Maine Council of Catholic Women—stayed elsewhere at the resort. (Red Smith interviewed one "twittery old doll" from the Council, who told him, "We've been coming here nineteen years, and this is the most exciting year so far." She added that she should have been upstairs dressing for dinner at that point, "but I can't leave now. They told us Mr. Liston would be coming over.")

Despite Maine's warm acceptance, Liston remained as guarded as ever. He insisted on cutting his own steaks in the Mansion House kitchen. ("Who are we to disagree?" a member of the hotel staff said.) And, as stark evidence of his growing paranoia, he also used a food taster.

Nevertheless, he ate well. During his first day at Poland Spring he gained two pounds. Liston & Company ate in a private dining area called the Oak Room, accompanied by the Feldman family. "Here he was, a sharecropper's son, and he's up there with a bunch of Jews in Maine," Mike Feldman recalled later. "It was him and his wife and the sparring partners and the trainer and the manager and their wives—all black. And my family was eating dinner with them."

As predicted, Liston and young Mike Feldman formed a bond. Their shared "otherness" might have contributed to it. "The whole picture is, we moved to Maine when I was five and we were the first Jews to live in the town. Poland Spring Hotel didn't allow Jews for many years. I was the first Jew in the history of Poland School. Most people in Poland then knew one black person, and she had had an unfortunate, tough life. She was the mother of a mixed-race son whose father we didn't know, and who was in my class. Nice guy, but he had a lot of issues."

Young Mike wanted to spend as much time as possible with Liston. "One of the bellhops or one of the drivers or somebody would come and pick me up from school and take me to watch him train at like 2:30 in the afternoon every day," Mike recalled. "So one day I was watching him train and I said to my grandfather, 'Do you think Sonny would come to my school and meet my friends?' [Saul] said, 'We'll go in the locker room after he trains and ask him.' So I went in the training room after and asked him. He said, 'Let me think about it and I'll let you know.'"

When Sonny didn't mention it at dinner that evening, Mike was disappointed. "But that night at eleven o'clock he called my mother and said, 'Tudi, we want to go to the Poland School and see Michael tomorrow. We'll get the three limousines and we'll pick up you, your father-in-law, and your husband at 11:30. So would you call the principal in the morning and tell him we'll be there?'

"I don't think my mother slept a wink that night."

For the school visit, Feldman recalled, "My mother and my father and grandfather were dressed like normal Maine people. Everyone in [Liston's] group had on suits and fancy dresses. They were dressed in their best."

Liston didn't restrict his visit to Mike's class. "He talked to the kids in every single classroom," Mike recalled. "They took a mimeograph of his hand and sent one home with every kid. And because he didn't decide until eleven o'clock the night before, nobody knew he was coming. So all of a sudden, there's the former heavyweight champion of the world in your classroom."

Years later, Mike said that Sonny Liston was, hands down, the nicest of the handful of celebrities who stayed at Poland Spring during the Feldman family's tenure—a list that included Joan Crawford. "Everyone [on the staff] hated Joan Crawford," Mike recalled. "But when my grandfather, the hotel owner, would walk into the room, she would look at him and smile and say, 'Saul, would you escort me into dinner, please?' He thought she was the nicest woman and the most modest woman he had ever met in his life. The rest of the people hated the ground that she walked on. When the movie *Mommie Dearest* came out, everyone I knew who had been there that summer said, '*Exactly!*'

"Having seen how nasty some of these [famous] people were, and remembering the effect on me, it's rather astounding that I remember how *nice* Sonny Liston was. He could not have been nicer."

While Liston might have adjusted socially to the switch from Dedham to Poland Spring, his training appeared to suffer, along with his focus. He seemed prone to distraction. On Monday, during his first session of roadwork since arriving in Maine, Liston was jogging on the Poland Spring golf course when he happened upon a bird with a broken wing. Liston insisted on bringing the bird back with him, turning his training run into a rescue mission. "The bird is [now] in a cage at the Mansion House . . . with a fresh supply of worms and Poland Spring water," the *Evening Journal* reported.

More and more, boxing insiders questioned Liston's workout regimen. He fixated on developing pure strength rather than on addressing his most urgent need—finding a way to counter Ali's quickness. It was as if Liston still held out some vain hope that he could get Ali to stand still and fight *his* kind of fight. In one drill, a trainer repeatedly threw a medicine ball at Liston's midsection to strengthen his abdomen. Even the previous fall, when Liston was in peak condition, Angelo Dundee had questioned the value of that. "Why don't they throw it in his face?" Dundee said. "That's where my guy is gonna hit him."

By the time he got to Poland Spring, almost all of Liston's workout— skipping rope, standing on his head, that medicine ball bit—seemed designed more for show than anything else. And for many of the locals, who had never seen anything like it, it was a terrific show indeed. Each afternoon, Lewiston High School sophomore Bill Johnson headed to Poland Spring with a group of friends to watch Liston train. "He was just so imposing," Johnson recalled later. "He was the biggest human being we had ever seen. Massive neck. Huge hands. He never smiled, never said anything. It was an hour of drudgery, going from one [exercise] to the other. Everyone watching him was very quiet. They were in awe of him—scared, I think."

Johnson said that he and his friends all reached the same conclusion: "There's no way Muhammad Ali can beat this guy."

Johnson's group tried to meet Liston once, but security shooed them away. As long as they kept their distance, however, they had the run of the place. "His sparring partners hung out in a separate building, where they would play cards and stuff," Johnson recalled. "That's where we hung out, too. There were three sparring partners there. One was a guy named Big Train Lincoln—a big heavyweight. So one day we said to him, 'Who do you think will win the fight?'

"He said, 'Oh, there's no doubt in my mind that the champ will win.' Ali. And we thought, *Are you kidding me?* He said, '*I* could knock Liston out.' He said Liston was old, he was slow, and he didn't even *want* to fight."

Johnson dismissed Lincoln's comments as professional jealousy: "We thought that was just smack talk."

Compared to an average person, any heavyweight boxer in his final days of training would be in extraordinary physical condition. The difference would have been particularly pronounced in the 1960s, when a significant proportion of adults smoked, ate high-fat diets, drank to excess, and got little exercise. So, six days before the fight, when press accounts quoted Dr. Ralph Turgeon, the Maine Boxing Commission's appointed physician, describing Liston as "the fittest man I ever examined," there was little reason for anyone to raise eyebrows. (Except, perhaps, for Dr. Turgeon himself, who later denied that he ever said those words. Plenty of others, from fellow champions Jim Braddock and Joe Louis to distinguished members of the press, also went on record in declaring that Liston appeared to be in fine physical shape. Afterward, of course, it would be only the doctor—another Maine rube—whose opinion would be held up for ridicule.)

Dr. Turgeon said a couple of other things that were more relevant, although few papers reported them. According to the *Portland Press Herald*, Dr. Turgeon found no evidence of a lingering injury to Liston's left shoulder. "There's no indication of any carry-over," said Dr. Turgeon. "It appears to have healed completely and he has 100 percent mobility."

The only question from the press that flummoxed Dr. Turgeon concerned Liston's age. At that Dr. Turgeon turned to the ever-present Harold Conrad and whispered, "I don't know whether that's for publication."

Conrad's reply: "No secret. Sonny's thirty-one."

That was the Liston camp's story, and they were sticking to it.

The week wore on for the aging fighter and the aged resort. The ambiance at the Mansion House was like something out of a bad art-house film. Curiosity seekers pounded on locked doors and windows. Guards yelled at them to go away. A promenade of bit players clogged the parlor, with its Oriental rugs and leather chairs, its stately fireplace and chandeliers, and other vestiges of Victorian elegance. There, for example, was Ted King, a Liston assistant with a nebulous function. He answered a page by shouting into a phone: "You know better than to call me now. You know I'm busy as all hell now. Call me back in an hour, but don't, *don't* bother me now!"

There was Mrs. Sam Margolis, trying to straighten out a ticket snafu, looking up in time to greet TV announcer Steve Ellis, who was flapping his arms like a bird. "Hello, dear," said Ellis, "I just flew in."

But the Mansion House's star attraction was Geraldine Liston. Brandishing a diamond that one writer said "could flash a ship into safe harbor on a foggy night," Geraldine sat with a parade of reporters, handling their obtrusive questions with relaxed grace. When the *Boston Globe*'s Bud Collins asked if the repeated references to her husband's prison record bothered her, Geraldine said, "No. That don't make me no difference. He was in jail. He was there—that's the truth. Maybe you have to refer to it to make a point in a story. Lots of people been in jail, and if Charles wasn't a big fighter and get all this publicity, nobody would mention the jail."

She never called her husband Sonny—it was always Charles "because that's the way we was introduced. Charles Liston."

At the time, Liston worked in a bullet factory in St. Louis. "I was coming home from work in 1952 and got caught in a hailstorm," Geraldine said. "He was in a car with some fellows and they stopped and offered me a ride. I didn't want to get whacked by that hailstorm, so I accepted. Later he asked me out for a malt and we started dating. We married in six months."

Arch Soutar, who edited the *Lewiston Evening Journal*'s magazine section, had the most bizarre take on the scene at the Mansion House. "This story must be a hodgepodge," he wrote, "just as the afternoon was."

Soutar wondered aloud if Poland Spring's founders, "the bewhiskered Ricker brothers," were "spinning in their nearby graves."

He elaborated: "The changed humanity of the place! Handsome Negroes of the Liston entourage were everywhere. Once unthinkable at the Hilltop? Of course. But as I said to Mrs. Liston after saucily inquiring of her if she had encountered any 'race problem' (No, she said, she hadn't), 'Do you know, Mrs. Liston, it is but a few years since Jewish guests have been welcomed here? Yes, strange as it may seem, our Jewish brothers were not welcomed by the old Ricker management. Time changes all things.'"

Geraldine's response: "Change, yes. But for the better. We are all brothers. We are all God's children."

Soutar also said that he was driven to distraction by a vase of wilted carnations. "When I had stood them as long as possible," he wrote, "I wrenched them out and threw them into a nearby wastebasket. The setting seemed better now, and the future blasted into strong light. All right for the famed Poland Spring Orientals to be a bit faded, for age makes these floor coverings more precious and glowing somehow—but not faded flowers, not at this moment when two eager young men are fighting to decide which one is to be World Champion."

His conclusion: "It all blends so happily. So sensibly. Jews and Negroes. Priests and Protestants. One whole, entire union of humanity. And it took prizefighters; the 'fight game'; to bring this happy blending of all races, and creeds, and colors of humanity to my attention. Perhaps—after all—the Ricker boys, in their nearby graves, are content, too."

Another *Evening Journal* reporter, Rose O'Brien, was in the middle of interviewing Geraldine when Sonny arrived. But before she could ask Sonny anything of substance, a phone call interrupted them.

Geraldine answered the page. The caller was Willie Maxwell, the young man with cerebral palsy who lived in a nursing home. After speaking with him, Geraldine covered the phone and turned to Sonny. "He's just a young fellow, Charles. For twenty-nine years he's been bedridden and all he wants in the world is to see you."

Sonny didn't answer right away.

"It's just off Ash Street in Lewiston," Geraldine continued. "I know how to get there. You'll go, Charles?"

"He nodded," O'Brien reported, "and they both smiled."

CHAPTER SEVENTEEN

From Boyhood to Manhood in a Year

Meanwhile, in western Massachusetts, Ali was rounding into amazing shape—for a dead man. Rumors of a murder plot persisted, although the details were consistently sketchy or just plain wrong. (One Associated Press account claimed that "Before the title fight was postponed in November, there had been talk of a possible attack on Clay to avenge the assassination of Malcolm X." Malcolm X wasn't assassinated until three months after the fight was postponed.)

Syndicated columnist Milton Richman captured the vague sense of foreboding. Richman reported that "a stranger in a black sedan pulled up near a deserted field where Clay was doing his early morning road-work in Chicopee. The stranger silently watched each move Clay made and the champ's handlers became apprehensive but Clay laughed off the entire episode."

When Richman asked about the incident, Ali replied that he "was not scared of anything." Wrote Richman: "Malcolm X proclaimed to the world that he wasn't frightened of anything. Look where he is today."

Those in the Liston camp who saw through the hysteria had to be troubled by the more substantive reports out of Chicopee. By all accounts, Ali had improved as a fighter over the last fifteen months. And Angelo Dundee declared that he was in the "best condition of his career."

One wire-service story reported, "It is not uncommon, his early-morning companions agree, for him to shadowbox his way throughout four to five miles of roadwork. Clay even keeps up his quick-motion system at the dining table, [making] several quick jabs with either hand in the general direction of a passing waiter or a seated newsman. Even the breeze of his practice shots can be unsettling.

"By contrast . . . Liston has a 'Neanderthal' style in which his stance is nearly flat-footed."

Portland Evening Express sports editor Blaine Davis, continuing his series of informative previews, reported that Ali's sparring rounds lasted four minutes instead of the usual three minutes, to increase his stamina. "Most agree," wrote Davis, "that Liston couldn't hit the champion with a handful of rice."

Sam Silverman concurred. For all of his failings as a businessman, Suitcase Sam knew boxing. He reminded a *Boston Globe* reporter that he had picked Ali in Miami, "which is what I'm doing again at Lewiston."

He explained why: "I have been looking at fighters all my life, and Clay is the fastest big fighter I ever saw. . . . Here's something I've been thinking about a long time—and now I gotta say it: Clay is a better fighter at this stage of his career—twenty bouts—than anybody else, including, yes, Joe Louis. . . . There are many times when I read the papers about Cassius Clay and I don't recognize the guy they are talking about. . . . I think Clay will handle Liston easily this time. Inactivity kills all fighters. It did it to Dempsey and Sharkey, and all of them. Liston's had no fights. He has fought only ten rounds in five years. At his age, that's trouble. I've never seen a man train harder than Liston has. He is the most solemn, determined fighter I remember in training.

"But you gotta remember that Clay is a kid who fought Liston a year too soon, and still beat him. He'd been rushed and overmatched, and pushed to a title fight. He was an inexperienced fighter faced with all the tension that builds up before a title fight. This time you will see a Clay who has gone from boyhood to manhood in a year."

New York Times columnist Arthur Daley asked Ali about his deceptively powerful punching style. In Miami Beach, said Daley, "Clay had flitted about with what appeared to be powder puff punches. The wicked gash under Liston's eye was a puzzler. How did Cassius do it?"

The answer: "'A sharp right with the snap of a karate punch,' said Cassius, swinging his right arm and twisting his fist."

In his syndicated column, Joe Louis said Ali had the psychological edge as well. "Apart from his natural ability and his size and strength, which a good many people keep on underestimating, Clay is one of the smartest strategy boxers I've ever come across," Louis wrote. "When I say strategy, I mean how he works up to the fight as much as how he fights an opponent. When he pops off he isn't talking for publicity alone. He's trying to put ideas in the minds of the fellows with Liston. Willie Reddish, Teddy King, and Al Braverman, they are only human, and when Cassius puts out the bait they go for it.

"The danger for anybody against Clay is the state of mind he'll put you into before a glove is lifted. He aims to jolt your outlook off balance and keeps you jittery by what he says or does next. This is something new, to my experience. It's tough to listen to and tough to ignore. I know that I bruised kind of easy inside when guys needled me."

Finally, the hometown *Evening Journal* brought back an intriguing nugget from Chicopee to Lewiston. Ali, the paper wrote, "informed the group gathered in the second floor training facility, converted from a motel banquet room, that his friend Stepin Fetchit, former actor and vaudevillian and member of the old Jack Johnson camp, has taught him an 'anchor punch' which will drop the Bear.

"He would comment no further on the secret weapon."

Ali betrayed not a trace of concern over the upcoming bout. He bought ten $100 tickets for the doctors in Boston who had treated him for his hernia, including the anesthetist. "He's the only one able to knock me out," Ali joked.

"I feel sorry for [Liston] and I'll feel sorrier after I whup him," he said on another occasion. "We've got a temple in Denver. I'll have a couple of hundred brothers visit him afterwards and then we'll convert him."

He said he would take a different approach when he fought Floyd Patterson: "I'll buy the first three rows at ringside and let [Muslim brothers] sit there staring at him. Boy, that'll freeze him. We'll scare him to death."

That he was talking openly about fighting Patterson showed he was already thinking about life after the Liston era. During a conference call with reporters—which, in addition to Ali and Liston, included Joe Louis and Joe Walcott—Ali spoke as if Liston wasn't even on the line. "I'm going to win by a knockdown," he said, "but I'm not picking the round, because then no one would come to the fight. . . . [Liston] takes me a lot more seriously now, and he has trained a lot harder. He lost a lot of respect after he lost the last time. He sees how it is to lose, and he's hungry. He needs the money.

"But only a fool would pick Sonny Liston. A wise man would pick me. I'm taller, by two inches, faster on my feet, I can't be hit, and I know his style and his pace."

Also on the call was a promising amateur named Joe Frazier, who had won a gold medal at the 1964 Olympics. When all the fighters on the call were asked to offer predictions, only Frazier would bite. He picked Ali.

Asked if he had any advice for Frazier, whose professional debut would come that summer, Ali said, "Lose some weight and become a light heavyweight."

He was sizing him up already.

Another indication of the degree to which Ali was in control of things: He got his prefight physical in Chicopee rather than in Maine. "Clay didn't want to break up his training routine," said Duncan Mac-Donald of the Maine Boxing Commission, "so we decided to accommodate him."

The commission's physician, Dr. Leo P. Lemieux, made the 400-mile round trip to Chicopee for the exam. "In all my thirty-nine years of medical practice I never saw a more perfect physical specimen," said Dr. Lemieux, an osteopathic physician from Westbrook. "And that includes Charles Atlas."

Dr. Lemieux had examined Atlas, the "ninety-seven-pound weakling" who had transformed himself into a world-famous bodybuilder, when Atlas summered in Maine.

Dr. Lemieux called Ali's reflexes "surprisingly acute," declaring him "in A-1 condition and prepared to fight Liston or, for that matter, Jack Dempsey or anyone else. I find no defects whatever."

While the Maine contingent was in Chicopee, someone asked Ali how he felt about defending his title belt in Lewiston. The Champ said he was looking forward to seeing "the little one-horse town with courage enough to tackle and put a world heavyweight fight across."

He finished the session by requesting a private meeting with Sam Michael.

That must have been quite a trip to Chicopee and back—Sam sharing the car with Dr. Lemieux and Duncan MacDonald. That would be the same Duncan MacDonald who had gone after Sam with such zeal thirteen years earlier, during the Rocky Marciano flap. And the same Duncan MacDonald who had refused to expunge Marciano's suspension from the record.

The Ali–Liston fight was the greatest testament to Sam's ability as a diplomat and a negotiator. He had to work with people in both the City of Lewiston and the Maine Boxing Commission with whom he had had bitter disputes. He had to convince Saul Feldman that Sonny Liston would be a gracious guest at Poland Spring. He had to assuage whatever private concerns Muhammad Ali had. He had to be everywhere at once, and all things to all people.

The day after driving to Chicopee to meet with Ali, Sam was in Augusta, accompanied by three members of boxing's aristocracy. As part of the promotional tour they visited Governor Reed in his office and also appeared at the State House, where their visit was documented in the Legislative Record:

> The Chair will request the Sergeant-at-Arms to have this very distinguished group come to the rostrum if they so desire. (Thereupon, Mr. Sam Michael, Joe Walcott, Jim Braddock, and Joe Louis were escorted to the rostrum amid prolonged applause of the House, the members rising.) The Speaker: "On behalf of the House, gentlemen, I want to say that we are most honored to have such a distinguished group in our presence and we hope that you will enjoy your stay here in Maine and we hope that you will all return again. Is there objection at this time if the gentleman from Lewiston, Mr. Michael, addresses

the house very briefly? The Chair hears none, the gentleman may proceed."

Sam approached the microphone. "Thank you, Mr. Speaker," he began. "Members of the Legislature, friends: First I would like to apologize. President Bob Nilon of Inter-Continental Promotions Incorporated was unable to be here with us today. He does send his best wishes to the group. I'd like to say that this has been an honor for me to be associated with such a group to put on this world's heavyweight championship fight. I'd like to take this opportunity to thank Governor Reed, Attorney General Dick Dubord, the boxing commission, the local officials at Lewiston, Mayor Couturier, and everyone else concerned."

Then he concluded like the veteran fight promoter that he was: "I hope that we can see you all at Lewiston on the night of the twenty-fifth. I thank you very much."

CHAPTER EIGHTEEN

Big Red Rides Again

The experts agreed. *Too old*, they said. *Too broken down. Will never go the distance. Suffered too much abuse at the hands of Muhammad Ali last time out.*

They were wrong.

Big Red made a triumphant comeback.

After going out in an inglorious blaze along the back roads of North Carolina, en route from Miami, Ali's private bus rose from the ashes—or, in this case, burned-out bearings—to ride again. Its vital signs stabilized in Fayetteville, and bearing a fresh coat of paint from a young Ludlow, Massachusetts, auto-body man who labored four days and three nights for free for the honor of having his name (Harold Bennett) go down in obscurity, Big Red departed the Schine Inn at 11:13 a.m. on Sunday, May 23, 1965, carrying Muhammad Ali on the final 200-mile leg of his long and tortuous journey from Louisville to Lewiston.

So much for security concerns. "They say a car with six guys is coming here from New York City to get me—Malcolm X's boys," Ali had said the day before. "The hell with Malcolm X. . . . It's only three hours from New York to here. What took Malcolm's boys so long to get here? Why is it that three days before the fight all this news breaks? . . . Somebody planted this. I wonder who's behind it."

And so, after all the dire warnings that he carried a bull's-eye on his back, that he would be a marked man as he made his way to Maine, Ali took fewer precautions than a chaperone on a junior high school field trip. He and his entourage even made a twenty-minute pit stop at Howard Johnson's—which was then America's ubiquitous fast-food franchise—at the Kennebunkport exit along the Maine Turnpike.

Harold Conrad had done his best to keep the paranoia at a boil, planting the most outrageous rumor yet: A group of crazed pro-Malcolm X radicals planned to take out Big Red with an antitank gun. The handful of reporters aboard the bus—including the *Boston Globe*'s Bud Collins—scoffed at the absurdity. Nevertheless, when a couple of suitcases toppled from a luggage rack and hit the floor with a bang, the writers ducked for cover.

Ali laughed and assured them that Big Red was not taking artillery fire. "We just being attacked by men on horseback," he said. "It's Jesse James after us."

But whether he knew it or not, Ali had an escort riding shotgun. A couple of New York City detectives, William Confrey and John Keeley, followed Big Red in a convertible, keeping a discreet distance. What they were doing so far outside their jurisdiction was anybody's guess.

At any rate—and in Big Red's case the rate turned out to be about fifty miles an hour—Muhammad Ali finally arrived at the Auburn Holiday Inn at three o'clock Sunday afternoon. In one sense he was late; the fight was just two days away. But in another sense he was early. The promoters hadn't expected him until that evening. In order to let the champion have the spotlight to himself, the Maine Boxing Commission had scheduled a press conference at Poland Spring for a time that was supposed to have been well before Ali got to town: three o'clock Sunday afternoon.

Like every other blunder connected with this fight, the miscommunication wasn't just a mistake. It was a mistake that produced the worst possible outcome. Ali's arrival in Auburn and the boxing commission's press conference at Poland Spring happened at exactly the same time.

What's more, the Pine Tree Warriors drum-and-bugle corps was also practicing at Poland Spring at the same time as the press conference, which made it difficult for reporters to hear. Meanwhile, over at the Holiday Inn, Angelo Dundee was furious. "This is dirty pool," he said. "The meeting with the commission has been moved up and I wasn't told. I could have been here earlier. Among other things I want to see the gloves to be used in the fight and weigh them."

Dundee also wanted to inspect the ring at St. Dom's, but that didn't happen, either. "The Dominican Fathers who run the arena staunchly turned aside all appeals with a reminder that it was Sunday," the Associated Press reported.

As usual, the hullabaloo didn't faze Ali. Although his early arrival surprised the fight's organizers, about 200 fans were already waiting. Seeing the crowd, Ali said, "They act like the Beatles are in town."

Truck driver Lucien Dagneau saw things differently. "We figured it would be more fun than taking the kids down to the animal farm at Bath," he said.

Two other early arrivals were twelve-year-old Michael Boulanger of Lewiston and his father, Bill, an accountant. As soon as Ali stepped off the bus, the younger Boulanger asked for an autograph, and the champ complied, signing his name *M. Ali.* Boulanger also snapped a picture with his Kodak Instamatic.

Half an hour later, at a press conference, the Boulangers presented the local security force with its first test. The force failed. "My father knew the police officer who was at the door taking credentials," Michael Boulanger recalled years later. "They used to play softball together. So my father took a postcard and showed it to the officer, and he waved us in. I just remember my father telling me to be quiet."

With Ali holding court, this was not a problem. "He was a show," Boulanger recalled. "But nobody believed that he was for real because he hadn't caught on as the popular champ at that point. He was still the bad guy."

Even so, Boulanger, a Liston fan, found himself warming up to Ali. The Boulangers, like many other Lewistonians, were dismayed at the way their town was being portrayed in the national press. "We resent the Hicksville treatment," the *Daily Sun* wrote in an editorial.

So Ali scored points with the locals at his introductory press conference when he said, "I like Maine. I have never been here before—it's a beautiful state." (The next day, he was considerably less kind when asked how he felt about holding his first title defense at St. Dom's: "It's a disgrace. This is the biggest fight of all time and it's gonna be held in a little country arena.")

One thing Ali declined to do during his Holiday Inn press conference was make a prediction in rhyme. Sticking to a theme that he would repeat ad nauseam, he said, "I've got a big surprise. But if I told you, you wouldn't come to the fight."

After the press conference, Ali went to his room, number 252. The Auburn Holiday Inn was not a high-rise hotel. It was built in the "motor court" style popular at the time, with just two floors and a parking lot that ran around the entire building. Ali's entourage had sixteen rooms on the second floor, several of which had balconies overlooking the swimming pool in the courtyard.

It was a forum that perfectly suited Ali at age twenty-three. From the balcony he addressed the crowd. "I am the savior and the resurrection of boxing," he declared. "You're looking at history's greatest fighter. There'll never be another like me."

When his parents appeared, he introduced them as "other members of boxing's royal family."

Some fans had items that they wanted autographed. The best Ali could do was to sign slips of paper and let them flutter from the balcony. "I'm sorry," he said. "I just can't reach that far."

It was one of the few times he acknowledged his limitations.

The next morning Ali was relaxing by the pool. His training complete, he had no schedule to speak of. So he was just hanging with Angelo Dundee. But he wasn't used to inactivity. He wanted to *do* something.

He had an impulse. "Man," he said, "let's go raid the Big Bear's camp."

Dundee shot the idea down. "You don't want to go up there," he said. "It's old-fashioned and it looks just like the Munsters' house."

Besides, Dundee knew there was no need for such shenanigans this time. Ali agreed to stick to the script. "We're worrying Liston more by staying away from him this time," Ali said. "It's reverse psychology. We're *not* raidin' him."

So he stayed put. And he soon became distracted by a distant fighter jet from Brunswick Naval Air Station. He posed another question that betrayed his youth: "How long you think it would take me to catch up to him in my bus if he stopped right there?"

"Oh," Dundee said absently, "about two hours."

Ali's parents spent some time poolside as well. ("Hello, bird," Ali greeted Odessa.) Both expressed pride in their son and confidence in his abilities. "He will knock Liston out cold," said Cassius Sr. "He is the most fastest, most shrewdest, most accurate fighter boxing has ever known."

But there was also something poignant in the way the Clays spoke about their boy. Like many other middle-aged American couples in the 1960s, they couldn't comprehend the forces that were tearing their children away from them. For some families the wedge was drugs or long hair or rock music or antiwar protests. For the Clays it was Islam. "We know he can take care of himself—against everybody except Elijah Muhammad," Odessa said. "I'm afraid Elijah has him in his clutches right now."

Added Clay Sr., "We have tried to tell Cassius about his mistake. We think it's hurting his image nationally. But he is stubborn. After all, he is only twenty-three. We must wait for him to find out for himself."

"We brought the boys up in a Baptist church," Odessa said. "They went to Sunday school every Sunday. I don't know how in the world they got caught up with these new ideas.

"Poor, misguided boy."

Also among the onlookers at the Holiday Inn that Monday morning were the two New York City detectives who had followed Big Red from Chicopee. At least nine different law-enforcement agencies were now involved in the fight's security effort—ten, if you counted Ali's bodyguards, "the Fruit of Islam." Or, as columnist Jim Murray called them, "the Gestapo in blackface."

Strange bedfellows. The FOI and the FBI were working toward the same objective—although the FBI's operation was supposed to be covert. "We don't talk about that," said Joseph Farrand, Lewiston's police chief.

Farrand walked a fine blue line. He made it clear that his department took the threats seriously. He implemented procedures that would become standard under the Department of Homeland Security, such as issuing special ringside credentials, searching the bags of everyone entering the building, and setting aside a special detention area in the arena for anyone who seemed suspicious. But such precautions were extraordinary in the 1960s.

At the same time, Farrand tried to reassure the townspeople and their guests that everything was under control. "We do not expect any violence," he said, "but we must be prepared because this is an unusual event, something we've never had in this area."

He was blunt in expressing his ultimate objective: "I don't want [Lewiston] to go down in history as the place where the heavyweight champion was killed."

Reporters were equally candid in wondering aloud whether he could achieve that goal. Ali, wrote Murray, "may be the first heavyweight champion to lose his title by assassination."

Murray's closing line in his Ali–Liston preview column: "And may the better man live."

Harold Conrad must have smiled when he read that one.

Farrand did an admirable job resisting efforts to portray him and his department as overmatched. He noted that the most outrageous reports all seemed to originate with New York newspaper columnists such as Jimmy Cannon. Said Farrand, "If the reports came from an authorized agency, rather than a rumor from a reporter, I would be concerned."

Blaine Davis pointed out that chief Farrand's men would have to overcome a more insidious threat on fight night. Noting that the forty-seven-man ringside security force would be facing the crowd rather than the fighters, Davis wrote: "It will be an unusually dedicated cop who won't want to sneak an occasional peek."

It appeared, as Ali had predicted, that the rumors were beginning to unnerve Liston. When one report prompted tighter security at Poland Spring, Liston sought reassurance, asking, "They're after Clay, aren't they? Not me."

Ali continued to insist that the threats didn't bother him. "I am not scared of nothin' but the living god," he said at one press gathering. "I move too fast to get hit [by a bullet] anyway. Let 'em bring the Army in, the Navy. I don't need it. The American Negro has been here 400 years. You know the American Negro and you know fear is his biggest problem. That's why you picked up this story. . . . What kind of law is it that makes a fool of itself and lets them pick on a clean, righteous man like me that hurts no one? . . . How's come they can let armed men roam the highways and nobody can do a thing about it?"

In hindsight, it's obvious that Ali had the surest grasp of anyone of what was going to happen on fight night. There would be no violence at the arena—and very little in the ring. He said so over and over.

To Deane McGown of the *New York Times*: "I can only say this: Come early. There will be a lot of excitement for those who dare to dare. Just wait and see. I may not throw a single punch in the first round. Then again, I may go right out and get him. . . . That man Liston is scared. He's scared of me. He's scared about all of this security talk. He's scared he'll get hurt."

To a photographer who tried to snap a picture of him shadow boxing: "Don't bother—you can't do it. My punch is too fast. That's what Sonny's afraid of—my speed, my terrible punch."

To Arthur Daley of the *New York Times*: "It's gonna be a shock. If I was to predict what was to happen no one would come to see the fight. That's how shocking it will be. They might even say the fight was fixed."

To Mort Sharnick of *Sports Illustrated*: "I'm just gonna go backwards and Liston will pursue and then finally, *Bam!* I'll hit him with the right hand and it's gonna be over. . . . It will be a short fight."

Ali was on the money in another regard: He had reservations about Jersey Joe Walcott serving as the celebrity referee. Walcott, in previous bouts, had showed signs that he was too diffident, and perhaps too easily influenced by ringsiders. He should have stopped Floyd Patterson's 1961 fourth-round knockout of ten-to-one underdog Tom McNeeley earlier than he did. But with the Maple Leaf Garden crowd egging the plucky McNeeley on, Walcott allowed the fight to continue through eight official knockdowns and several unofficial stumbles. (He also failed to usher Patterson to a neutral corner after the seventh knockdown.)

But the Ali camp's primary objection stemmed from a lightweight title bout that Walcott had refereed in Panama City, Panama, just a month earlier. Walcott had sided with a Panamanian judge in awarding the bout to hometown favorite Ismael Laguna in an upset of Carlos Ortiz. (The third judge, New Yorker Ben Green, called the bout a draw—and "left the stadium under heavy police protection, which he requested prior to the fight when he claimed he had been told he would be lynched if he had an anti-Laguna decision," according to UPI.) Afterward, Walcott claimed he had scored the bout much closer than the 143–132 decision that was officially announced.

If the Lewiston fight came down to a decision, the Ali camp didn't want any discrepancies. They wanted a ref who could keep up both in the ring and on the scorecard—and who wouldn't be unduly swayed by a pro-Liston crowd.

Under Maine rules, however, the referee did not have a say in the decision. Three appointed judges would decide the bout; the ref's only function would be to keep the bout clean and deliver the count in case of a knockdown. Thus assured, Ali's camp eventually rescinded its objection. (Walcott also met one of the other stipulations that both sides had agreed to: The referee had to be black. That eliminated, among others, Barney Felix from the original list of nine prospective referees submitted to each camp.)

Liston, for his part, said he didn't care whether the referee was involved in the scoring or not. "It don't make no difference," said Liston. "All we need is a referee who can count to ten."

But as Joe Louis pointed out in another of his prefight columns, the referee's job was more complicated than that. "Don't let anyone tell you it's easy," Louis wrote. "When you have two big men in there, each looking to get an edge, you've got to be on the ball to keep everything moving as fair for one as for the other. . . . The thing is that either fighter could do something wrong—not intentionally, just in the heat of battle—and the ref must be on the alert to catch it."

Like not retreating to a neutral corner after a knockdown, for instance.

In truth, there was no way to predict what would happen once the bell rang. "That's the way fights are," Ali said. "There's no plan. It's like no other sport."

In this case, with so many things already having gone wrong long before the opening bell, a strictly-by-the-book bout would have been a welcome change. "Let it be a good fair fight," wrote the *Boston Globe*'s Harold Kaese, "so that forty years from now, one of the principals will not claim his coffee was drugged, or his opponent was wearing gloves padded with plaster of Paris. May there be no short count or long, foul claim, or foreign substances where they shouldn't be.

"And for their courage, let the yokels of Maine who took the fight have the last laugh on the yokels of Boston who did not want it."

CHAPTER NINETEEN

"I Counted Him Out,
I Counted Him Out!"

Lewistonians had a variety of entertainment options on the evening of May 25, 1965. The TV schedule featured *Petticoat Junction, The Fugitive*, and *Peyton Place*. (The movie version of *Peyton Place* had been filmed in Camden, Maine, in 1957; despite its scandalous nature, the film helped increase staid old Camden's allure as a tourist destination.) On the radio, the Red Sox hosted the Twins at Fenway Park.

For those who preferred to get out of the house, the Lewiston Fairgrounds had a full card of harness racing. The Lewiston Drive-in was showing Elvis Presley in *Kid Galahad*, a B movie whose implausible plot revolved around a small-time boxing promoter, a rustic resort, and the Mob's scheme to fix a fight. (Preceding the feature attraction were a couple of newsreels that put the *short* in selected shorts: Sonny Liston's two victories over Floyd Patterson.) And a sign on a downtown church promised: BEANO AS USUAL TUESDAY NIGHT, 7:30.

But there was nothing usual about this spring Tuesday in Lewiston.

Those Toots Shor types who didn't want to spend a long weekend in Maine all showed up at once. So many visitors flew in just for the day that the Federal Aviation Administration took over the control tower at Auburn–Lewiston Municipal Airport to handle the additional air traffic. Private planes were scattered like toys.

There was heavy traffic on the roads, too, and in restaurants. At Poland Spring, the wait staff was so overwhelmed during the morning rush that Kelly Bishop, wife of syndicated columnist Jim Bishop, went to the kitchen to get their order herself.

It was a hectic day at the Michael household, too. And possibly a life-altering one. Bob Nilon had promised Sam Michael that Inter-Continental would bring Liston back for his first title defense if he managed to beat Ali. And why wouldn't they? Lewiston had been as accommodating as could be. Sam had to secretly be rooting for a Liston victory, but he wouldn't admit it, not even to his family. All he said was: "If the fight is a corker, Lewiston will be the fight capital of the world."

Sam had a job to do—and so did his teenage son, John, thanks to Bob Nilon's penchant for snap decisions. "We need a round-card boy or a round-card girl," Nilon had told Doris Michael at one point.

"Well, Johnny's fourteen," she said.

Done. Wearing a tuxedo, like his dad, John Michael would watch the fight from the ice rink's penalty box, holding a stack of numbered round cards with a silhouette of the state of Maine on them.

The 12:30 weigh-in had a similar feel—equal parts pomp-and-cir-cumstance and theater-troupe improv. And while it lacked the drama of Ali's tour de force performance in Miami, it was not without incident. The crowd, estimated at anywhere from 500 to 2,000, cheered Liston as he arrived, accompanied by Willie Reddish, Teddy King, and Ash Resnick. (Also on hand was Jersey Joe Walcott, who climbed into the ring for the ceremony, adding weight to the rumors that he had been chosen as referee.)

Ali was accompanied by his bodyguards and his brother Rahaman, who was scheduled to fight on the undercard. The crowd, which included a bunch of townies on their lunch hour, heckled the champion.

"Who's the greatest?" shouted one. "Sonny Liston!"

"You'd better bring your pillow, Clay!" shouted another.

Another addressed Ali by his Muslim name—although it was hardly a show of respect. "Hey, Muhammad!" he yelled. "Your camel's double-parked!"

To keep everything nice and official-like, the Maine Boxing Commission had its two physicians, Dr. Ralph Turgeon and Dr. Leo Lemieux, on hand to oversee the proceedings, along with Charles Tuttle, Lewiston's sealer of weights and measures. There was really no need for any of this; unlike other classes, which required fighters to stay below a certain weight, heavyweights had no limit.

Even so, a minor controversy ensued. Commission officials had placed the scale inside the ring. When Liston stepped aboard, commission chairman George Russo announced his weight as 219½, considerably above his target weight of 211.

"Fat!" Ali hooted.

Liston and Reddish immediately challenged the reading. They pointed out that the canvas under the scale wasn't stable. So officials stuck a sheet of plywood under the scale and tried again. This time the reading was a more respectable 215¼. Still a little higher than anticipated.

Ali, on the other hand, came in much lighter than expected— lighter, even, than he had been in Miami: 206. It was another indication of just how much fitter—and faster—he was than Liston.

Afterward there was some halfhearted jawing and pantomimed outrage. "Clay again went into his dancing jig-step and began shadow boxing furiously," the *Portland Press Herald* reported, "coming close enough to Liston's dour visage as to frighten the heart out of co-promoter Sam Michael and publicist Hal Conrad."

And just in case this little bit of stagecraft distracted anyone long enough to forget the threats of violence, Rahaman stood in the background holding up a newspaper whose headline implored local police to guard his brother against "avengers."

Although St. Dom's was far from sold out on fight night, streets were clogged throughout Lewiston. In the lingering spring twilight, revelers gathered along the hill on the south side of Birch Street outside the arena, captivated by the sheer spectacle of it all. "It was as if the World Series had moved to New Gloucester," John Michael said later.

Many of those who entered the arena did so without paying. Despite the elaborate precautions, "security was really no good," John Michael said. "If [an assassin] had really wanted to shoot Ali, all he would have had to do was put on a delivery uniform and carry in a case of Pepsi like half my friends did."

Everyone, it seemed, had an angle. Ray Lebrun, who ran a local real estate business, scored complimentary tickets through his brother-in-law, Bert Cote. "He was playing the organ for the national anthem," Lebrun said later. "I helped him carry the organ in."

Tapped to accompany Cote on the national anthem was Las Vegas crooner Robert Goulet. Before the night was out, his reputation would take as big a hit as Sonny Liston's, at least around Lewiston.

Goulet, who was born in Lawrence, Massachusetts, and later moved to Montreal, had roots in Lewiston—although that apparently had slipped his mind. He suddenly remembered his local connection during an interview with the *Lewiston Evening Journal*'s intrepid reporter, Rose O'Brien. When O'Brien arrived, unannounced, at his room in Poland Spring, Goulet told her, "I can't give you an interview now, dear. I'm not even awake. Come back later. Oh, in about forty-five minutes."

O'Brien, on deadline, returned in fifteen. "You really want this interview, don't you?" Goulet said. So he consented—on the condition that O'Brien remain in the hall and ask her questions through the door, left slightly ajar, while he got dressed. And it was during this rambling exchange that Goulet suddenly declared, "Say, my mother was *born* in Lewiston, come to think of it. *Lewiston*. I didn't really think of that before."

After this visit he would never forget Lewiston again because Lewiston wouldn't let him.

During the interview Goulet sang snatches of the anthem—"trial runs on how he was sounding," O'Brien reported.

This would be Goulet's first public performance of that notoriously difficult song. He was not, as later accounts claimed, drunk and ill-prepared. During a cocktail reception for Governor Reed at Poland Spring that night he stepped outside three times to practice on the balcony. He then rode to St. Dom's with the Feldmans, which was when the trouble started. Knowing how anxious Goulet was about performing the anthem, Tudi Feldman tried to take his mind off it by singing "America the Beautiful" instead. "I take the blame," she said later. "I put the wrong tune in his head."

The second problem: Amid the crush and confusion at St. Dom's Goulet lost the crib notes he had made to help him remember the words. He didn't realize the notes were gone until just before he stepped into the ring.

"What am I gonna do?" he muttered.

St. Dom's was still practically empty when the program started at 8:30. The undercard featured the Ali and Liston sparring partners against a ragtag assemblage of pugs who would have been right at home on one of Sam and Joe Michael's weekly cards at City Hall. Jimmy Ellis—who had bruised Ali's ribs in their final sparring session—knocked out Joe Blackwood at 1:04 of the first round. It was the last of Blackwood's sixty-six professional fights, ending a career that had begun in 1944.

Rahaman Ali squared off against Louisville's Buster Reed, who, like Blackwood, was making his final appearance as a pro. It was also Reed's first appearance as a pro. His career lasted less than four minutes, with Rahaman kayoing him in the second round. Two other bouts—Mel Turnbow over Cody Jones and Mike Bruce over Abe Brown—went the six-round distance. About the only one who benefited from those fights was John Michael, who got in some practice being the round-card boy.

As the preliminaries dragged along, the hubbub outside St. Dom's reached a crescendo. Each fighter arrived late, detoured by heavy traffic that consisted mostly of people who were "just curious to see what was happening," said Lewiston police captain Andre Roux. (Also among the onlookers outside the arena were seven Nation of Islam members who had requested permission from Lewiston police to do video surveillance for Malcolm X loyalists.)

Liston left Poland Spring at 8:22, accompanied by seven members of the Androscoggin County Sheriff's Department. He reached St. Dom's at 8:45. Ali arrived five minutes later, aboard Big Red. Taking no chances, the state police had stopped traffic in both directions on the Maine Turnpike during the short drive between the Auburn and Lewiston exits. Ali's wife Sonji rode in a state police cruiser, along with his parents. Ali entered St. Dom's through a rear door, singing "Let's Dance."

The preliminary bouts complete, there was little to do but wait for the choice of referee to be announced. While he waited, former champ Jack Sharkey, whose name had been on the list submitted to each camp, turned to Joe Louis and said, "Want to go a fast ten, Joe?" Said Louis, "You can't go ten anymore, Jack."

Sharkey's stamina wouldn't be an issue. To no one's surprise, Jersey Joe Walcott was officially named referee.

Most of the politicians and other dignitaries straggled in late. Governor Reed arrived at 9:50. Congressman William D. Hathaway, a prominent Lewiston lawyer who had received the Purple Heart and Distinguished Flying Cross during World War II, landed at Auburn at 9:45. He reached St. Dom's at 10:10, accompanied by representatives from Iowa, New Jersey, and Connecticut.

To the right of Governor Reed and his wife Cora sat Edwin W. Weston, Maine's adjutant general (he wore a white uniform with epaulets and a black bowtie) and Weston's wife Virginia. To the Reeds' left sat Rhode Island governor John Chaffee. To Chaffee's left sat former Massachusetts governor Endicott Peabody, the man who, the previous September, had set in motion the chain of events that culminated with this circus of the surreal. (The promoters had also extended an invitation to Suffolk County D.A. Garrett Byrne, the man who had run the fight out of Boston. His response: "Not interested.")

Also in the house was Robert Couturier, Lewiston's twenty-four-year-old mayor. He was there against his better judgment. "I had said that I probably wouldn't attend," Couturier said later, "but Sam Michael convinced me that because I was the mayor I should be there."

Sam worried about every aspect of the fight. As the big moment drew near, he bounced around St. Dom's, a bundle of nervous energy. He checked on the concession stands, where fifteen-cent sodas were selling briskly. The evening was cool, but it was warm and stuffy inside St. Dom's. Secondhand smoke wafted to the rafters, creating a halo in the glare of the hot television lights. Also in the rafters were several sets of strobe lights set up for the photographers who formed a cordon at ringside. Twenty-two-year-old Neil Leifer, who was on assignment for *Sports Illustrated*, had spent several days working with local technicians at St. Dom's to get his lights positioned just so. He'd also installed a remote camera with a wide-angle lens at the far corner of St. Dom's, and another remote camera with a fisheye lens directly above the ring. His plan was to get an overhead shot that would transform the ring canvas into an artist's canvas. A fallen fighter would be silhouetted against a plain background, with the ring ropes forming a frame.

Getting a memorable picture often required meticulous planning and hours of effort. Other times it was simply a matter of being in the

right spot at the right moment. In Lewiston, Leifer accomplished all of
the above. After installing his remote cameras, he chose a position at
ringside that, by sheer luck, was the perfect place to shoot with a hand-
held camera. "If I had put an X on the canvas where I hoped the fight
would end," he said later, "that was the spot."

The crush at ringside grew as 10:30, the starting time of the closed-
circuit telecast, approached. Among the madding crowd was LeRoy
Nieman, the handlebar-mustached watercolorist on assignment for
Playboy. He flitted around the ring, drawing sketches on Western Union
pads that he grabbed from reporters' tables. So many people were filter-
ing in and milling around that it was hard to tell who belonged where.
Sam Michael did his best to chase interlopers from the restricted area
and maintain order, but it was difficult. Some people simply abandoned
their seats on the floor and tried to squeeze in ringside, right alongside
the VIPs.

One VIP was seventy-seven-year-old Nat Fleischer, dubbed "Mr.
Boxing Himself." Fleischer, who saw his first fight in 1899, had founded
Ring magazine in 1922; he was still its publisher and editor-in-chief. In
ranking the greatest boxers of all time, he acknowledged a bias toward
those who had fought before World War II. "Any of the clever boys of
the past would stand the fighters of today on their ears," he had said
recently.

And, if anything, Fleischer had even greater contempt for modern
boxing officials and referees. Mr. Boxing Himself had been a referee himself in his younger days. He wasn't shy about letting the fighters know
who was boss—even if it meant overstepping his authority. Take the bout
he refereed at Toledo, Ohio, in 1942 between Billy Conn and Henry
Cooper, a journeyman from Brooklyn (not to be confused with the British Henry Cooper that Ali fought twice). In his most recent fight, for the
heavyweight title, Conn had been knocked out by Joe Louis. Conn took
the Cooper bout just to get in a little work and collect some money while
he angled for a rematch with Louis. So, not wanting to risk suffering a
knockout that would have killed his chances, he spent the first five rounds
dancing. The crowd became restive and began to boo.

Before round six Fleischer grabbed the microphone and addressed
the crowd. "Unless there is more action," he said, "I am requesting the

police department to return your money and I am declaring [this fight] no contest."

When Conn, who went on to win what became a lively battle, complained afterward, Fleischer said, "Don't you think you should earn your money, Billy?"

That was how you refereed a fight. "Now," Fleischer had complained recently, "we have many men of incompetence, with political affiliations. And they are too timid, too often afraid to act."

Fleischer sat at the end of a ringside table, next to Francis McDonough, the knockdown timer. There was a gap between that table and the next. As fight time approached, that space was filled to overflowing by an ample man who squeezed the 5' 2" Fleischer uncomfortably close to McDonough.

On McDonough's other side was fight timer Russ Carroll, head of the business and audio-visual departments at Edward Little High School in Auburn. Carroll, fifty-five, had recorded the time of Shiner Couture's reputed world-record knockout at City Hall back in '46. Carroll had his own stopwatch, but because this was no ordinary fight the Maine Boxing Commission had given him a fancier one. Among other things it had a function that made it easier to reset the watch to zero.

Later, Carroll claimed that, as he struck the bell to start the fight, he had a premonition: *Something is going to go wrong.*

Despite his obvious talent, Robert Goulet originally resisted the idea of becoming a singer. When he was five, some of his French Canadian aunts darkened his face with burnt cork and made him do an Al Jolson impersonation. Their uproarious response frightened him. It took him years to get over the resulting performance anxiety.

Goulet might have flashed back to that nightmarish family gathering when he took the microphone, sans cheat sheet for the lyrics, inside the twenty-by-twenty ring at St. Dom's, in his mother's hometown, to sing "The Star-Spangled Banner." The acoustics in the smoky, cement-block ice arena were terrible. Goulet had a hard time even hearing organist Bert Cote, let alone following the melody. And he may well have had Tudi Feldman's rendition of "American the Beautiful" stuck in his head. In any case, he missed his cue, came in late, and flubbed the first line, singing "by the dawn's early *night*" instead of "by the dawn's early light." And although he got the rest of the words right, more or less, he never did get synched up with Cote's organ. This discordant opening colored the way seemingly everyone in the arena would remember the evening. In the *Boston Globe*, Bud Collins summarized Goulet's performance: "Clay hit the wrong guy."

Years later Goulet said, "I walked into Lewiston, Maine a hero because I had a French–Canadian background and I spoke their language. . . . I walked out of town a bum."

Sonny Liston would go through a similar transformation, almost as quickly.

At the outset, Liston was the clear fan favorite. The crowd cheered when he entered the ring (looking spaced-out and sweaty, some observers later claimed) and booed lustily as Ali danced into the ring a few minutes later.

Ring announcer Johnny Addie's heavy New Yawk accent added a splash of color to the festivities. "Ladies and gentlemen, here are some introductions," Addie began. "From the nightclubs, Billy Daniels. Singer Billy Daniels."

To judge from the tepid applause, Daniels was only slightly better known in 1965 than he is today.

Addie's next announcement: "May we have the gloves into the ring, please? The gloves. Come into the ring with the gloves, please."

The lurid-red, eight-ounce boxing gloves, like the boxers, had taken a circuitous route to Lewiston. The previous fall a Chicago company called Frager had custom-made the gloves—a necessity in Liston's case, because of his huge hands—at a cost of $154. At the time of the postponement, the Massachusetts Boxing Commission had the gloves in a safe, and that's where they stayed until the Massachusetts commission transferred custody to the Maine commission, which then kept the gloves in a different safe until fight night.

While Ali and Liston got their gloves laced up, Addie introduced, in order, Canadian heavyweight champion George Chuvalo, who was lobbying for a title shot (and who worked out at the Portland YMCA during his stay in Maine); retired featherweight champion Sandy Saddler; another of the all-time great featherweights (and Sam Michael's good friend), Willie Pep; newly crowned light heavyweight champion Jose Torres; James Braddock; Floyd Patterson; Jack Sharkey; Rocky Marciano; and—in Addie's delivery—"the Brown Bomb-uh, Joe Louis!"

Of these, Patterson got the loudest applause.

Next, Addie introduced all the Maine boxing officials. Then: "And the referee, ladies and gentlemen, the former heavyweight champion of the world, Jersey Joe Walcott!"

The crowd applauded warmly as Walcott made his way into the ring. It took him almost thirty seconds to get there.

Finally, after fifteen months of hype and hysteria and hernias; of speculation and cynicism and conspiracy theories; and of Mobsters and Muslims scattered from Miami to Massachusetts to Maine, it was time to settle things decisively, definitively, and once and for all. "Ladies and gentlemen," Addie intoned, "Inter-Continental Promotions, Incorporated, Robert A. Nilon, president, and Arena A.A.* present the main event. Fifteen rounds for the heavyweight championship of the world. The principals: Introducing, from Denver, Colorado, he's wearing black trunks, he weighs two-fifteen and a quarter, the former heavyweight champion, and now the challenger, Sonny Liston. Liston!"

Addie's voice drowned in a swell of applause.

Addie continued: "His opponent, from Louisville, Kentucky, he's wearing white trunks, he weighs two-oh-six, the heavyweight champion of the world, Muhammad Ali!"

It was the first time Ali was introduced before a fight under his Muslim name—even if Addie pronounced it "Muhammad Alley."

St. Dom's resounded with boos.

On the SportsVision closed-circuit telecast, announcer Steve Ellis felt compelled to cut in: "Muhammad Ali," he said, "*better known* as Cassius Clay."

This was the first US fight broadcast live in Europe. At that moment in France—where it was approximately 3:30 Wednesday morning—about 1,000 Parisians gathered at the Radio House, where

---

*Although Sam Michael had once had an attorney named Benjamin Arena, that's not why his promotional outfit was called Arena A.A. "I think he just liked the sound of the word," his son John said. "And the three A's made it the first listing in the phone book."

they had paid the equivalent of sixty cents apiece to see this little bit of history as it happened. The fight also aired live in London, where the House of Commons was in an all-night session. A few members of Parliament reportedly sneaked out to catch the fight. (Not that they would be gone very long.) Later that day, viewers from Asia to Australia would also see the fight. Some of those viewers might have wondered why America seemed so unsettled by a young boxer's new name.

After assuring viewers that this was in fact Cassius Clay they were watching, Ellis turned the call back to Addie just as Addie turned the microphone over to Jersey Joe Walcott for the fight instructions. Walcott spoke so softly that it was hard to hear him. But among the things he muttered was this: "I'm not gonna go with a lot of preliminaries—I know you both know the rules of Maine."

The question would become: Did Walcott know the rules of Maine?

At the opening bell, as the ringside photographers ducked under the bottom rope, resting their elbows on the canvas, Ali surprised Liston. Rather than keep his distance as everyone—including Liston—expected, Ali charged and bopped Liston on the head with a wild, looping right, like he was driving a nail. Liston ducked, but the punch got through. A moment later Liston started to throw a left hand but aborted the punch and ducked when Ali threw a left-right combination and scored again. Just five seconds had elapsed.

That start couldn't have helped Liston's jitters.

After that initial flurry the fight lapsed into a more conventional feeling-out period. Ali, following the same pattern he had established in Miami, began circling the ring clockwise. Liston stalked him like a man trying to swat a fly. For all his movement, Ali maintained good balance and kept his shoulders square. His description of his style—dancing—was more accurate than Liston's description of it—running. There was never a moment when Ali appeared compromised or vulnerable or in harried retreat.

Liston approached tentatively, like a fencer, repeatedly stepping toward Ali with his left foot. About forty-five seconds into the round he drew a rise from the crowd with a right jab as Ali's head snapped to the side. But Ali had snapped his head on purpose, ducking out of range. He hadn't been hit. (ABC Sports later determined that Liston missed with all seventeen jabs that he threw.) This was the phantom punch's inverse; Ali's quickness had fooled some spectators into thinking they had seen something that they hadn't.

Liston wasn't the only one having trouble keeping up with Ali. Walcott gave the fighters a wide berth, frequently backpedaling or moving at a trot while glancing over his shoulder, trying to stay out of the way.

At just over a minute Ali lowered Liston's defenses with a quick left to the midsection, then drilled him on the chin with a roundhouse right. Had Liston been planning an early departure, that would have been an opportune time. There would have been no talk of a phantom punch after that blow, which had a full wind-up and follow-through. "Beautiful right-hand shot," Ellis said on the SportsVision broadcast. "That was the best punch thus far, landed by the champion."

Later, longtime trainer Chickie Ferrara—who was stationed near Liston's corner on orders from Angelo Dundee to keep an eye out for anything suspicious—said: "That shot shivered Liston. He blinked his eyes three times, like he was trying to clear his head."

Jim Braddock also was impressed by that punch. "It was a right to Liston's jaw and it was a beauty," Braddock said the next morning. "It shook Liston to his shoe tops."

Braddock, who had picked Liston to win, also said this: "That guy Clay is a pretty fair fighter. I have a feeling that he's a lot better than any of us gave him credit for being."

Over the next thirty-five seconds Liston threw a succession of body shots, none of which actually reached the body; Ali blocked them with his arms. At 1:32 Liston fired a left jab at Ali's head that missed. He tried and failed again a second later. Ten seconds after that, after missing with his left jab yet again, he pitched forward and then crumpled to his knees. The phantom punch, Ali's right-hand counter over Liston's jab, had flashed so quickly that few people to Liston's rear saw it. This group included the closed-circuit TV audience.

It also included the referee. At the precise moment Ali threw his quick, short, decisive right, Walcott had just circled directly behind Liston. He was in the worst possible position to see the punch. He was also the shortest man in the ring. He was fifty-one years old. He had fought seventy-one times in his twenty-three-year career and had absorbed a brutal knockout from Rocky Marciano in his penultimate bout. And his history as a referee showed that he gave the benefit of the doubt when it was unclear whether a fallen fighter had been knocked down or had merely slipped.

Did Walcott think Liston had just lost his balance? Marciano, seated ringside, thought so. "He acted that way," Marciano said later, "because he just didn't start the count at all."

Walcott was so far out of position that it took him three seconds just to get between Ali and Liston. Ali's animated reaction during that time could have reinforced Walcott's assumption that Liston had stumbled. Ali stood over Liston, yelling at him to get up and fight (a blink-of-the-shutter moment that Neil Leifer captured in what became the iconic Ali photograph). Why would a man who had just floored his opponent with a potential knockout punch want to keep fighting? But if Liston had simply fallen down and was taking his time getting back up, Ali's anger would have made sense. He could have thought that Liston was exploiting his own clumsiness to catch a breather.

In any case, Walcott had an obligation to protect Liston until Liston regained his feet. Walcott tried to do so—and Ali's refusal to go to a neutral corner flummoxed him. Walcott spent the next nine seconds preoccupied with just one of his multiple responsibilities as he chased Ali around the ring. He neither tried to start the count nor suspend it, even though knockdown timer Francis McDonough had begun banging his gavel the moment Liston went down. (Though muffled, McDonough's count was audible on the SportsVision broadcast.) Nor, during all this time, did Walcott take a second look at Liston, who appeared lost in a private Greek tragedy.

What was going through Liston's mind—a mind at least somewhat clouded by the phantom punch? He could have had any of many different thoughts—or all of them at once. Consider, for starters, Liston's frame of reference when it came to heavyweight title fights. He had been in three of them before Lewiston. In two of them he had destroyed Floyd Patterson in the first round. Patterson had fought foolishly—playing to Liston's strength by trying to mix it up rather than make it a bout of attrition. Nevertheless, the press remained sympathetic to Patterson. Not only had those first-round knockouts failed to tarnish

Patterson's reputation—they hadn't significantly diminished his prospects, either. Since the last Liston bout Patterson had had five fights and won them all, including a TKO of Tod Herring in Sweden earlier that month. Now he was in Lewiston angling for yet another title shot, against Ali. And Liston knew that he would probably get it.

So Liston might reasonably have deduced that a first-round knockout wasn't the worst thing that could happen to a fighter.

In his third title fight, against Cassius Clay in Miami Beach, Liston had persevered through six tough rounds with a debilitating arm injury. (He might have torn the tendon as early as the first minute, when he tried for a quick knockout.) Then, with his eyes swollen nearly shut and his left arm feeling like it was "full of water," he did something that had to be incredibly difficult. He conceded that he was a beaten man. Beaten by an opponent he had dismissed as a joke.

Facing that truth took a certain kind of courage. In fact, you could argue that it took even more courage than Floyd Patterson had shown because it required a conscious decision, as opposed to the unconscious decision occasioned by a first-round knockout. But Liston was crucified for his perceived cowardice. *He quit on his stool.* That's what they all said—over and over. (Google "Sonny Liston" and "quit on his stool" and you'll get more than 15,000 hits.)

So imagine you're Sonny Liston. Halfway through round one in Lewiston, you have no confidence, no heart for going through another six rounds of what you endured in Miami Beach. Your head's already swimming from a sharp right. And on top of all that you're worried that at any moment some lunatic might pull out a gun and start shooting. You just want this nightmare to be over, one way or another, as soon as possible. So maybe you figure, why not go the Floyd Patterson route? Just wade right in there and give Ali your best shot, that notorious left jab. Maybe you'll get lucky and catch him on the button. And if you miss and he turns out your lights with a solid counterpunch? Well, at least they'll say you went out like a man this time.

So you recklessly throw that left lead, which comes up short, and. . . .

Wham!

You take another lightning-bolt right hand to the jaw.

That's the most important thing to keep in mind about the phantom punch. Liston might not have seen it coming, but he certainly felt it when it arrived. So from his perspective, the punch's "realness" was never in question. He knew he got tagged, and he would have had no reason to believe that anyone watching thought otherwise. How could he have known that so many people, in the arena and at theaters around the world, didn't see it?

After bracing himself with his gloves on his way to the canvas, Liston pivoted on his right knee and landed on his back. He stayed that way for three seconds before rolling over onto his stomach. He then drew himself up until he rested unsteadily on his right knee and tried to stand by planting his left foot—whereupon he toppled onto his back again.

Twelve seconds had elapsed since the phantom punch landed.

At that moment Walcott, still caught up in a slapstick chase scene, almost tripped over Liston's outstretched arms. Walcott's aspect abruptly changed. He abandoned his pursuit of Ali (who jogged alongside the ropes, his arms raised, as if on a victory lap). Walcott looked down and seemed surprised to find Liston in what appeared to be extreme distress—way more distress than if he had simply slipped and fallen.

Walcott appeared to experience a dawning. It might have been this: *I missed a knockout punch!*

For the first time since Liston went down, Walcott glanced in McDonough's direction. He leaned over Liston, hands on his knees, as if he were about to begin a better-late-than-never count. But in another instance of tragicomic timing, McDonough had just stopped banging his gavel.

That was a huge mistake on McDonough's part. As Blaine Davis explained in the next day's *Portland Evening Express*, "Maine ring rules allow the knockdown timer only one function, and this is to guarantee with the aid of a stopwatch that the fallen boxer is given the benefit of ten full seconds, since in the excitement and confusion which normally attends such an occurrence, the referee often inadvertently tolls the ten count in fewer than nine, or even eight seconds. The knockdown timer's count could reach 100 and still have no bearing on the outcome, except to inform the referee that every time the timer's hammer hits the ring floor one second has elapsed."

Then, to compound Walcott's troubles, Liston struggled to his feet. In other words, just when it finally occurred to Jersey Joe that he ought to pick up the count, there was no longer any count to pick up; just when it finally occurred to Jersey Joe that Liston had legitimately been knocked down, Liston got up.

Now what?

Walcott moved between Liston and Ali (who, for some reason, had just jumped into the air) and wiped Liston's gloves, glancing with what appeared to be growing urgency toward the timekeeper. Ali stood behind Walcott, pumping his fists, champing to resume. It was a pathetic scene. Walcott, the only man who had the authority to stop the fight under Maine rules, was buying time, waiting for somebody else to take charge and make a decision.

And Nat Fleischer, Mr. Boxing Himself, was happy to do so.

This is what happened next, according to Fleischer's later account: "I was watching the timekeeper. I was sitting on half of his bench because my seat had been taken by someone else. Contrary to the general statements of most of the newspapermen that no count had been made, he definitely was hitting the gavel against the boards, because he also hit my thumb. When he counted to ten, he automatically shut off the watch and then immediately put it on again for two more seconds. Then he tried to gain the attention of the referee, but since his body was hemmed in and he could not possibly move around there, he asked me if I could help him by getting Joe Walcott's attention. So I jumped out of my seat and I yelled to Joe. When Joe looked around for the first time toward the timekeeper, which he should have done a long, long while ago, I said, 'He's out!' And the official timekeeper was yelling the same thing: 'I counted him out, I counted him out!'"

Again, declaring Liston out was not the timekeeper's responsibility—much less Fleischer's. It was Walcott's. But Walcott didn't want it.

Walcott had one last chance to salvage a little credibility, both for himself and for the bout. All he had to do was stand by his initial assumption that Liston had slipped. He could have ignored Fleischer and McDonough and allowed the fight to continue. In all likelihood Ali would have scored a more definitive knockout within a round or two, and the confusion over the phantom punch would have been relegated to a footnote, like Ali's temporary blindness in Miami.

Or, if Walcott had determined that Liston was incapacitated—for whatever reason—he could have ended the fight by declaring a technical knockout. Although it would have been only slightly less controversial, this outcome would at least have been defensible under Maine rules.

Instead, Walcott surrendered any slender thread of credibility he might have had left by leaving the fighters, running across the ring, and ducking through the ropes to confer with McDonough. In his absence, Ali quickly resumed his assault, throwing another half-dozen punches during this six-second limbo in which the bout continued with all the supervision of a barroom brawl.

Fleischer: "Joe let the two fighters remain where they were and raced over to Mr. McDonough and he said, 'What happened?' Mr. McDonough said, 'I counted him out twice. . . . I counted twelve . . . and then twenty.'"

Only the final part of Fleischer's account would not be open to dispute: "Joe ran back and separated the two fighters—then re-engaging in fighting—and held up the hand of the winner, Cassius Clay."

Thirty-five seconds had elapsed between the moment Ali had thrown the phantom punch and the moment Walcott briefly clutched his left arm (which was already raised). That was the nearest indication anyone got that the fight was over.

CHAPTER TWENTY

A Not-So-Instant Replay

How people saw all of this depended on their physical perspective as well as their philosophical one. Those facing Liston at the time of the phantom punch were more likely to take the outcome at face value. This group included Sam Michael, who was watching from the fifth row with an unobstructed view. Although the reach of his ambition often exceeded his grasp, Sam was a realist. He accepted the punch's legitimacy. "I saw it," he said later. "Liston came lunging with a left and Muhammad Ali threw a right over his left and got him on the cheek. If it had hit him on the chin, Liston would still be out."

As for the debacle that followed with Jersey Joe and Francis McDonough and Nat Fleischer—yeah, that had looked really bad, but none of it changed a simple fact: Ali had knocked Liston out. And Sam immediately grasped the implications. "When Liston fell to the canvas," he said, "my heart fell to my stomach."

He knew. This was not the corker he'd hoped for. Liston would not regain the title. Lewiston would not become the fight capital of the world. The dream was over.

Contrary to a mythology that developed, many journalists also saw the punch clearly and called the knockout legitimate. This group included:

Jim Murray, syndicated columnist: "This is the second time this fight has ended with several thousand people looking at each other and asking, 'What happened?' Well, I'll tell you what happened. Sonny Liston got the hell beat out of him is what happened. This time I was looking for it and I saw it. . . . [Liston] should have

199

worn a catcher's mitt on his face. I counted three times when Cassius staggered him."

Bud Collins, *Boston Globe*: "No fake, baby. This was a beautiful short right hand that went in over Liston's hands like a sword going over a bull's horns for the kill. It arrived at Sonny's jaw like an anchor from the Queen Elizabeth. Suddenly the bear was rolling around as though his body were on fire and he was trying to put it out. No use. It was a holocaust."

John Gillooly, *Boston Record American*: "We have a religion editor. Cassius can go to his church; I'll go to mine. All I know is that he's a great fighter and that Liston was lucky to be legitimately kayoed in [the first round] or his head might have gone rolling with the logs in the Androscoggin River."

Tex Maule, *Sports Illustrated*: "Muhammad Ali, born Cassius Clay, retained the heavyweight championship of the world by knocking out Sonny Liston with a perfectly valid, stunning right-hand punch to the side of the head, and he won without benefit of a fix."

Blaine Davis, *Portland Evening Express:* "Though scores of fans yelled 'Fake!' after the weird ending, most fighters on the side of the ring where the action occurred contended it was a solid right smash that floored Liston. We saw it as a punch of which any heavyweight could be proud."

Despite the testimony of these and other credible eyewitnesses, most observers refused to believe what they did not see. This resulted in a mass occurrence of confirmation bias, reinforced by the farcical sequence of procedural errors that followed the knockout punch (including the announced official time of one minute even, an obvious discrepancy that resulted from Russ Carroll's having inadvertently reset his stopwatch during the round).

To those who didn't see the knockout punch, the fight looked like a staged performance—and a poorly staged one at that. After all the negative prefight publicity, the quick, chaotic conclusion yielded a toxic cocktail of anger and embarrassment. No one likes to hear *I told ya so*, but that is effectively what many of those at St. Dom's heard in their heads. They felt like they had been played for suckers—and they reacted accordingly.

Take Michael Boulanger, whose twenty-five-dollar seat in the second-to-the-last row up in the balcony was a twelfth-birthday present—the only present he got, because it was so expensive. (At least he *thought* it was expensive; years later, he found out that his father had scored the tickets for free.) He had bragged to all his friends that he was going to the big fight—and this ridiculous burlesque was all he ended up with? "I got kidded terribly about the whole thing for a while afterward," he said years later. In addition, "Everybody thought it would bring glory to the community, the city, and the state, and it turned out to be just the opposite."

He felt swindled, and he was furious. "I stood up on my seat and I started yelling, 'Fix!'" he recalled later.

He was not alone. "For about a minute people were yelling 'Fix!' and then it looked like the security people were starting to run around a little bit," Boulanger recalled. "People were jumping in and out of the ring—it was like a mob scene there." Among those inside the ring were a handful of Lewiston police officers who were trying in vain to lock arms and form a human shield.

"After about a minute of yelling 'Fix!' everybody shut up all at the same time," Boulanger recalled. "At least that's my memory of it. It was really weird. It just stopped all at once, as if we got a signal to do so. And the rumor was going through the crowd that people could get shot because the Black Muslims were there. They were going to shoot anybody that wasn't in favor of the verdict—that sort of thing. Totally absurd. But it was that type of mob mentality when you're not thinking clearly."

This mass confusion was broadcast around the world live, without any narration. Unlike today's blanket sports coverage—a modern fight telecast includes a blow-by-blow call, color commentary, ringside reporters, and studio analysts, not to mention multiple camera angles and immediate super-slow-motion replays—SportsVision's production of the Ali–Liston fight was bare bones. Poor Steve Ellis was left to fend for himself. To his credit, Ellis called the punch as it happened. "A knockdown, ladies and gentlemen!" he said. "A right-hand shot! A right-hand shot on the chin!"

During the ensuing chaos, Ellis didn't speak again for eight seconds. When he did, all he said was, "Jersey Joe Walcott. . . ."

Four seconds later: "Sonny cannot move. . . ."

Eleven seconds later: "Let's check the time. . . ."

And then—nothing. For well over a minute, as Ellis tried to climb into the ring, all the TV audience could hear was the ambient noise of disorder—including those chants of "Fix! Fix! Fix!"

When an explanation finally came, it was delivered not by Ellis but by ring announcer Johnny Addie. The bell tolled three times, and then Addie gave the verdict. "Now, ladies and gentlemen," he began.

He paused five seconds before continuing: "Ladies and gentlemen! The timekeeper. . . . The timekeeper counted out Liston in one minute of the first round." There was a swell of boos. "One minute of the first round," Addie continued. "The winner by a knockout, and still heavy-weight champion of the world, Muhammad Ali!"

Addie's announcement was correct in one sense. The timekeeper *had* counted Liston out, and the official time *was* one minute. But that announcement did nothing to dispel doubts about the punch or explain why the knockdown timer had rendered the decision instead of the referee, or how the official timekeeper had arrived at a time that clearly was erroneous.

Nor did it help that by the time Ellis finally caught up with Ali, the champion himself was unsure what had just happened. "Cassius. . ." Ellis began.

"Muhammad," Ali replied.

That set a tone. Ellis had one agenda, Ali had another, and rarely did the twain meet.

After repeating the "better known as Cassius Clay" disclaimer, Ellis led off with the obvious question. "Muhammad, what was the punch that won it for you?"

"Well," said Ali, "the punch that won the fight for me, I believe, was a left hook or a right cross. One of the two. But I really can't think because I was moving too fast."

Ellis: "A left hook or a right cross?"

Ali: "That's right."

Ellis: "Did you think you were gonna be able to do it in the first round? You did it in six rounds last time, Cassius."

Rather than provide much-needed insight, Ali slipped into Gorgeous George mode: "Well, now, didn't I tell the world that I had a *surprise*? And if I *told* you the surprise you would not come to the fight. With me was Almighty Allah and his messenger, and I've been saying my prayers regular, living a righteous life, and you see what happened."

Ellis tried again: "Wait a minute, let me ask you this if I may, Cassius . . . ."

"Muhammad."

"Muhammad, all right. . . ."

After a little more dancing, Ellis again tried to pin Ali down on an explanation of the phantom punch: "Did you really knock him out with the left hook or the right smash?"

Ali: "Well, I would like to see the videotape, if you have it."

Ellis, to the production crew: "Do we have the videotape?" Then: "Yes we do. We have the videotape and let's try, for viewers all over the world, to see what we have."

By then, no doubt, many of those viewers all over the world had already headed home, convinced that what they had seen had all the authenticity of professional wrestling.

As Ellis and Ali looked down through the ropes at a ringside monitor, the crowd behind them squeezed closer. There was Howard Cosell, whose WLAM "engineer" had indeed gotten him into the ring. There was Bundini Brown, in black tie and a white shirt with his name in script. Bundini, who had massaged Ali's shoulders with Vaseline just before the fight, now gripped Ellis's shoulders, leaving greasy fingerprints on Ellis's tuxedo. "Where did you get that after-dinner jacket?" Angelo Dundee asked Ellis, drawing a laugh. "That's a beauty—just like the knockout."

Everyone in Ali's camp was giddy, eager to show the world proof of their fighter's greatness.

But television replay technology was still in its infancy. CBS had introduced instant replay during coverage of the 1963 Army–Navy football game, using a videotape machine that director Tony Verna said was "the size of two Frigidaires." When CBS used it for the first time to replay, at full speed, a touchdown run moments after it happened, announcer Lindsey Nelson groped for context. "Ladies and gentlemen," Nelson exclaimed, "Army did not score again!"

In May 1965, slow-motion instant replay of isolated moments was still a couple of years away. The only way to show the phantom punch in slow motion was to replay the entire round at about half speed. That frustrated Ali. He wanted to get to the knockout as quickly as possible. "We don't need no slow motion!" he said.

"We want to entertain the folks," Ellis replied. "We want them to see what you just told us."

"Oh, I understand. I ended so fast you want them to get something for their money, huh?"

As the slow-motion replay unfolded, Ellis and Ali were again on two different planes of reality. Ellis, dutiful reporter and proxy for the American everyman, wanted straightforward answers to obvious questions. Ali, despite whatever initial misgivings he might have had about the knockout's legitimacy, had realized by now the importance of selling it. He had to defend his reputation—and by extension the Nation of Islam's. And so, as ever, he hawked his point of view with cartoonish zeal. "Look at that beautiful grace, fellas!" he said, beginning his own narration and ignoring Ellis's questions. "You've never seen a man in history move like this! *Notice* that! Ain't that beautiful? Dodgin' all those powerful punches. Notice that I'm floatin' like a butterfly and stingin' like a bee. That's my old sayin'."

"That is your old saying," Ellis said. "Now. . . ."

Before Ellis could finish, Ali was away again: "Look at that beautiful work. Joe Louis, Marciano—none of 'em was no prettier. Look at the timing. *Look!*"

Ellis tried again: "All right. Now, Cassius. . . ."

"Muhammad, Steve. . . ."

Finally, Ellis managed to penetrate the champ's defenses and land a question with a semblance of substance: "There's Sonny moving toward you with what he considers his big bombs. Did you think he'd be able to lower the boom?"

Ali: "Yes, Sonny have big bombs. And as you see, with those bombs he couldn't find nothin' to hit."

The slow motion made plain just how ineffective Liston's punches were. "I notice you got out of close range pretty fast," Ellis said. "Was that your battle plan?"

Ali didn't answer.

Ellis tried again: "Muhammad, tell us now, what was your battle plan?"

Ali: "I'm just watchin' him, letting him throw a few punches. He's strong, he's got a lot of energy, let him tire hisself out a little, miss a few. . . . When a man misses his punches he loses confidence. As you see I'm just floatin' around, taking my time, watching him, listening to the people boo me. As you know . . . Liston was a gangster, a criminal, but now, as you know, everybody was for him. I guess I was the villain, although I live a righteous life, I'm the villain. So I guess God just wanted the world to see that no wicked, evil criminal can whip a righteous man. . . ."

Ellis, suddenly excited, interrupted: "What did you do there with your feet?"

The slo mo revealed that, as Ali ducked another jab, he executed what soon became known as the "Ali shuffle." "Beautiful footwork," Ali said. "I was getting ready to come in there with a pretty right, but he was in the way."

In Ali's telling, Liston's presence in the ring was incidental, and detracted from Ali's demonstration of unsurpassed pugilistic proficiency.

Even Ellis had to laugh. "He was in the way?" he said, chuckling.

"Yes," Ali said. "I must say, this was an easy payday. My shape was so good, it really surprised [even] me."

And so it went. The irony was that, at that point, Ellis had a clearer understanding of what had happened than Ali did. Ellis was certain that the right-hand counter, not the left hook, had dropped Liston. So when he saw the roundhouse right that Ali threw just past the one-minute mark, he got excited, thinking it was the knockout punch. "There it is!" Ellis said. "That was the right-hand counter!"

But his call was premature. The jousting continued, both between Ali and Liston in slow motion and Ali and Ellis in real time. Ellis, after

Liston made minor contact with a right to the belly: "He hit you under the heart there."

Ali: "I didn't feel it."

Ellis: "You didn't?"

Ali: "I thank Allah and his messenger, Elijah Muhammad, for giving me the confidence to conquer all of this spirit that they've tried to put in me here tonight."

Ellis, still thinking the punch was imminent, tried to stay on point: "Now watch this. Here it goes, in my opinion. Halfway through this first round, or a little better. He's off balance. . . ."

Ali: "I'm glad you're showing this in slow motion. I see why now. I'm so fast, I don't guess you can see me in real action."

"You're too tough for *me* to see," Ellis said. "Let's be looking closely. A long time in slow motion for this to happen."

Dundee called the phantom punch first: "Right hand!"

"Right hand," Ellis repeated. "A right hand hurt him." Then, to Ali: "What was it?"

Ali didn't answer. Instead he said, "Watch this! Watch this!"

Ellis: "Did you think he was getting up?"

Ali: "I knew he would fall early, but I wanted it to be about three or four minutes later."

Ellis: "Why are you standing over him?"

Ali: "I'm trying to tell the bum to get up and fight!"

Ellis: "Why are you doing that? Tell me why!"

Again Ali ignored him: "Didn't I tell ya?" he said. "Didn't I tell ya?"

Ellis tried yet again to get Ali to clarify, but Ali cut him off: "Hold it—don't say nothin'! Didn't I tell ya in my poem: 'Liston said, "This time I'm a bigger fool/I'm flat on my back instead of a stool!"'"

Ali's entourage dissolved into laughter, and Ellis joined in. It was obvious that he would get no concrete answers.

As Ali donned his robe and made his way to the locker room, the chant of "Fix! Fix! Fix!" briefly resumed. Addie implored the stragglers to clear the ring. "We're gonna have another bout—four rounds," Addie said.

It was true—the Ali-Liston fight was not the last one on the card. One more remained: Liston's principal sparring partner, Amos "Big

Train" Lincoln, versus Abe Davis, a boxer of legendary ineptitude. After starting his career with five victories in his first eight bouts, Davis never won again in twenty-five attempts. He would last just thirty-eight seconds against Lincoln.

As Lincoln waited for the ring to empty, a reporter approached with a question: "Could you have done what Clay did tonight?"

Lincoln's response: "Any time for the last six weeks."

L ater, during a press conference, Ali offered a more detailed explanation of the phantom punch, if not a more plausible one.* His explanation further strained reporters' credulity. For one thing, Ali had said right after the fight that even he didn't understand how he had knocked Liston down. Now, in short order, he had concocted a revisionist history—and an outlandish one at that. Ali repeated a story that he had told a handful of reporters back in Chicopee, about how he had learned a secret punch. "This is a punch that Jack Johnson took to the graveyard with him," Ali said. "Nobody knew it but Stepin Fetchit. And it's a twist-like chop, right hand that is hard to see. . . . It's a snap punch. And you can't punch it until the man is coming in at you. It's like a head-on collision. One car doing fifty hitting the back of [another] car going fifty, going the same way, it's not much shock. But you turn the car around and bring them together head on, it's a shock. So I had to time the man with my rhythm and bouncing to where he was coming at me and where I was meeting him, and just. . . ."

Here Ali's twisting right hand became a blur as he smacked his left palm, demonstrating. "That's all," he said. "A twist." He demonstrated again. "And you can't see it, but if you were hit with it, *all* of you would be out."

Stepin Fetchit later explained that it was called the "anchor punch" because "it sinks anybody."

---

* It was Ali himself who coined the term *phantom punch*. He meant it in the stealthy sense—a punch that did its damage faster than the naked eye could detect. The press put its own spin on *phantom*, suggesting that the punch was a figment of Ali's imagination. And, as with every other aspect of this fight, it was the negative interpretation that stuck.

And so, in Ali's telling, he had floored Sonny Liston, one of the most fearsome heavyweights of all time, with a mere flick of the wrist, thanks to a tip from a seventy-three-year-old actor who had made a career of providing politically incorrect comic relief in such films as *Charlie Chan in Egypt*. It all sounded so ridiculous. Journalists from around the world, like the ticket-buying public, felt that they were being played for fools. Hostility flowed from hard-boiled urban reporters (Dick Young of the *New York Daily News* on the phantom punch: "Chances are you've hit your wife harder"); from the heartland ("The world's most publicized puppet show," the *Kansas City Star*'s Ernest Mehl called the bout); and from overseas (A PIFFLING FARCE, a *London Evening Standard* headline declared). It even came from behind the Iron Curtain. "There is complete incomprehension by the spectators," said TASS, the Soviet news agency. "Clay's punch could in no way have been decisive."

Nor did local journalists pull their punches. "One of the most ridiculous masquerades ever foisted upon a gullible public under the guise of a sports event took place in Lewiston last night," declared an editorial in the *Portland Evening Express*.

And in the Nilon Brothers' hometown paper, the Delaware County *Times*, columnist Ed Gebhart wrote: "Promotion of boxing bouts no longer will be entrusted to such firms as Inter-Continental Promotions. Henceforth, all heavyweight championship bouts should be staged under the auspices of the Ringling Brothers, Barnum and Bailey."

Liston's demeanor during his post-fight press conference did little to allay suspicion. It wasn't so much what Liston said—he called the punch "fair" and claimed that the real issue was that he never heard a count—it was how he said it. The man who had so often sounded surly in victory now appeared at ease in humiliating defeat. "You seem to be in good humor," a reporter said.

"Ain't no sense in being in bad humor," Liston answered.

There wasn't? Liston had just lost any hope he might have had of regaining the only thing that had ever really mattered to him— the heavyweight championship of the world. And he had done it in the most ignominious way imaginable. Beyond that, boxing was his sole method of making a living, and now there was a serious question whether he would ever get another decent-paying match. When a reporter asked who he might fight next, Liston said, "It don't make no difference. I'm in a position now where I can't squawk."

Then he laughed and added, "I might have to fight *you*."

The public's first impression of the phantom punch became the lasting one. It didn't have to be that way; those with an open mind had an opportunity to reconsider the fight just four days later, when ABC rebroadcast the bout in its entirety (such as it was) on *Wide World of Sports*. In addition, ABC provided a detailed breakdown of exactly what had happened, using the best available technology.

A clock superimposed on the screen established, first of all, that the official time was bogus. "One minute," Howard Cosell intoned as the fight continued past the sixty-second mark. "The time officially proclaimed by the Maine Boxing Commission as the end of the fight."

The commission, under siege since fight night, did itself no favors by neglecting to correct this error. Russ Carroll seemed willing enough to own up to his mistake. "I'm going to be honest," he said. "I'm not going to argue with something on film."

But Duncan MacDonald, the same man who had refused to expunge Rocky Marciano's dubious suspension, would. "Films can lie," MacDonald maintained. He added that "we've got to go by what our officials say, and I understand they are sending reports and affidavits that the bout lasted one minute."

Granted, the official time was a secondary issue. But by stubbornly insisting that the bout had lasted just one minute, MacDonald called the commission's competence into question at a time when the commission could least afford it. If the Maine Boxing Commission couldn't provide a satisfactory explanation of why the official time was so far off, how could it possibly provide a satisfactory explanation of the chaos surrounding the knockout? In standing by an obvious mistake, the commission reinforced suspicions that something was fishy.

But there was nothing especially fishy, it turned out, about the phantom punch. The *Wide World of Sports* presentation made that clear. After replaying the bout in real time, ABC isolated the knockout punch in slow motion. "I trust that time you saw the blow cleanly," Cosell said.

His tone was matter-of-fact, with good reason. Any objective observer would have had to concede that Ali's counterpunch had landed, and landed with enough force to turn Liston's head. To reinforce this, ABC also showed a video of the punch from the opposite angle, which demonstrated that the punch traveled farther than the six inches many observers had originally claimed—and with substantial velocity.

In addition, ABC showed still photos of the first two solid rights that Ali had landed. Acclaimed sports photographer Robert Riger also provided a frame-by-frame breakdown of the knockdown punch. Riger asserted that it might have been a karate punch—"which Clay can do because he has this great balance and this great speed, which you need in karate, and the twisting motion at the waist, which a karate fighter always has. And the way when you bring the glove up, you turn your fist over. The karate people call this 'focusing the punch.' . . . No one says that Clay planned this punch, but because of the nature of his style of fighting—it's perfect for throwing such a punch."

ABC also had isolation footage of Jersey Joe Walcott, which made plain his dereliction of duty. Ruby Goldstein, a respected referee, sat with Howard Cosell and broke down every error that Walcott made. That segment made it obvious that Walcott's incompetence, more than anything else, had led to the chaotic ending.*

But the most revealing portion of the broadcast was a panel discussion that Cosell moderated. It featured two of the greatest heavyweights of all time—Jack Dempsey and Rocky Marciano—along with journalists Jimmy Cannon and W.C. Heinz. All four panelists acknowledged that the phantom punch had landed. And three of the four conceded that it might have been sufficient to knock Liston out.

The sole remaining holdout, predictably, was Cannon. The cantankerous syndicated columnist loathed the very idea of Muhammad Ali

---

* It hadn't been a good week for Walcott. He declined an invitation to a post-fight press conference, which looked bad. Then, according to Steve Cady of the *New York Times*, Walcott just sat and watched when a fistfight broke out between two waiters during breakfast at Poland Spring the next morning. Two other guests broke it up. "Even with amateurs," wrote Cady, "affable Jersey Joe didn't behave like a take-charge referee."

and Sonny Liston fighting for the heavyweight championship. He had invested fifteen months in trashing the bout's legitimacy, airing every negative rumor he heard (including all those threats of Muslim violence— violence that, of course, never came to pass). He wasn't about to change his story now—even though, as Cosell pointed out, he'd had an ideal ringside vantage point. "Yes, there was a punch, Howard," Cannon began, "but I didn't think it was hard enough to crush a grape."

In trying to defend his point of view, Cannon actually undermined it by revealing his bias. "Now, I'm not jumping on the bandwagon after the fight," he said. "Before the fight I refused to pick a winner because I didn't like the circumstances of it—the people connected with it."

He spent the rest of his segment rehashing the same old insinuations about Liston's background.

Dempsey also acknowledged a bias. He hadn't even bothered to watch the fight live; the first time he'd seen it was in the ABC studio. But when Cosell asked if he thought Ali had landed a knockout punch, Dempsey said, "Well, I don't know how hard [Liston] was hit. Not being on the receiving end, you never know just how hard these punches come over."

Also unknown was exactly how much head trauma Liston had suffered over the years, and the degree to which that might have compromised him. John Doherty, a captain with the St. Louis police, had told writer Nick Tosches that once, while arresting Liston, officers "broke hickory nightsticks over his head." And while that was a striking example of Liston's toughness, it also suggested a possible history of concussions that could have left him vulnerable.

Consider what happened in a 1933 bout between Ernie Schaaf and Primo Carnera. Schaff, the favorite, suffered a thirteenth-round knockout after what the *New York Times* called "a straight left to the face which did not appear to carry much power." The punch looked so innocuous, in fact, that many among the Madison Square Garden crowd of 20,000 booed, and some chanted "Fake!"

Four days later Schaaf died of a cerebral hemorrhage.

After an autopsy, medical examiners concluded that Schaaf probably entered the ring suffering from some undetected brain trauma, a result of either illness or damage from an earlier bout. Some witnesses later said that Schaaf hadn't looked right from the opening bell, appearing sluggish and out of sorts.

Sort of like Sonny Liston—who, as Heinz said, "looked like an old man. And as the two pros here can tell you, when you get to a certain age, you just don't live under a punch the way you did when you were young."

That led Cosell to segue to Marciano, whose comments were the most insightful. Earlier, Marciano had admitted that seeing the videotape had altered his opinion. When he had seen the punch in real time, he didn't think it had anything behind it. Now he did.

Cosell also pointed out that Marciano himself had once been floored by a short right from Archie Moore. And although Marciano contended that the Moore punch was very different, his explanation echoed Ali's description of the anchor punch. "I missed him with my own right hand and had the full force going," Marciano said. "And Archie, the clever man, stepped back just about three inches and hit me with the best counterpunch you ever saw." Through the combined momentum of his miss and Moore's direct hit, said Marciano, "I just went straight forward."

Marciano, who had retired undefeated, added that the psychological effect of being dropped by such a short, sharp counter was almost as unsettling as the physical impact. "You realize that you *can* be put down," he said, "and it's a frightening thing. . . . You say to yourself, 'He can do it again. . . .'"

Wide World of Sports made a compelling case that Ali had legitimately knocked Liston out—or at worst, that Ali had knocked enough starch out of Liston to make him quit. No one on the broadcast, not even Jimmy Cannon, contended that there was anything overtly underhanded about the outcome. "I don't think it was a fix in the sense that money was passed," said Cannon. "But I don't think that Liston tried as hard as he should. He just took a punch and got out of there—that's the way it looked to me."

While quitting due to a lack of heart is far from commendable, it hardly rises to the same level as taking a dive for the Mob. But by then the notion of a fix had already taken a firm set in the public's mind. The *Wide World* segment—which aired just once, on the Saturday of Memorial Day weekend—had little impact. The *Boston Herald*'s Bill Kipouras, who had watched the fight at Boston Garden, was one of the few writers who admitted that the segment changed his mind. "Perhaps I was influenced by the bazoo of the crowd," he wrote the next day, "but on closed-circuit at the Garden it looked to me that the income tax people hit me harder than Clay hit Liston. However, I must now add my name to the list of 'believers.'"

But cold logic rarely prevails in a contest with heated emotion. As Joseph M. Sheehan wrote in that Sunday's *New York Times*, "A startling outcome, such as the latest Clay–Liston fiasco, evokes a mob-psychology reaction of disappointment and chagrin that beclouds reason. Has it occurred to anyone that the magnificently proportioned, magnificently conditioned twenty-three-year-old Clay just might be the 'greatest' fighter, as he claims?"

Yes it had, actually. And that enlightened opinion originated right in Lewiston, with one of the oldest of the old guard. Wrote Norman Thomas, who had manned the sports editor's desk at the *Evening Journal* since Babe Ruth wore red socks, "Liston lost to a mitster who, whether you like his Muslim connections or not, has demonstrated that he doesn't get too far out on a limb when he shouts, 'I'm the greatest.'"

Thomas was neither disgusted by the outcome nor aghast at how it might reflect on Lewiston. "It was a great fight," his account began. "Why so? Well, because it gave food for argument for years to come, for one thing."

Still, he was glad that Lewiston's moment in the spotlight was over. "It is the day after the day that was," he wrote, "and now Lewiston and the surrounding territory can go back to living their lives in a [sedate] and otherwise leisurely manner, while the rubes from the cities of the land can wander back from whence they came, with their tales of adventure from up here in God's country. It has been nice meeting some of them and the money of all of them was good. It has been a milestone in the fight business, one which despite the kicks isn't going to hurt a bit."

Epilogue

Sam Michael didn't dwell on the disaster that the Ali–Liston fight turned into. There was no time; he had to start his new job as the industrial development director of Oxford County. Brooding wasn't his style anyway. "When you're in the promotion business you have a lot of wins and losses," his son John said. "So he took it in stride, pretty much. I remember Jack Sharkey, the former heavyweight champ, called the next morning. I took the call, and Jack said he had missed seeing my dad at the fight. Then he said, 'I just wanted to congratulate your dad on a great promotion.' He couldn't believe that he had pulled it off in a couple of weeks. So within the industry everybody was pretty amazed at what had happened."

For a day or two the next winter, it looked like it might happen again.

Ali had fought once since Lewiston, against Floyd Patterson in Las Vegas on November 22. Patterson, who was already a far more popular boxer than Ali, also tried to claim moral superiority. Unlike Sonny Liston, who never made an issue of Ali's religion, Patterson made it the *only* issue. As Patterson wrote in a first-person *Sports Illustrated* article, "I say it, and I say it flatly, that the image of a Black Muslim as heavyweight champion disgraces the sport and the nation. Cassius Clay must be beaten and the Black Muslims' scourge removed from boxing."

Add the bad aftertaste from Lewiston, and Ali stood no chance in the prefight popularity contest. Patterson, on the other hand, stood no chance in the ring. And because Ali was so rankled by Patterson's attacks on his religion, he fought without his characteristic flamboyance. Instead, he toyed with Patterson for twelve rounds, taunting him and prolonging an ugly spectacle that even his closest supporters found difficult to watch.

Then, just when it seemed Ali's stature couldn't get any lower, it disappeared down a Florida sinkhole. In February 1966 Ali was at home in Miami, preparing for a bout with World Boxing Association champion Ernie Terrell, scheduled for March 29 in Chicago. With the Vietnam War escalating came the news that the U.S. Army had reclassified Ali 1-A, making him eligible for the draft.

The press pressured him to comment. So Ali said, among many other things, "I ain't got no quarrel with them Vietcong."

After that, Chicago disinvited the Ali–Terrell fight. Ali, explained Illinois State attorney general William G. Clark, "has made statements that he was unwilling to serve in the Armed Forces of the United States and would take action to avoid the draft."

Seeing another opportunity to capitalize on a major city's about-face, Sam Michael floated the idea of holding the Ali–Terrell bout at Bangor Auditorium. Notwithstanding the overwhelming public outcry against Ali, he said, "The fight would still be an asset to the State of Maine."

Besides, Sam said, "I feel a man has a right to say what he wishes. This should not be considered a moral issue."

Sam's outlook was reasonable from a civil libertarian's perspective. But given the political climate of the times, it was tone-deaf. Governor John Reed made it clear that he would no longer endorse any bout in which Muhammad Ali was a participant. Ali, said Reed, "should be held in utter contempt by every patriotic American. Maine sons and daughters are fighting and dying in Vietnam and I don't think Maine people want our state to be used to further the ambitions and gains of an individual of Clay's character."

That was that. Ali would not fight in Maine—nor would he fight anywhere else in the United States for the foreseeable future. His next bout, against Canadian champ George Chuvalo, was in Toronto. Two bouts in England and one in Germany followed. Ali finally fought on U.S. soil again in November 1966, defeating Cleveland Williams at the Astrodome in Houston.

Houston, Ali's new legal residence, was also the setting for a much more important fight, which played out in 1967. On April 28, Ali refused induction into the U.S. Army, citing his standing as a Muslim minister. He was indicted in May and tried in June. A jury deliberated just twenty-one minutes before finding him guilty. He was sentenced to five years in prison. And although he remained free while his legal team filed a series of appeals, Ali spent more than three years—at the height of his athletic prime—in boxing exile.

T he tide turned slowly. In a 1965 Gallup Poll, just twenty-four percent of Americans said they thought the Vietnam War was a mistake. By 1971 that number had risen to sixty percent. Violent responses to antiwar protests—most notoriously at Kent State University, where the Ohio National Guard fired on a crowd of students on May 4, 1970, killing four—fueled the backlash.

Against this backdrop Ali's draft resistance looked different than it had three years earlier. Refusing induction wasn't merely a way to save his skin. He could have accepted a deal to join Special Services. He could have allowed himself to be used as a shill—visiting the troops to bolster morale. That would have allowed him to remain heavyweight champion. Instead, he refused on principle. And that principle cost him dearly. He was stripped of his heavyweight title. No boxing organization in American would grant him a license. And because his passport had been confiscated pending the resolution of his appeal, he was not allowed to leave the country and fight elsewhere. (Despite his criminal background, Sonny Liston faced no such restriction. Contrary to what many people had anticipated, the Lewiston travesty did not mark the end of Liston's career. Between July 1966 and April 1967 he fought four times in Sweden, winning each time by knockout.)

Ali's refusal to join the Army earned him the respect and admiration of millions of young Americans—young urban black Americans in particular. And if the rest of America didn't necessarily think Ali's stance was admirable, many no longer considered it contemptible. By then a majority had realized that they had no quarrel with them Vietcong, either.

This gradual thawing of Ali's public image allowed him, eventually, to resume his career. On October 26, 1970, he fought Jerry Quarry in Atlanta, winning by a third-round technical knockout. He scored another TKO, against Oscar Bonavena, in December. That set up a title bout with the current heavyweight champion, Joe Frazier, at Madison

Square Garden on March 8, 1971. It was dubbed "The Fight of the Century."

Ali lost. But less than four months later he won the fight of his career. The Supreme Court overturned his conviction for draft evasion.

From there, Ali's popularity reached a level beyond anything that he could have envisioned, even during his most self-aggrandizing early '60s phase. He regained the title, lost it, and got it back a third time. In 1975 he left the Nation of Islam and distanced himself from the NOI's separatist views. And he made the world heavyweight championship an event of truly worldwide significance. His bouts took on mythic proportions. The Rumble in the Jungle in 1974 against George Foreman, in what was then called Zaire. The Thrilla in Manila, a rubber match against Frazier in 1975. He also fought in Zurich, Tokyo, Dublin, Jakarta, Kuala Lumpur, San Juan, Munich, and Nassau, as well as Yankee Stadium, the Superdome, and Caesars Palace.

And he made a triumphal return to Lewiston.

It was September 1995. Lewiston was marking its bicentennial. The city invited Ali to the celebration, which included a boxing card called "Night of the Young Heavyweights," televised on ESPN from St. Dom's—which now went by yet another alias, the Central Maine Civic Center.

Ali had been retired for fourteen years. In 1984 he had been diagnosed with Parkinson's disease, which in time would silence one of the loudest voices of the twentieth century.

Before the fight there was a banquet at the Lewiston Ramada Inn. Ali was there. So was former governor John Reed, the man who had once effectively banned Ali from boxing in Bangor, and Floyd Patterson, who had once declared that Ali's heavyweight title disgraced the sport.

Patterson had long since healed his rift with Ali. He had begun calling him by his Muslim name after their Las Vegas bout (although he still slipped occasionally and called him Clay). En route to the banquet, Patterson stopped to visit Tom Callahan, a longtime Lewiston fight fan afflicted with ALS. When Callahan expressed disbelief that one of his heroes, the great champion Floyd Patterson, was right there in his living room, Patterson said, "The real champ's on his way." Ali walked into Callahan's house moments later.

Another guest at the bicentennial banquet was Sam Michael. His ninetieth birthday (which would be his last) was less than four months away. After the Ali–Liston fight Sam never promoted another live bout (although he did a few more closed-circuit telecasts).

Sam, like the rest of America, rolled with the changes during the 1970s. When the Augusta Civic Center opened in 1973, Sam brought in *Godspell* and roller derby. He also co-promoted some Evel Knievel stunt jumps around New England. (Sam shared a Knievel connection with Harold Conrad, who did the publicity for the infamous 1974 Snake River Canyon jump. One of Conrad's assistants in Idaho was Margaux Hemingway, granddaughter of his old Havana drinking buddy.)

Sam also had a tangential connection to another infamous Lewiston promotion. On September 6, 1980, the Grateful Dead drew 25,000 people to Lewiston Raceway. Traffic backed up for three miles on the Maine Turnpike, and "the neighbors went through a very difficult ordeal," said Lewiston mayor Paul Dionne.

Ever the opportunist, Sam, who was seventy-four years old at the time, managed to cash in on the Grateful Dead's visit. He rented some vacant lots on Main Street and charged ten dollars a car for parking.

Sam's son John was the concert promoter.

At the bicentennial banquet in 1995, John spoke on his father's behalf. He noted that his own introduction to the promotion business, way back in May of '65, couldn't have gone much worse. He had looked so forlorn—stuck in the St. Dom's penalty box, cheated out of a chance to appear on worldwide television—that he became an object of pathos in a column by acerbic *Boston Record American* writer John Gillooly. "The only person I felt sorry for," Gillooly wrote after the Lewiston bout, "was the round-card boy."

Because it was self-evident that the fight began with round one, John didn't enter the ring before the opening bell. Resplendent in his tuxedo, he planned his grand entrance before round two. "I was going to be a star," John, now forty-five, told the banquet crowd at the Ramada Inn. "Talent scouts would discover me. I was going to date the 'little red-headed girl.' I was on my way to the big time."

He paused and turned to Ali, seated a few feet away. "And then *you* blew it for me!"

Ali stood and began peeling off his jacket, reprising his old "Lemme at 'im!" routine.

John Jenkins, Lewiston's first black mayor, then called Ali to the dais. It was the kind of occasion that called for the presentation of a ceremonial key to the city—the kind JFK had once received. But, for whatever reason, Lewiston no longer had such a key. So Jenkins presented Ali with a commemorative pin instead.

The room fell silent as Ali slowly approached the microphone. His voice was faint. "I come all the way to Lewiston," he said, "and this is all I get?"

Lewiston laughed as readily as it had once booed.

A key figure was missing from the banquet, of course: Sonny Liston. He had been dead for almost twenty-five years, the victim of a drug overdose, heart failure, murder, or a combination of all three. His death at his Las Vegas home was neither adequately investigated nor explained.

Liston had also enjoyed a measure of redemption, although on a much smaller scale than Ali's. After resuming his career in Sweden, Liston began fighting again in the U.S., eventually stretching his winning streak to fourteen. One of those victories was a second-round knockout of his former sparring partner Amos "Big Train" Lincoln, who had boasted in Lewiston that he could have kayoed Liston as easily as Ali did. That bout, in December 1968, took place at the Baltimore Civic Center, perhaps in the same ring that Dorothy Lamour & Co. had loaned to Lewiston.

Liston even got another title shot, for the vacant (and lightly regarded) North American Boxing Federation heavyweight championship. It came in December 1969, against another former sparring partner, Leotis Martin. Liston was the favorite and was comfortably ahead in the ninth round when Martin floored him with a left hook followed by a right cross that clearly was *not* a phantom punch. "This fight will be over," Howard Cosell declared as Liston lay face down on the canvas, "and with it Charles 'Sonny' Liston's career!"

But it was actually Martin's career that was over. He suffered a detached retina and never fought again. Liston fought one last time, winning his swan song against the "Bayonne Bleeder," Chuck Wepner, at the Jersey City Armory on June 29, 1970. The referee was Barney Felix, who had presided over Liston's bout with Cassius Clay at Miami Beach in February of '64.

Had he lived, would Liston have returned to Lewiston for the bicentennial banquet in 1995? (Robert Goulet, a good sport, sent a video of himself singing the national anthem—flawlessly.) And if Liston had returned, how would Lewiston have received him?

Another question that can never be answered.

D ue to the convoluted nature of the Ali–Liston fight contracts, Inter-Continental Promotions ended up with the 1965 Ali–Patterson bout in Las Vegas. Mostly, however, when Inter-Continental's name appeared in the papers after Lewiston, it was in connection with one lawsuit or another. Liston sued Inter-Continental alleging unpaid funds; Inter-Continental sued Miami Beach promoter Bill MacDonald for the same thing. Ultimately the lawsuits outlived both Liston and MacDonald. And bad feelings lingered in the Nilon family. "There's no question that that whole Liston experience was hard on my father and my uncles," said Terry Nilon, son of the late Inter-Continental president, Bob Nilon. "There's no way it couldn't be. Boxing was not a topic that they warmed to after that. I think they got a real education in the dark side of boxing. I don't think they had any idea. Boxing's a tough business.

"But they recovered and they put it behind them. And I think this is pertinent: They went on to their greatest success *after* the whole Sonny Liston experience. They loved sports from the bottom of their heart, which was one of the reasons they got involved with Sonny Liston in the first place. But their business, their forte, was food concessions."

When Philadelphia's Veterans Stadium opened in 1971, Nilon Brothers landed the contract for the concessions and the parking. "They spent the next fifteen years of their lives, into old age, managing that," Terry said. "That was a magnificent contract and it really put them on top in that industry."

Despite the negativity associated with the Inter-Continental Promotions experience, Terry Nilon has remained a lifelong fan of boxing—and of Sonny Liston. "He came to our house for Sunday dinner a number of times," Terry said. "It was always a big thing in the neighborhood. All the local kids would see that big car pull up and come running over. And of course Sonny liked kids. He had that soft side.

"But in the ring he was absolutely a wrecking machine. . . . He had *incredible* power. People forget, with all the bad press and the 'phantom punch' and all that crap, people forget what a dominant force Sonny Liston was in his prime. Even now, when people introduce me to old fight fans and they say, 'This is Terry Nilon—his family had Sonny Liston,' that stops them in their tracks. Not that it had anything to do with *me* being anything, but the name Sonny Liston still has cachet in the fight field. He was something. And it's a shame that his name has been so tarnished."

It's standard procedure, whenever a fight ends in controversy, for the supervising authority to impound the gloves. That's what Maine Boxing Commission chairman George Russo did immediately after the Ali–Liston fight in Lewiston. "He seized the gloves, both pair, right out of the dressing room," George's nephew, Bob Russo, said.

George took the gloves home to his house in Portland. His inspection revealed nothing suspicious. After that he basically forgot about the gloves and was on to more pressing matters. Contrary to the doomsayers' predictions, the Ali–Liston fight did not spell the end of boxing in Maine. In fact, it sparked a revival. "Sam Silverman, the promoter from Massachusetts, started to do a couple of events at the end of '65 at the Portland Expo," Bob Russo said. "That kicked off an unbelievable run that supposedly made Portland the busiest fight town in the world. They went fifty-one weeks a year for many, many, many years."

Predictably, Suitcase Sam had to navigate some turbulent waters during his time on the Maine coast. In 1968 the FBI charged him with offering a forty-year-old stiff $100 to throw a fight on a Portland Expo undercard. It was a ridiculous accusation, and after a mistrial in 1970, charges were dropped. How Silverman intended to profit from paying a sure loser to take a fall—in a bout that generated zero interest among bettors—was a question the FBI apparently never thought to ask, let alone answer.

Less than six months later, Silverman was the one going to court. He filed a lawsuit claiming that the rights holder for the Ali–Frazier closed-circuit broadcast reneged on a handshake deal and instead offered the fight to a concert promoter (or "rock and roll hippie," in Silverman's words) who came in with a higher bid. The fight game was changing and Silverman, the boxing lifer, was struggling to keep up. In 1977, late on a July night, he was in his roving office, a Cadillac, coming home from a bout in New York. Driving too fast, as usual. He lost control near his birthplace, Cambridge, and broadsided a service-station signpost, suffering massive internal injuries. He died at the hospital two hours later.

George Russo was gone by then too. He died in 1975. And those gloves, the ones from the Ali–Liston fight that he'd taken home and forgotten about? His nephew ended up with them. "I basically just had them on a hook down in the cellar," Bob Russo said. "People would look at them and try them on."

Bob Russo had attended the Ali–Liston fight as a ten-year-old, and got hooked. The weekly fights in Portland became an obsession. "I was the glove boy at the Expo," he said. "And I've been a boxing fanatic ever since. I remember waiting every Thursday at the window for my uncle to come and pick me up. We did that every week for years."

Because of George Russo's influence, Bob Russo devoted his life to boxing. He founded the Portland Boxing Club. He's promoted more than 100 bouts. He has a list of coaching credits at every amateur level, including the Olympics.

Over the years, Bob made connections with those at the sport's highest level, including Roberto Duran and Buster Douglas. And, inevitably, the provenance of the Ali–Liston gloves, and their prospective worth, came up in conversation. So Bob Russo had the gloves authenticated, with Ali furnishing an affidavit. In 2010 Bob sold them to Seth Ersoff, a Hollywood producer, for an undisclosed sum. In February 2015, in advance of the fight's fiftieth anniversary, Ersoff sold them through Heritage Auctions to an unnamed collector for $956,000. Said Chris Ivy, a spokesman for Heritage Auctions, "It's not out of line to place these gloves among the most important pieces of memorabilia to ever come to market. These transcend sports. The drama and outrage that swirled around the Ali–Liston fights were a microcosm of America's growing pains of the mid-1960s."

"That photograph," Bob Russo said, "is what makes those gloves so iconic." That photograph is, of course, Neil Leifer's. And even the image of that image has evolved.

AP photographer John Rooney, who was standing to Leifer's immediate left, captured the same moment. But Rooney's shot is black and white and Leifer's is in color. That's made all the difference over the years. Because it's black and white, Rooney's photo, like most from that fight—along with all the archival footage on YouTube—feels dated. Leifer's photo, with its vivid color—including those bright red gloves—feels ageless. There are no antiquated advertisements in the background, nor are there any of the other conspicuous visual cues that date fifty-year-old sports photos, like single-bar football helmets, flannel baseball uniforms, or basketball short-shorts. The lack of an obvious historical timestamp has given the photograph an indefinite shelf life. "Nobody went crazy over the picture in 1965," Leifer said in 2004. "In the National Press Photographers [awards], it did not win first, second, third, or honorable mention."

Nor did it appear on *Sports Illustrated*'s cover in 1965. But it did in July 1999, with the cover line "The Century's Greatest Sports Photos."

People knew too much about the fight in 1965 to fully appreciate the photograph. Back then it was a straightforward piece of photojournalism that documented a travesty. It expressed visually what knockdown timekeeper Francis McDonough expressed verbally: "If that bum Clay had gone to a neutral corner instead of running around like a madman, all the trouble would have been avoided."

Time has altered the context. In 1999, SI's readers instantly recognized Muhammad Ali as the cover subject. But many probably didn't know where the photo was taken, when it was taken, who the vanquished opponent was, or what was going on. Instead of seeing a moment they saw a legend. And Ali's Parkinson's added a retroactive poignancy. What was once a mere news photo had become a defining portrait. Said Leifer, "The picture became the image that most conveys the way people want to remember Muhammad."

It is now a point of pride in Lewiston, Maine, that the picture was taken at the local hockey rink. An enlarged, framed copy hangs in City Hall. Two floors above it, in dim light that filters through dusty windows, are the remnants of the auditorium where Sam Michael hitched his ambition to Lefty LaChance, believing against all odds that Lewiston could be a championship-caliber fight town.

Notes, Sources, and Bibliography

On August 9, 1969, Bill Butler of the expansion Kansas City Royals pitched a one-hitter against the Indians at Cleveland's Municipal Stadium. I was there. I was ten years old. It was the first major league baseball game I ever went to. And one measly single kept me from seeing a no-hitter.

For years I cursed Cleveland second baseman Dave Nelson because I thought he had ruined Butler's no-hitter—*my* no-hitter. Then, not long ago, I looked up the box score of that game on baseball-reference.com. I was surprised to discover that Dave Nelson went 0–for–3. The guy who got the hit was Indians shortstop Eddie Leon.

I checked the play-by-play. Nelson had reached on an error in the third inning. Leon got the hit two batters before. I remembered the error—Royals centerfielder Joe Foy dropped a shallow pop fly. I also remembered that the Royals won 10–0, that first baseman Mike Fiore hit a home run, that Steve Hargan was Cleveland's starting pitcher— and on and on and on. Hell, I even remembered how mournful Burt Bacharach's "This Guy's in Love with You" sounded between innings in the damp, nearly empty stadium, and that a parking lot attendant kicked some drunk in the ass.

But the name Eddie Leon? A complete blank. For all the stuff I remembered about that game, I had forgotten the only thing that mattered.

I kept that experience in mind as I sorted out the sometimes contradictory accounts of events related to the Ali–Liston fights. People forget. Worse, they misremember. That is, they *think* they remember— but they're wrong. So whenever an account from a contemporaneous source—i.e., a newspaper, magazine, film, or photograph published during the time covered in the book—differed from a later account, I went with the original source. Many eyewitnesses, relying on their memories years after the fact, said things about events surrounding the Ali–Liston fight that I knew from my research to be wrong. This applied not only to some of the interviews I conducted myself, but also to interviews published in other sources. So if a first-person account published in, say, 1995 differed materially from accounts of the same incident published in 1965, I went with the 1965 version.

Also, one style note: I referred to Muhammad Ali as Cassius Clay during the portions of the narrative that predated his name change in March 1964. Thereafter I referred to him as Ali in the narrative. The vast majority of Americans still called him Clay rather than Ali at the time of the Lewiston fight, however, and many quotes reflected this. I let those quotes stand rather than insert the name Ali in brackets—both for historical accuracy and to convey the degree of resistance to Ali's conversion to Islam.

What follows is a partial list of sources that I used, which I cross-checked and verified to the best of my ability. (It isn't possible for me to list *every* source that I consulted; I picked up some information by osmosis during an informal research phase before I ever decided to write a word about the topic.) I tried to flag instances where no second source was available to verify an eyewitness account by using attributives such as "according to," without disrupting the narrative too much.

BOOKS

Barrows, Gridley, and O'Halloran, Ruth Libbey. *Historic Lewiston: Its Architectural Heritage.* Auburn, Maine: Lewiston Historical Commission, 1997.

Bingham, Howard. *Muhammad Ali: A Thirty-Year Journey.* New York: Simon & Schuster, 1993.

Bowden, Mark. *The Best Game Ever.* New York: Atlantic Monthly Press, 2008.

Bryson, Bill. *One Summer: America, 1927.* New York: Doubleday, 2013.

Conrad, Harold. *Dear Muffo.* Briarcliff Manor, New York: Stein and Day, 1982.

Ezra, Michael. *Muhammad Ali: The Making of an Icon.* Philadelphia: Temple University Press, 2009.

Gallender, Paul. *Sonny Liston: The Real Story behind the Ali–Liston Fights.* Pacific Grove, California: Park Place Publications, 2012.

Hauser, Thomas. *Muhammad Ali: His Life and Times.* New York: Simon & Schuster Paperbacks, 2006.

Kirk, Geneva, and Barrows, Gridley. *Historic Lewiston: Its Government.* Auburn, Maine: Lewiston Historical Commission, 1982.

Leamon, James. *Historic Lewiston: A Textile City in Transition.* Auburn, Maine: Lewiston Historical Commission, 1976.

Mee, Bob. *Ali and Liston: The Boy Who Would Be King and the Ugly Bear.* New York: Skyhorse Publishing, 2011.

Michaud, Charlotte, and Janelle, Adelard. *Historic Lewiston: Franco-American Origins.* Auburn, Maine: Lewiston Historical Commission, 1974.

Miller, Davis. *The Tao of Muhammad Ali.* New York: Warner Books, 1996.

Myers, Walter Dean. *Malcolm X: By Any Means Necessary.* New York: Scholastic, Inc., 1993.

Patterson, Floyd, and Gross, Milton. *Victory Over Myself.* New York: Scholastic Book Services, Inc., 1962.

Remnick, David. *King of the World.* New York: Vintage Books, 1999.

Tosches, Nick. *The Devil and Sonny Liston.* Boston, New York, London: Little, Brown and Company, 2000.

Yost, Mark. *Tailgating, Sacks, and Salary Caps: How the NFL Became the Most Successful Sports League in History.* Chicago: Kaplan Publishing, 2006.

NEWSPAPERS

Baltimore Sun
Berkshire (Mass.) *Eagle*
Biddeford-Saco Journal
Boston Globe
Boston Herald
Boston Record American
Chester (Pa.) Times
Chicago Tribune
Delaware County Times
El Paso Herald–Post
Hayward (Calif.) Daily Review
Kansas City Star
Kennebec Journal
Kentucky New Era

Lewiston Evening Journal
Lewiston Daily Sun
Lewiston Sun-Journal
London Evening-Standard
Lowell Sun
Los Angeles Times
Maine Sunday Telegram
The New York Times
Portland Press Herald
Portland Evening Express
Santa Cruz (Calif.) *Sentinel*
Washington Post

WIRE SERVICES

Associated Press
United Press International
TASS

SYNDICATED COLUMNISTS

Jimmy Breslin
Milton Gross
Joe Louis
Jim Murray
Drew Pearson
Milton Richman
Robert Ruark
Red Smith
Dick Young

MAGAZINES

ESPN
Esquire
Jet
Playboy
Sports Illustrated
Yankee

WEBSITES

Baharris.org ("The Historic Poland Spring")
Baseball-Reference.com
BoxRec
Hell's Acre's blog (photo of Ali's Schine Inn itinerary card)
polandspringps.org (Poland Spring Preservation Society)
YouTube

MISCELLANEOUS

Ali–Liston fight program
The American Presidency Project: Transcript of JFK's Lewiston speech
The Edmund S. Muskie Archives and Special Collections Library, Bates College
State of Maine Legislative Record
University of Southern Maine (usm.maine.edu): Recording and transcript of
    Robert Couturier's inaugural address, January 4, 1965

TELEVISION SHOWS

Eyes on the Prize II: America at the Racial Crossroads 1965–1985, 1990
Sonny Liston: The Mysterious Life & Death of a Champion, HBO, 1997
Wide World of Sports, ABC-TV, May 29, 1965

INTERVIEWS

Dr. Michael Boulanger, 2014
Irene Bureau, 2014
Normand Bureau, 2004, 2014
Robert Couturier, 2004
Mike Feldman, 2014
Fred Gage, 2014
Bob Gardner, 2014
Bill Johnson, 2014
Ray Lebrun, 2004
Neil Leifer, 2004
John Michael, 2004, 2013, 2014, 2015

Guy Nadeau, 2004
Terry Nilon, 2014
Bob Pacios, 2014
Bob Russo, 2014, 2015
Dr. William Heinz (via email), 2013

Acknowledgments

Any work of narrative history is a mosaic, made of thousands of tiles from many sources. A suggestion here. A fact there. A direct quotation from a first-person interview. A detail gleaned from a newspaper photograph.

No writer can assemble that mosaic without plenty of assistance. What follows is a partial list of those who helped me.

Thanks to Down East Books editor Michael Steere for suggesting this book, and to former *Down East* magazine editor-in-chief Dale Kuhnert for green-lighting my original story proposal. Thanks to Phil Nadeau, deputy city administrator for the City of Lewiston, who provided sufficient background information, contacts, and enthusiasm to get me started in the right direction, and for showing me the old City Hall Auditorium. Thanks to former Lewiston mayor Robert Couturier, who invited me to his office a decade ago to talk about the fight. I was sorry to learn that he had died by the time I began working on this book; I'm sure there's so much more he could have told me about Lewiston's mid-'60s political climate. Thanks to Norm and Irene Bureau for inviting me into their home and sharing their differing opinions on the outcome of the fight.

Thanks to Bill Johnson for sharing his memories of what went on behind the scenes at Liston's training camp at Poland Spring (and for showing me his copy of Ali's *I'm the Greatest* album). Thanks to Mike Feldman for sharing an eight-year-old's perspective on Sonny Liston, and to Dr. Michael Boulanger for telling me how the fight looked from the perspective of a twelve-year-old boy in the cheap seats. (And while I disagree with Dr. Boulanger and trooper Bureau that Liston took a dive, I respect the steadfastness of their convictions.)

Thanks to Fred Gage for providing the "Howard Cosell Comes to Lewiston" story that the book needed. Thanks to Dr. William Heinz for providing a modern medical expert's opinion on the phantom punch. Thanks to Neil Leifer for sharing his memories of May 25, 1965, and for his insights into why his photogaph became an icon. Thanks to Terry Nilon for sharing his memories of the men behind Inter-Continental Promotions. Thanks to Bob Russo of the Portland Boxing Club for sharing his memories of his late uncle, Maine Boxing Commission chairman George Russo. Thanks also to Norm Rosseau, Bob Pacios, Ray Lebrun, Guy Nadeau, Fern Masse, Bob Gardner, and to everyone else I might have overlooked who returned a phone call or answered an email. Thanks also to the staffs of the public libraries in Portland and Lewiston, at the former Holiday Inn in Auburn, and at the Colisée for assisting me during my visits. Thanks to everyone who posted old fight films on YouTube, which allowed me to study Ali and Liston (and even Gorgeous George) in detail.

Thanks to my son Will for sharing his offbeat theories on the phantom punch. Thanks to my wife Tammy for her support throughout this project—and for being from a large French Canadian family, which enabled her to speak with authority about important matters like creton sandwiches. Thanks also to Tammy's father, Jeff Francoeur, a boxing nut whose offhand comment during an Ali marathon on ESPN first prompted me to dig deeper into the reasons why a world heavyweight championship fight ended up in Lewiston.

And thanks especially to John Michael, Sam Michael's son, for sitting through my lengthy interviews, for answering my frequent emails, and for taking me on a tour of Lewiston, both present and past. It was mostly through John's assistance that Sam Michael became more to me than just a name in some old newspaper clippings.